Endorsements

With impressive command of both the scriptures and church history, Gray Fitzgerald demonstrates how far we have fallen away from Christian teachings about the perils—and the distractions—of affluence. This is an important and timely book, reminding us that Jesus warned about camels negotiating the eye of a needle.

Randall Balmer

John Phillips Professor in Religion, Dartmouth College

Author of *Saving Faith: How American Christianity Can Reclaim Its Prophetic Voice*

"I love to tell the Story, "sings Katherine Hankey's old hymn about a far older story. The power of Gray Fitzgerald's *Capitalism Converts Christianity,* a prophetic reflection on the failure of faith to resist temptations of wealth and the violence it inevitably breeds is in his story-telling. Alive on the page are, indeed, the stories of Jesus, as Fitzgerald lets Zacchaeus invite readers to consider the implications of his ways of making a living. The longer biographies of Francis of Assisi, John Woolman, and Dorothy Day engage a heart of empathy that is never toxic, while dramatic retellings of world and US history tragedies become Capitalism's rite of confession, and short poignant stories like Xernona Clayton's transformation of Calvin Craig bring the book to conclusion in unexpected hope.

Maren Tirabassi has been a UCC pastor since 1980 and is the author of twenty-four books, from faith-related topics to cozy mysteries. Maren is a former Poet Laureate of Portsmouth, NH, and the 2023 recipient of the New Hampshire Humanities Council Lifetime Achievement Award. She loves hiking, swimming, quilting, beagles ... and mostly facilitating groups explor-

ing their own faith horizons. Her most recent book is *Death in Disguise* in the Rev. and Rye Cozy Mystery series.

In stark contrast to the reluctance of most Christians to talk about money and possessions, these were among the foremost topics at the heart of the teaching of Jesus. In this bold and much needed critique of the ways in which Christianity has sacrificed its values on the altar of unfettered capitalism, Fitzgerald invites Christians into the radical power of taking Jesus seriously enough to transform our society back to the generosity and mutual concern for the common good essential to building the Beloved Community on earth as it is in heaven.

Rev. John M. Gregory-Davis

Former Chair of the NHCUCC Economic Justice Ministry Team, Former Chair of UCC Justice and Witness Ministries, Founding Member of the United Valley Interfaith Project

Capitalism Converts Christianity is a prophetic word from a passionate prophet. Rev. Fitzgerald hammers home the point that the church and Christians are largely comfortable in our golden chains, but Fitzgerald is clear that serving the god of wealth in this society is to create chaos and violence and death, including spiritual death for us Christians to whom he is appealing. It is a work of the heart, an inspired word. He calls us back to faithfulness and to the scriptures we would rather explain away—as sources of hope and life. It will make you think and maybe even pray. He provides powerful examples and well thought out study guides. It's a book Christians should take seriously.

Chad Hale, Pastor of Georgia Avenue Church, Founder of Urban Recipe and author of *Forgive Us This Day Our Daily Bread; Can a Comfortable Church Remember Jesus?*

James H. Cone wrote that "Any talk about God that fails to make God's liberation of the poor its starting point is not Christian". Walter

Brueggemann wrote of the importance of "interpretive literature concerning the interface of Gospel and economic reality." Fitzgerald's book has done both. It offers the reader a comprehensive analysis of the gospels pertaining to wealth and inequality, potential models for addressing major economic and justice issues, and the social forces and dynamics in play that make resistance to the power of capitalism challenging. The art of the book is that it written not as strictly political or economic work but more as a focused and direct conversation with the reader concerning the Christian Church and its disregard for the teachings and life of Jesus related to economic reality, the poor, and the outcast. I see this book as excellent for personal reflection, Adult Sunday School study, and Bible study groups.

Robert Doyle Jones

Former Coordinator of Mennonite Central Committee Voluntary Service Unit, Atlanta, Georgia

CAPITALISM CONVERTS CHRISTIANITY

Capitalism Converts Christianity

GRAY FITZGERALD

First Printing, 2025
Published by Santos Books LLC, Elizabethtown, PA 17022
Conrad L. Kanagy, Executive Publisher/CEO
ISBN: 979-8-9994186-0-9

This book is dedicated to “the least of these.”

CONTENTS

Preface

Capitalism Converts Christianity features a variety of writing styles and diverse stories. There are vignettes based on events in history, as well as narratives rooted in Biblical stories. There are stories from history and accounts from modern times. Saints are portrayed, but also sinners. There are stories of those who embrace God's call and others who remain defiantly locked in destructive lives. There are conversion stories that seem impossible but open our minds to possibilities we hadn't imagined. Considering the book's diverse range of writing and stories, I suspect that some readers may strongly resonate with certain parts but not others. Given this, if you start one section but don't feel that it is speaking to you, skip over to a different part of the book that is telling a different kind of story. You don't have to read straight through. I encourage you to pick and choose.

INTRODUCTION

In my late teenage years, I dated a girl whose mother would say unusual things at unexpected times. Sometimes, I would be invited to dinner with the family. During the meal, we would be having a conversation, and without warning, her mother would interject something totally unrelated to what we had been saying. It was frequently bizarre. Maybe in the middle of the conversation, she would calmly say, "The moon just jumped over a cow." The rest of us at the table would sit there as if she had just stated a perfectly normal, rational thing appropriate for the conversation. I think the family and I didn't have a hint of what to do or how to respond, so we just kept going with the conversation like she hadn't said a thing.

As someone attempting to follow Jesus, I have started to believe that we are participating in a similar experience in the Christian church. Our scripture contains extremely radical sections about money, wealth, and possessions. These parts of our scripture challenge us to a drastically different way of life from our mainline North American culture. They depict a life of faith that is completely opposite to the dominant values in our culture today. However, when we read or hear these scriptures, their extremely challenging nature seems to glide comfortably past our consciousness. We keep going as if we had never heard anything out of the ordinary.

"If you want to be perfect, go sell everything you own! Give the money to the poor, and you will have riches in heaven. Then come and be my follower." (Matthew 19:21) We hear or read this and sit placidly as if thinking, why of course, what could be more logical? What should be happening in our heads is, Yikes! Selling everything you own and giving it to the poor!!!??? Now, that is an outlandish idea as we clutch our wallets.

Jesus and his disciples were sitting in the temple near the offering box, watching people put in their offerings. A poor widow came and put in all she had, and Jesus said, "I tell you that this poor widow has put in more than all the others. Everyone else gave what they didn't need. But she is destitute and gave everything she had. Now she doesn't have a cent to live on." (Mark 12:43-4) What should be going through our heads is that she gave everything she had! Nothing to live on! Who in their right mind is going to do that?! Are we really following this guy?

It gets worse. In Luke, it says, "Jesus called together his twelve apostles and gave them complete power over all demons and diseases. Then he sent them to heal the sick and to tell about God's kingdom[1]. (For those who don't prefer the use of the language of kingdom, please see the extended endnote in the back.) He told them, "Don't take anything with you! Don't take a walking stick, a traveling bag, food, money, or even a change of clothes." (Luke 9:1-3) What leader in their right mind would send his followers out on a mission with absolutely nothing? Think about it. He sends these guys out with no extra clothes, provisions, money, or even a walking stick. Of course, we don't want to consider the possibility that he is not just sending the twelve out like this, but rather giving the same directions to all who claim to be following him. If that is the case, the 2.2 billion people worldwide who believe they are following this guy seem not to have gotten the memo about these bizarre teachings.

The book of Acts tells the story of the early church members who, after Jesus' death and resurrection, sold their property and donated the money to the disciples for the care of the poor. (Acts 2:44-45, Acts 4:34-35) Despite the demanding nature of these teachings, the followers began to embody what Jesus had taught and practiced.

At another time, Jesus teaches that "when you have done it unto one of the least of these, you have done it unto me." (Matthew 25:40)

It's hard to imagine what it would mean if those of us who claim to be Christian took this verse seriously and lived by this directive with regard to money. We would be transformed. The world would be transformed!

I've read, heard, or been exposed to these verses, possibly thousands of times. Have I ever thought seriously about giving everything I've got to the poor? Not a chance. The uncomfortable truth is that during most of my life, like the rest of us, I have wanted to have more instead of giving it all away. My wife and I certainly give, but selling everything and giving it to the poor is not something that has been on the table.

Most of us don't think of ourselves as being wealthy. My wife and I certainly don't. Some of the work I've done can lead to poverty rather than wealth. We live in a small condo of less than 1,000 square feet, own one car, and live relatively modestly. Like many of our age, we are concerned about whether we have enough to last out our senior years. However, Credit Suisse reports that if you have assets valued at $93,170, you are wealthier than 90% of the world. That definitely includes us. Another website shockingly puts us in the richest 2.4% of the global population.

For years, I've been railing against wealth inequality and the wealthiest one percent of this country. Then, to realize that compared to the world's population, I'm incredibly wealthy is embarrassing and disconcerting. And when I remember the scripture about it being easier for a camel to make it through the eye of a needle than for a rich person to enter the kingdom of God, I reluctantly conclude that it may be me. I'm not at all pleased that the camel and I are looking at the same predicament.

Disturbingly, I find that a book about Christian scripture and money needs to start with confession and an awareness of my own complicity. I certainly have thought of myself as a Christian. However, after focusing on these verses, it is probably more accurate to say that I'm a Christian in belief but not practice. Gandhi's statement, "We must become the change we want to see," confronts me. In short, a book about the Christian scriptures related to money and wealth is inevitably and uncomfortably a call to conversion for all of us.

Those of us who have some possessions are shocked by the radical nature of being called to give them away. We automatically realize that living out these scriptures demands sacrifice and puts us at significant risk, so of course, we strongly resist taking them seriously. However, if we turn the tables and imagine ourselves being the ones who are homeless, hungry, and struggling to survive, we would see these scriptures very differently.

If roles were reversed, and we found ourselves as parents living each day with a sense of desperation, unsure how we would feed our children, these verses would carry a different meaning. If we were the ones trapped in a subsistence existence, constantly at risk of falling through the cracks, we would see others living out these verses as a way to prevent that outcome. These verses could offer hope if we were uncertain about our survival. If those who are more well-off took steps to embody these scriptures of sharing, those of us struggling would gain more courage. As we received their generosity, our lives would transform. Our family would be less likely to fall through the cracks. The sharing from others would help support our survival.

If we were the ones benefiting from the generosity inspired by these scriptures, we would experience them as a Godsend. From this perspective, these verses wouldn't feel like a threat that we recoil from and resist. We would be thankful for and embrace the incarnation of these scriptures as a source of hope, relief, survival, freedom, justice, love, and salvation.

These challenging scriptures about money and possessions are linked to essential parts of the Bible. They are foundational for those core verses of loving God with all your heart, mind, and soul and loving your neighbor as yourself. (Mark 12:30-31) They undergird the Golden Rule of treating others in the way we want them to treat us. (Matthew 7:12) The more we are able to live out the scriptures about money, the closer we come to loving God, loving our neighbor, and doing unto others as we would have them do unto us.

These scriptures are shocking and counter-cultural for practically all cultures. Nevertheless, parts of the early church remained faithful to them, and later Christian monastic communities continued to follow this early tradition by incorporating vows of poverty into their shared lives. Given that these scriptures were so challenging, they have largely been abandoned throughout much of Christian history. However, at various times, there have been followers of Jesus who recognized the centrality of these teachings to our faith. They resurrected these verses and in doing so, became a light to the rest of us. This book will remember three of those saints.

In developing these teachings about money, wealth, and possessions, Jesus drew heavily from the Hebrew Bible/Old Testament, which provides powerful insights on justice related to money. All the prophets were very adamant about protecting and caring for the poor, sojourners, widows, orphans, and all who were marginalized. Jesus was grounded in these teachings, but it appears that in what he taught, he was concerned about the power of money and viewed it as a threat to one's relationship with God.

To address these issues, part one of this book begins with Jesus developing radical beliefs about money, property, and wealth that shattered cultural norms in his time and throughout history. What Jesus taught about money seems impossible to live. Why did God need these scriptures to be so countercultural? What was God's intent in leading Jesus to make these teachings so radical?

The first part of the book also tells the story of three people who incorporated these impractical, seemingly unattainable teachings into their lives. What do we learn about how the world changed when they chose to live according to these scriptures? Are we witnessing the reign of God breaking out when these ordinary people embody these extraordinary teachings?

In contrast, part two of the book recounts stories of horrendous crimes, including two genocides that we rarely hear about. In these accounts, we do not witness the reign of God, but rather the reign of the kingdom of evil. When the scriptural teachings about money are abandoned, ignored, or hidden, does greed run free to fuel the proliferation of atrocities?

Lurking in the background is the question: Does our economic system set the stage for these atrocities? Few of us spend much time pondering capitalism. We don't think about it because, like fish swimming in water, we are immersed in it. Part two of the book examines capitalism's role in shaping our culture, thoughts, and values. If we are shaped by the values of capitalism and those values contradict Christianity, what does that say about the quality of our faith?

Jesus starts his ministry by reading from Isaiah about the release of prisoners and captives. (Luke 4:16-19) Are those who imprison and enslave others, in fact, captives themselves? Are there ways in which we are all captives, sometimes without our being aware of it, and if so, how does that captivity relate to money? Are the scriptures about money related to the way Jesus frees the captives?

To avoid leaving the reader focused on the dark side of humanity, including mass crimes and genocide, the third part of the book explores the hope of transformation, or conversion, even in situations where such a change seems impossible. This part of the book doesn't deal with money like the first two parts, but engages us with the transformation of evil into good.

The book suggests that our transformation regarding money, wealth, and possessions is essential for establishing God's vision for creation, the kingdom of God. It proposes that every step we take in that direction transforms us and helps realize God's kingdom coming on earth. When we take these verses about money, wealth, and property seriously, we begin to be transformed. We are in a process of conversion. We are participating in establishing the reign of God.

NOTES

[1]The Biblical language of kingdom is offensive to some people and for good reason. Kingdoms were hierarchical, arbitrary, masculine, and non-inclusive. Typically, there was little to no regard for human life. Crimes against humanity were the norm, especially against the poorest and weakest. Ordinary citizens were powerless and had few to no rights. Authority was maintained through brutality. The language of kingdom generates images of ongoing palace intrigue ending in bloody conflict. Struggles for supremacy typically involved lies, betrayals, vengeance, and violence. Power and wealth were worshiped. Our Declaration of Independence was a declaration of freedom against the arbitrary, dictatorial, intrusive regime of a colonial monarchy. Given this history, how does one write a book that frequently refers to what Jesus called the kingdom of God when the word itself implies the opposite of anything Godly?

Moreover, in Jesus' day, everything an individual did was affected by the kingdom in which one lived. The word bristled with power and authority. In today's world, our lives are also strongly impacted by the government under which we live. However, except for a handful of countries located mainly in the Middle East, most of the world does not live under a functioning kingdom. Except for a few countries, the word kingdom has lost the power and authority it had in Jesus' day. Rather than bristling with authority, it more often conjures up pomp, pageantry, tabloids, gossip, celebrities, and reminders of history long past. Not only does the word hold negative connotations, but it's a relic.

Given the above, many Christians understandably prefer a different choice of words to convey Jesus' intent when using kingdom. Ada Maria Isasi-Diaz promoted the use of kin-dom, implying that we are called to grow into being la familia, the family of God. Another good choice is Dr. Martin Luther King Jr.'s term, the Beloved

Community. Realm or commonwealth chosen by others automatically reminds us of how sharing money, property, and wealth is integrated into God's desire for us.

Sometimes the concern around language is addressed by rewording kingdom in the Lord's Prayer. The Anglican Church of New Zealand has chosen to replace kingdom with commonwealth of peace and freedom. Neil Douglas-Klotz, working from the original Aramaic, translates it as reign of unity. In his version of the Lord's Prayer, Parker Palmer has changed it to reign of peace. All of these alternative offerings represent qualities of the life Jesus was teaching and help us to understand Jesus' meaning when he spoke about the kingdom of God.

Jesus used the language of kingdom, even though he was far more aware of the negative, malevolent aspects of traditional kingdoms than we are. He lived under the cruelty and brutality of the Roman Empire. The Roman Empire may have functioned differently from a monarchy for those at the top of the power structure. Still, for the Hebrew people who were at the bottom, it functioned like an arbitrary, dictatorial, oppressive, occupying kingdom. Jesus was aware of rampant Roman executions long before his own crucifixion.

Jesus' way of dealing with the word was to completely change the meaning. He adopted the kingdom language but promptly picked the word up like a bucket, turned it upside down, and dumped out its traditional meaning. He dumped out the male-dominated hierarchy along with the implications of oppression, war, injustice, violence, and victimization of the poorest. Then, he filled the word with a new vision of how to live on Earth. He created a new word out of the shell of an old word.

In filling kingdom with new meaning, Jesus was projecting a vision of a kingdom different from any ever imagined. It was the polar opposite of a traditional kingdom. He gave the people (and us) the reign of God as God imagined and desired it. He promoted God's vision for a new creation distinct from any earthly concept it had held before. He called the people to imagine and live in a reality different from the culture in which they were immersed.

Even Jesus' disciples had trouble grasping that he had abandoned the conventional meaning. They persisted in asking Jesus questions that implied they were still thinking of a traditional kingdom. Jesus was setting up the kingdom of God over and against all other kingdoms. There were these different kingdoms, and then there was God's kingdom.

It appears Jesus didn't put energy into finding the perfect word. His focus was on redefining and living in a new kind of kingdom. Possibly, Jesus was even glad the disciples had difficulty understanding his concept of the new word he was creating out of the old one. The more the disciples stumbled over the new meaning, the more they were forced to struggle with what Jesus was teaching. Trying to comprehend his confusing concept of kingdom was part of how they grew. Maybe it's good that we also stumble over the word and look for different words or phrases as we attempt to absorb the meaning.

The Hebrew people Jesus was speaking to weren't concerned about the negative associations that many of us have about the language of kingdom. For them, it was simple. They hated the Roman Empire but desperately wanted a return to a replica of King David's reign, which had been their high point in history. They wanted a powerful king to protect them against foreigners like the Romans and restore their former independence and glory. They weren't against kingdoms. They wanted their kingdom.

That's not what they got. Jesus challenged the Hebrew people (and us) to live into God's vision of a world never conceived. For the Hebrew people who were suffering under Roman rule while yearning for a repeat of the Davidic reign, he gave them God's kingdom. Although the original meaning of the word implied the opposite of anything Godly, he filled it with God's vision for humanity. Then, of course, he lived the vision.

In the first three gospels, the word kingdom is used approximately 117 times, most often by Jesus. Frequently, Jesus would say something like, "The kingdom of God is like...." For Jesus, the kingdom of God was the unifying concept of his ministry. Kingdom was the concept Jesus used to draw all his stories, parables, healings, interactions, and teachings toward a unified vision of what he called the kingdom of God. Even when he wasn't using the word, Jesus was teaching and modeling how to bring into fruition the kingdom of God.

Arguably, there is no perfect word to replace kingdom. Given that all of Jesus' ministry points toward the kingdom of God, no one word or short phrase adequately captures the full meaning of what Jesus was communicating. All the alternatives are helpful and depict part of what Jesus meant by kingdom, but they are insufficient by themselves. Jesus didn't have a perfect metaphor. Neither do we. Given the above, this book will stay with the traditional language of kingdom.

PART ONE

This book begins with Jesus in the desert, beset by temptation, struggling to be faithful to God's call and the path. Following that, we remember three eccentrics, Francis of Assisi, John Woolman, and Dorothy Day, who actually took Jesus seriously about living the seemingly impossible scriptures about possessions and wealth. They are among the minority who recognized life in these verses and wholeheartedly embraced them. These extraordinary people believed the true path to God was found in responding to these scriptures, no matter how irrational and demanding they seemed. They grasped that to love in the way Jesus taught and lived, their lives had to be transformed by these teachings about money and wealth. Furthermore, they were willing to make the sacrifices needed to follow that path. They found God through these scriptures.

For those attempting to follow Jesus, these three are models; they are guides to our faith. Reflecting that they lived these challenging scriptures so faithfully gives us hope that we, too, can move closer to that path. These guides call us to allow ourselves to be challenged by these verses instead of dismissing them. Very few have lived these difficult parts of the gospel as faithfully as these three. Very few will, but we can accept that they lead us toward the truth of our faith and follow them in moving closer to the light they offer. Any step we take to follow their example transforms us and the world.

| one |

Jesus Chooses Poverty Over Wealth

Again, the devil took him to a very high mountain and showed him all the kingdoms of the world and their splendor. "All this I will give you," he said, "if you will bow down and worship me."

Jesus said to him, "Away from me, Satan! For it is written: 'Worship the Lord your God, and serve him only.'"

Then the devil left him, and angels came and attended him. (Matthew 4:8-11)

Jesus Chooses the Foolishness of God

When I was younger, I would read these verses about the temptation of Jesus and think, of course, Jesus knew what was going on all the time. It was easy for him to see through what evil was attempting to do. It would have been a piece of cake for him. After all, this was Jesus we are talking about. That's not what I think now. I think this was an extremely difficult time for Jesus, and he was very vulnerable to these temptations. Just before the temptation, the scriptures have Jesus coming from his baptism, where he has seen God's Spirit descending on him like a dove. He has heard a voice saying, "This is my beloved Son, in whom I am well pleased." (Matthew 3:17) It seems from this experience, Jesus was beginning to realize he was the long-awaited Messiah.

Jesus grew up surrounded by people who expected the Messiah to be a king in the model of Saul, David, and Solomon. They particularly saw David as the type of Messiah for whom they yearned.

David had been king when Israel was at the height of its glory. He was admired as a powerful military leader who protected the people from their enemies. He brought security to a people who longed for that. It was a time when the people were relatively unified. David was a flawed man who made mistakes but was still seen as a leader faithful to their God. His reign was a time of relative safety and strength. The Hebrew people saw it as a time that represented what they wanted their lives to be.

In contrast, during Jesus' time, the people were occupied, dominated, demeaned, and exploited by the Romans. They had no self-determination or autonomy. They hated the occupation. Therefore, for Jesus to consider fulfilling the role of an earthly ruler with David as a model to save them from their suffering would appear to be an automatic consideration. In Hebrew thought, there was no other model for a different kind of Messiah.

The temptation presented to Jesus was that if he worshiped the tempter, he would be given all the kingdoms he could see from the mountaintop. The tempter offered a power similar to being president. It was the power to order people to do things and have them carry it out. In Jesus' time, the authority would have been more far-reaching than that of a president, as there would have been no checks and balances. It would have been the power of a dictator to arrange things in the way he thought best. Automatically, great wealth would have accompanied this position. So, in this scenario, Jesus would have had both political and economic power.

Jesus was just coming out of his baptism. If the temptations were couched in terms of all the good things he could do if he were an earthly ruler, that would seem consistent with his call. He would have had the worldly power and wealth not only to rule but to rule out of justice as the prophets had taught. The temptation is that he could have had the earthly power to order things done to create a kingdom that would follow God's teachings.

Jesus would have been highly aware of the injustice and the cruelty of the Roman Empire. He had seen crucifixions and was fully aware of the tortures and imprisonments the Romans inflicted on the people. He was aware of the economic injustices imposed by the Romans and the upper classes. He knew his people were oppressed, and he longed for their release. He yearned to free them from their sufferings. In his struggle to be faithful and discern his path, it would have been natural to consider the possibility of having earthly power to enact these reforms.

It seems logical that as these temptations were besetting Jesus, he wasn't aware that some of these options were temptations. They could have seemed like alternative opportunities for ways to be faithful to God and to fulfill God's call. Evil doesn't come to us and announce, "I'm the source of all evil. Worship me." Evil is always more cunning, hidden, and deceptive. For Jesus, being a worldly ruler who sought to do good with earthly power could have appeared to be a viable way to respond to God's call.

The biblical story is a concise, black-and-white, matter-of-fact account of what happened. These few sentences of scripture about the temptations are probably a shortened, summarized version of days of struggle. Probably, the experience was a more protracted time of prayer, discernment, and searching in which there were many possibilities and pulls in different directions. Undoubtedly, Jesus was searching for clarity about fulfilling God's blessing and making sense of the call he had experienced at his baptism. We imagine that as Jesus was in the turmoil of being beset by the temptations, he didn't always know what God was and what was evil. The scriptures likely provide us with the conclusion of the struggle. At that point, Jesus could clearly distinguish between God and evil, but when he was in the midst of it, the struggle was probably not the case.

Only after an arduous struggle was Jesus able to see clearly that he was not called to be an earthly king and establish a traditional kingdom. Perhaps it was only after much difficulty and discernment that he realized the possibility of being a logical, earthly ruler was not coming from God, but from evil. At this point, he could see that choosing to be an earthly ruler would have been abandoning what God was asking him to do and worshiping evil. At this point, he was clear to emphatically command, "Go away, Satan! The scriptures say: 'Worship the Lord your God and serve only him!'" (Matthew 4:10)

The Narrow Gate Opens an Unseen Way

To become an earthly king would have been a far more logical, practical, and seemingly realistic path for Jesus than the call he accepted. It would have been far easier for him and the people to understand a messiah like David. The call Jesus accepted, however, was the polar opposite of being an earthly king. It was an unconventional, illogical choice to the point of being incomprehensible. By the world's values, it was a foolish decision.

It appears that Jesus not only taught, giving away everything, but that he lived what he taught. He chose the route of not having anywhere to lay his head. (Luke 9:58) We have no evidence that he owned anything. His disciples said they had left all to follow him. (Matthew 19:27). We have to assume that he was living out his words that if you have two cloaks, give one away to someone who has none. (Luke 3:11) We have to assume that Jesus had already given away his belongings, as he told the rich young ruler to do. (Mark 10:17-27) Toward the end of his ministry, he sent his disciples out without supplies. (Lk. 9:1-3) If Jesus didn't live out these teachings, one would have to conclude that Jesus himself was a hypocrite. From all we can see, he felt led to choose a life of poverty.

The path he felt called to could not have been more different from that of an earthly king with the wealth, power, authority, and privileges that come with that position. He had no worldly power to change anything. He lived and taught a downward spiritual journey of humility, self-effacement, and service. He chose the polar opposite of the pomp and power of an earthly ruler. This was definitely a different kind of kingdom.

Given the people's expectations of what the Messiah would be and that Jesus had been immersed in those same expectations, it's remarkable that he could discern that he was being led on such a different, irrational, obscure, counter-cultural path. Equally astounding is that, having had the wisdom to see how God was leading him, he then dared to make such a radical, difficult choice and live it out.

He separated himself from wealth and power while becoming completely reliant on God. He rejected earthly ways of understanding power and put himself on an uncharted path that would redefine the Messiah, God's power, and God's kingdom.

Through rejecting the world's values, Jesus was able to be malleable and compliant to God's leading. He forfeited the world's concept of power, placing him in a position to be a conduit for a completely different kind of power. His choices made him an open channel for spiritual power. God now had a willing subject to do the things God always wants to do on earth.

Jesus' rejection of a worldly kingdom allowed God and God's power to enter into the world through him. It allowed God's Spirit to be present in the world to heal, reconcile, and teach. Through Jesus, God was able to be on earth, repairing the breaches of hate and confronting the greed that caused such wounds. Jesus was now able to be a conduit of love, peace, and justice. His life was a channel of truth and wisdom. He offered salvation, not just salvation after death, but salvation from the ways we create hell on earth. Again and again, people were astounded at the power that came through him, but it was a very different kind of power than would come from an earthly king.

In the temptations, Jesus was given a vision of a unique kingdom with the potential to lead to a different kind of world. The vision of the kingdom God gave Jesus astoundingly did not value money and wealth in the way the world values them. The power of this kingdom is not seen or even imagined by the world. In rejecting the temptation of a worldly kingdom and in his teachings about money, wealth, and property, Jesus was pointing God's creation in a direction that had not been imagined before. In this kingdom, Jesus' power increases with a lack of wealth.

Rejecting the temptation of wealth and worldly power made a way for Jesus not only to challenge the people of his time but also to challenge and lead people through the millennia to a different kind of kingdom and a different kind of power. It opened people's lives and hearts to an incredible, saving, spiritual power through the centuries.

If Jesus had chosen the array of kingdoms offered by evil, we don't know if that would have ever come to fruition. Even if it had been realized, the old concept of kingdom would have just been a traditional king or messiah for the Hebrew people for a few decades. In contrast, Jesus was pointing not only the Hebrew people but the world toward a concept of an infinitely larger vision of the Kingdom of God, intended for all people for all time. Tragically, we have largely abandoned his vision. The state of today's world is evidence of that.

Jesus wanted the same social reforms that the prophets wanted. But he knew that it didn't happen just with changes of laws, policy, and institutions. He knew real change was rooted in a transformation of the heart through conversion.

| two |

The Saint Who Gave It All to the Poor

A man came to Jesus and asked, "Teacher, what good thing must I do to have eternal life?" Jesus said to him, "Why do you ask me about what is good? Only God is good. If you want to have eternal life, you must obey his commandments." "Which ones?" the man asked. Jesus answered, "Do not murder. Be faithful in marriage. Do not steal. Do not tell lies about others. Respect your father and mother. And love others as much as you love yourself." The young man said, "I have obeyed all of these. What else must I do?" Jesus replied, "If you want to be perfect, go sell everything you own! Give the money to the poor, and you will have riches in heaven. Then come and be my follower." (Matthew 19:16-27)

Living the Scriptures that Seem Impossible to Live

In Matthew 19, Mark 10, and Luke 18, we read what has commonly been called the story of the Rich Young Ruler. It is a story of a man who has lived an exemplary life, asking Jesus what he must do to have eternal life. The young man has followed all the commandments, including loving others as he loves himself. Any synagogue or church would be happy to welcome this man as a member. Jesus tells him, "If you want to be perfect, go sell everything you own! Give the money to the poor, and you will have riches in heaven." In our contemporary society, imagine the uproar if religious leaders were to sincerely preach and teach this to their congregants. It wouldn't matter whether the church was fundamentalist, evangelical, conservative, or mainline. It would be quite entertaining to be an outsider and watch a pastor urging his/her congregants to follow this scripture.

The early Christian church, monasteries, and convents have a history of living out these verses. But what could be more diametrically different from our present-day North American culture than selling everything one owns and giving it to the poor?

The Rich Young Ruler scripture is not an isolated passage. In Luke 12, we read, "Sell your possessions and give to the poor. Provide purses for yourselves that will not wear out, a treasure in heaven that will never fail, where no thief comes near, and no moth destroys." There is the story of what is called "The Widow's Mite" mentioned in the introduction. "A poor widow put into the offering all she had, and Jesus said, I tell you that this poor widow has put in more than all the others. Everyone else gave what they didn't need. But she is destitute and gave everything she had. Now she doesn't have a cent to live on." (Mark 12:43) The verses about not worrying about tomorrow (Luke 12:22-26) have a similar connotation as does the scripture about money being the root of all evil. (I Timothy 6:10) There are many Christian scriptures that don't have precisely the same words but are similar in meaning. Numerous Hebrew scriptures don't go quite this far but point in the same direction.

It's hard to state how outrageous these scriptures are to the culture of this country, or any country for that matter. If anyone but Jesus had said these things, we would be writing them off as deranged. Picture walking into a Wall Street office and announcing to the people there that they should sell everything they own and give it to the poor. Or, suppose a business consultant were to advise a corporate board to divest all their assets and give the proceeds to the poor.

It's not just the business world that would be shocked by these spiritual directives. What would happen in your household if you declared that, as a family, you were going to sell all that you had and give it to the poor? If a politician campaigned to sell all that we have and give it to the poor, we would think that deranged individual needed to get back on their psychiatric meds. Obviously, when we stop to think about these verses and consider living them out, they are shocking. Yet somehow, contrary to all logic, 2.2 billion people worldwide claim to be following the guy who taught these bizarre, irrational, impossible directives. What are those of us who understand ourselves to be part of that 2.2 billion thinking!?

These scriptures seem not only unrealistic but impossible and unattainable. However, the miracle is that some people did the unthinkable and lived them out, apparently starting with Jesus himself. It seems improbable that he asked the rich young ruler to do something he wasn't doing. Matthew, Mark, and Luke all have verses where the disciples tell Jesus they have left everything to follow him. (Matthew 19:27) In Acts, it says that "The group of followers all felt the same way about everything. None of them claimed that their possessions were their own, and they shared everything they had with each other. In a powerful way, the apostles told everyone that the Lord Jesus was now alive. God greatly blessed his followers, and no one went in need of anything." (Acts 4:32-35) It appears that at least part of the early church practiced these scriptures.

That tradition continued when, approximately 300 years after Jesus, the church joined with the Roman Empire. Some people became what we call the Desert Fathers and Mothers, who left the cities, moved into remote areas, and chose to live in poverty. They had loosely formed communities in which individuals supported each other but essentially chose to live with an absolute minimum of possessions. They believed this kind of relationship with a minimum of money and property was a critical part of following Jesus.

These desert fathers and mothers were the forerunners of Christian communities and religious orders, which frequently had a vow of poverty as a requirement for membership. These religious orders had different ways of defining and living out what poverty meant. The extent to which these communities lived out their vows of poverty varied greatly from community to community and depended on the time in their history. For some of these communities, poverty turned into wealth, and the earlier vows became meaningless. However, there were moments when these seemingly impossible vows were lived out in ways beyond our comprehension. One of those moments occurred when Saint Francis, one of the most faithful saints of all time, founded the Order of the Brothers Minor, more commonly known today as the Franciscans.

The people who have written about Francis usually have low regard for Francis' father. Here, we will give Francis' father more of a voice to state his perspective of how he experienced the highly atypical role of being the father of a young man in the process of becoming a saint.

It's Hell Being the Father of a Saint

You don't know me. I'm Peter Bernardone. I lived in the little town of Assisi, in Italy, 800 years ago. You probably know my son, the saint. They called him St Francis. St. Francis of Assisi. I called him Saint Crazy. They certainly didn't call me a saint. They called me the pompous, big-headed Bernardone, father of the saint.

We lived in Assisi, Italy, in the 1200s. I was what, in your culture, you call a self-made man. I was one of the most prominent and successful cloth merchants in the whole of Italy. My grandparents were peasants. Peasants, mind you. Nobodies. But at the precise time when we lived, trade between different parts of Europe was beginning to expand. It hadn't been possible in the centuries before, but during this time, if you had a little bit of money and you were really sharp, you could buy and sell and make more.

I was very sharp, and I took advantage of every opening. I bought, sold, and traveled to buy and trade more, maybe cheated a bit now and then. For this town, during the time I lived in, I made it big, quick. I went from being a nobody, from being everybody's underling to being somebody. We had our noble families with all their inherited wealth and land, but in my time, a few of us were becoming wealthy in a different way.

It even reached a point where the nobles needed us. The nobles who had always lorded it over all of us now were coming to us for help. Traditionally, they sponsored the town's big yearly festivals. Now, though, sometimes they were starting to come up a little short of the money needed for these festivals. They didn't like it; they were embarrassed, but they started coming to some of us who were now doing well financially. A few of us joined forces with the nobles and began to help sponsor these large festivals, and we gained status as a result. One might even say we were a little smug about it. A few of us weren't nobodies anymore. It was tense, and there were rivalries, but we were pushing our way in. Francis was to be the lever for our family to push our way in further.

I had big plans for Francis. I had plans for him to come into the business, and not only that, but to gain a position in running the town. I planned for him to expand our influence and our family's power, not only in Assisi but in this whole area. I had made significant steps, and it was going to be his role to expand our name and position. I had it all set up. The way was prepared.

It started well. He was very competent. He got along with others better than I did. I used to take him on business trips to France. He did great! He learned the language quickly, and people loved him. Back in the store in Assisi, he was a natural. I was excited that everything was going perfectly according to my plan. I could just imagine how it was going to unfold.

As a young person, he liked to party a lot with the other young people around here. They loved him. He was outgoing and what you would call the life of the party. Of course, part of the reason he was the life of the party was because he was doing it with my money. He spent my money very freely on throwing parties and carousing around with these kids. I didn't like him spending all that money, but there was an upside. He was spending it on the right people. These were the children of the nobles and other wealthy merchants. These were the kids who were going to be running things around here in a few years. I didn't like that he was spending so much of my money on these parties, but it did fit with my plan for his future. Our future! I let that money go.

There was this other oddity with money, though. He started giving money to beggars. Money for parties and his friends, OK. Money for beggars!? What do we get out of that?

And then there were his go-to war escapades. At that time, there were these useless wars with neighboring towns. Assisi and the nearby village of Perugia went to war. Who knows over what, but Francis went to fight with the others. I outfitted him. Well, he ended up getting captured and was a prisoner for a year. That was embarrassing. I paid a lot to get him released, I'll tell you.

Then, there was another time he was going to go to war. He spent a considerable amount of time and money preparing for that war. I bought the horse, armor, and all that stuff necessary to go to war. After weeks of him talking and parading around here and lots of talk about going to war, he and the others from Assisi finally left. However, after only one night on the road, he turns around and came back here to Assisi. We never did get the straight story on that, but again, it was pretty embarrassing.

About this time, the real craziness started. Francis started working less and less. I didn't have a clue when he was going to work or not. He would spend time out in the forests, nearby chapels, or caves. Who knows what he was doing? Communing with God or whatever. He certainly wasn't communing with me. Worse than that, when he was around here, he was wasting more money than ever on the beggars. I was not happy.

Then there was the story of when he went to Rome. While there, he went to the piazza in front of the great basilica in Rome, where a lot of people were out begging. He got one of the beggars aside and exchanged clothes with him. Then, he took the beggar's place and begged in the piazza for the whole day! My son!!! Begging!!! In rags. Out in public. What in the world was going on in my son's head?

You've all heard about Francis and the leper. Francis was out on his horse on the road near Assisi when he rounded a turn and was face to face with a leper. He was terrified of lepers, absolutely petrified, so immediately, he jerked his horse around and started off at a gallop in the other direction. The story we heard is that he became so ashamed of his cowardice that he turned back toward the leper, went up to him, got off his horse, kissed the leper's hand, and gave him all the money he had with him. Who goes around kissing a leper's hand like he's some bishop or something?

None of us had a clue what was happening with him. In later years, people talked about this series of experiences as being part of his conversion. Well, I'm a merchant. I buy, sell, and trade. I don't know anything about spiritual experiences and conversions. These people say that these experiences were of the old person dying and a new person being born. I didn't want the old person to die. That old person was more like me. Just give me back my fun-loving, partying, drinking, carousing, charismatic, spendthrift son. This new person wants rags, poverty, beggars, and lepers. What kind of a new person is that? This is a son I don't recognize.

All this had to come to some kind of ending. One day, when I wasn't there, he went into the store, took a lot of fabric, put it on his horse, and went to a market in a neighboring town. He sold not only the fabric but also the horse, then went to one of the chapels he frequented and tried to give the money to the priest. The priest knew something was wrong and wouldn't accept it. Francis threw the money on a pew and left.

I eventually got the money back, but no more of this nonsense for me. No more patience from me. I went to the bishop and told him that I wanted it to be official that Francis would get no inheritance from me. I needed to make sure that he couldn't mess me up any more than he had. I told the bishop I wanted this settled. We set a date for Francis, the bishop, and me to meet in the town's main piazza. The whole village heard about it and was gossiping for days. So, when we got there, of course, everyone was there for the big show. The show they wanted to see was for me to be embarrassed and humiliated.

The bishop asked Francis if he would publicly renounce all his inheritance from me. Francis stood there, not saying a word. Then he went inside the bishop's palace. Very soon, he came back out--- completely nude, holding his clothes in his hands along with the little bit of money he had left. He handed it all to me and said to everyone, "Until this time, I have called Peter Bernardone my father, but now I desire to serve God. This is why I'm returning to him this money, as well as my clothing and all that I have from him. From now going on,I desire to say nothing else than 'Our Father, who art in heaven." I grabbed the stuff he was handing me and marched out of there. The townspeople had gotten the show they came for.

The bishop, man of God that he was, didn't offer any of his clothes to Francis but instead told his gardener to give Francis something old of his to cover himself. People said that Francis left joyfully. There he was in hand-me-down clothes from a gardener, with no place to live, no money, and no way of providing for himself. Yet he left, singing, happy, and joyful. I raised a lunatic!

So, before you go judging me -- how would you have liked raising the saint? If you were the parent, what would you have done when he was doing nothing productive and giving away all your money? How would you like your child to take off the proper clothes you had provided, put on rags, and start begging in the streets? What would you have done when he started spending all his time out in the woods, caves, and chapels and then came home looking like a madman with the children chasing and teasing him?

Of course, at this point, no one was calling him a saint. At this point, they were all saying what I was saying: this guy's crazy. He didn't care. He started working on restoring one of the chapels near Assisi. He would beg for materials, sometimes for food. He would come into Assisi and sometimes preach in the piazzas. People laughed and made fun of him. He just kept on, apparently happy.

Then, strangely, it began to change. A few people started to help a little. Then more. There was something about him that attracted people. It started slowly, but some seemed to find themselves even admiring him a bit. Not me. We didn't see each other much anymore, but occasionally, our paths would cross out in the streets, and when we did, I told him what an ingrate he was. I berated him and told him he was a terrible son. I yelled at him out in the street.

But more and more, some of the others were attracted to him. Some of them pitched in on the work on the chapel. I didn't talk to the people about this, but my wife talked with them. She told me that when they work out there, he is happy. He even sings. He has rags for clothes and doesn't know where his food is coming from, but he sings. She said people enjoy working with him.

If this wasn't enough, it got even more bizarre. Instead of just helping him, a few of the young people around here started accepting his way of life. They joined him and lived out there with him. It began with a few of the young guys. Now, get this. Before they could join him in this community they were forming, they had to give away all their possessions. They had to give it all to the poor!!! They sometimes had a big celebration of giving away their wealth. Most of the young guys who joined him were from well-to-do families. They gave up a lot!! Their families were like mine. They didn't understand it and were sometimes very angry. Craziness was contagious. However, in the minds of his followers, I believe they saw this outward renunciation of wealth as reflecting their inner conversion and transformation. Francis believed that to follow God, one needed to be changed. Not a change I would make, I tell you.

Then, there was a teenage girl who came from nobility who wanted to join. That caused a massive fight in her family. Then, her younger sister wanted to join. It was messy. They beat and threatened her. But in the end, both girls stayed with the community. Maybe a third sister came; I can't remember. In the end, a new group was formed for the women with their own separate convent.

During this time, my wife kept telling me that they were happy and joyful. How can you be joyful when you don't own anything? It defies all logic. It turns the world upside down.

They were creating a whole new social order. Our entire society around here was starting to change because of what they were doing. Some families were torn apart, but others felt like some of the changes were good. I wasn't changing. When I ran into him in the street, I still told him what a terrible son he was.

With all these new people coming in, a rule was needed for how they were to live. All these religious communities have a rule. I guess it's what guides their life and mission. So, they tell me the core of Francis' rule came from three scriptures. The first went something like, if you wish to be perfect, go and sell all your possessions, give the money to the poor, and you will have treasure in heaven, then come, follow me. (Matthew 19:21). Sell everything and give it to the poor. That's a recipe for disaster! My grandparents were peasants, and now he wants to be more destitute than they were. That would be my worst nightmare!

A second scripture of their so-called rule was one in which Jesus sent his disciples out and told them not to take anything for their journey. He sent them out on their mission and told them not to take a staff, no bag, no food, no money, not even an extra tunic. He was sending people on a mission with no provisions, no change of clothes, and no money. No one can live out madness like these verses. Why in the world would people follow a Jesus who said things like this? Who would be so crazy? Right, my son would be so deranged.

The last verse at the core of their rule was, "If any want to become my followers, let them deny themselves, take up their cross, and follow me. Those who want to save their life will lose it, and those who lose their life for my sake will find it. For what will it profit them if they gain the whole world but forfeit their life? Or what will they give in return for their life?" (Matthew.16:24-26) Well, this last scripture is a little better. It's not so concrete, know what I mean? It's vague. You can find a bit more wiggle room.

After I heard about this ridiculous rule, I ran into Francis in the street. Along with my usual tirade about what an ungrateful son he was, I also asked him how he could possibly think that people were going to commit to his absurd, outrageous rule. Maybe a few of the most crazed fanatics around here might hold to it, but most people aren't going to live like that. I told him he was trying to make people do the impossible.

Exasperated, I blurted, "Come to your senses, boy. Come back and make something of yourself. Go to Mass on Sundays; put a little in the collection. You can even give some to the beggars, but then come back and have a good life working with me. Let's be something in this town! Living with beggars and lepers is no life. Think about it. Wake up."

He was quiet. Finally, he replied. "People are desperate for the truth. They're lost, and I'm showing them the way. Someone has to light their way."

"Francis, that talk doesn't feed anybody. You can't live on truth and light. Truth and light don't feed your belly, put a roof over your head, or keep you warm in the winter. Be realistic, son!"

"People need the truth." Francis was quiet again for a second before continuing.

"Father, I'm not sure you will understand this now, but I hope someday you will feel the Lord's love as I have. Until then, please try to understand this: you sell people cloth for their bodies, but what is clothing for the body when the soul is starving? What is a bolt of colored fabric to a person whose soul is in darkness? I don't want to sell people fabric; I want to give them food for their souls—to give them what they most hunger for."

Frustrated, I responded, "What happens when the belly is empty, the babies are crying, and there is nothing to give them?

"I'm not just giving them a rule for a religious community but a path that gives what in the deepest part of their hearts they most hunger for. They want to experience God's love in their hearts and then share that love with the world. They want to be connected to the creator of all life."

In total frustration, I shouted, "Live in the real world, Francis! Live in the real world!"

"Your world is not the real world, Father. I am living in the real world. I don't want to live in your world. That's exactly what I don't want to do. I've left this world and its values behind. I've left what appears to be real to you."

This conversation was going nowhere. I was shaking. "This so-called path you are on is a path straight to misery," I screamed. "Open your eyes!" But he was beyond reason. I stopped wasting my time and returned to my business, which was my true path. It's hell being the father of a saint.

At some point, his community worked less repairing chapels and began to attend more to the beggars and the lepers. I can tell you that no one else was helping those people. Definitely, I wasn't. I don't understand why they wanted to fool with them. Well, I guess those beggars and lepers felt differently about it than me. But he and his companions sought them out. I think they gave them love in the ways they could. My wife said that people started to think about and understand love differently than they had before. They began to think differently about what it meant to be a person of God.

Francis and his companions didn't just beg. They actually worked most of the time. They would work in the skill or trade they had before they joined his order, or work in the fields for the peasants. However, here's the remarkable part: when they worked, they wouldn't accept payment for their labor. They would only take food. Maybe it was just food for the day; I don't know. I just know it was ridiculous. Francis said that money was evil. He wouldn't touch it. How could I, of all people, have had a son who hates money!? A son who thinks money is evil! I can't tell you how incomprehensible that is to me. But that's the way they lived. And if he thinks money is evil, what does he think of me? Am I evil?

Increasingly, people followed and supported them. They were a religious order by now, and by the authority of the Pope, many young people were joining. People were joining from other places in Italy and from Europe. The order was proliferating. It later turned out to be a problem. These people joining must have had some kind of romantic fantasies about what this life was like because once they got in, most weren't too happy and became grumblers and complainers. That life was too hard for them. No surprise to me.

However, his core companions stayed; they remained loyal to the rule. And the people around here in Assisi seemed to admire him more and more. They continued to respect and support him. My wife said they felt a spirit in him and his companions different from anything they had ever known. She said he was like a light that seemed to spread. Something kinder, gentler. People seemed to accept each other more.

Not me! I stayed hard as a rock toward him. I still yelled at him if I saw him. My wife said it hurt him badly. So that he could stand it, he got help. He would find a beggar in the street to bless him in my place. He would tell the beggar, "Take the place of my father. When I'm in the street, and you see Bernardone cursing me, if I say, bless me, my father, then you bless me in his place. Make the sign of the cross over me and bless me in his place." So, there we were in the street: the saint, the beggar, and me. Me cursing, -- the beggar blessing, -- and Francis in the middle. It was quite a scene we put on.

But then, he and his companions helped negotiate peace in the city and surrounding area. It's hard to understand, but remember, I told you there was a war between Assisi and Perugia. Hate and anger lingered from that. It was complicated because some people from Assisi fought with Perugia. Others here didn't forget that. And despite the fact that the nobility and the merchants occasionally worked together, we really hated each other. I don't know how he did it, but Francis helped broker a peace agreement between these feuding factions. He brought peace to a lot of people and in a lot of situations. -- But peace never came to the two of us.

He even went on a mission to stop the Crusades. Imagine! The bloody Crusade wars had been ongoing for a century. And my son, the ragamuffin, and a few of his friends set out to stop this war. They were gone for a long time. Maybe it was around a couple of years. He first tried to get the Crusaders to stop. That was unsuccessful. Then, somehow, he managed to make his way over to the other side, through all the armed forces and chaos, until he eventually reached the Sultan, who was the commander of all the Muslim armies. Some say he even tried to convert the Sultan. Fat chance of that happening. I really would like to know, though, what the Sultan thought of this strange group of young guys in rags, with no authority from anyone-- except their God, coming to him wanting to end this war that had been going on for a century. I really wonder what was going on in the Sultan's head. I wouldn't say it to Francis, but trying to make peace to end that bloody, senseless butchery was a noble act.

After this, the world began to cave in on Francis. The living conditions on this trip had been terrible. His health began to fail. He began to go blind, and the others had to take care of him. The order that he created was rebelling. They said the rule was too strict, and they wanted to change it. Some of them were starting to be very angry and critical of him. He didn't understand it. It hurt him– a lot. He didn't know why they joined and then got angry and wanted to change what they had committed to. He couldn't go back on his commitment to God. It was conflicted, complicated, and messy.

I don't remember when it started, but for a long time, people had been talking about him being a saint.

When he was young, I wanted him to be important in Assisi. I wanted him to extend the power of our family around Assisi. Now, in a different way, he was influential in many parts of Europe. Through the centuries, he influenced people all over the world. Here we are eight centuries later, and we are still talking about the poor man from Assisi. I don't understand it. How is it that he didn't own a thing but was so incredibly influential? I try to comprehend it, but it escapes me.

Saint or no saint, he was still human. He was sick and dying, and the people in the order were rebelling and angry. I think they hurt him even more than I had. I didn't see him during this time. Many people around here have changed. One could say they became new people because of Francis. They became better people. They began to think and live differently. They saw the world through a new lens because of him. They loved more fully.

I thought about him a lot. These knights around here wound and hurt each other with their lances and swords. My son and I wounded each other in a different way. I wanted him to commit to my values and my way. He chose the precise opposite of my way. Of course, I felt rejected. I wanted him to love what I loved, to want what I wanted. He wanted God and poverty. It hurt me. Maybe the world gained a saint. But I'm his father; I lost my son. So, I called him an ungrateful wretch whenever I got the chance.

Other people here changed. I wish I could have changed. Toward the end, when some of these people in his order started rejecting and hurting him, maybe I could have changed. When he was dying, I wish I had given in and been more caring as a father. He was sick, dying, feeling rejected, and depressed--I wish I could have given him more. I'm not talking about one of those big-time all-or-nothing about-face conversions, but I wish I could have softened a little. I wish I had gone to see him in those last days. I wish I had hugged him.[1]

Inside the Chrysalis

Surely Francis had been baptized at birth, but the conversion he went through as a young adult was a baptismal experience. It was a washing away of the old, making way for the new. It was a death followed by rebirth and a new life. It's hard to imagine a more complete death and rebirth in a person's life than the one Francis went through.

No one would have accused Francis of being a saint in his early life. During his late teens and early twenties, he was the equivalent of a playboy for that time and culture. He was the son of one of the wealthiest men in Assisi, and his father was willing to provide money for the merrymaking. He was fun and entertaining and entered into this life with gusto, enthusiasm, and enjoyment. One biographer says "He was forever in the streets with his companions, compelling attention by his extravagant or fantastic attire. Even at night, the joyous company kept up their merrymakings, causing the town to ring with their noisy songs."[ii] In his early adulthood, Francis reminds one more of the Prodigal Son than of a saint.

However, there was something in Francis that was pulling him in a different direction. Not all at once, but sometimes in small steps and sometimes leaps, Francis separated himself from his partying companions and his old life. Over several years, Francis went through a process of conversion, though present-day usage of the word conversion connotes something far too anemic and mundane for the dramatic change taking place in him. Francis's transformation seems more akin to a Monarch butterfly's complete transfiguration. A Monarch lays an egg on a milkweed plant. The egg emerges into a caterpillar, a very colorful, attractive caterpillar, but nevertheless, a caterpillar whose primary objective is to eat. Then, it has the incredible inner wisdom to create a chrysalis and to fold itself into the outer shell. Then, a miracle happens. Everything inside the chrysalis breaks down into a substance without shape and then reforms itself into a completely different creature, a beautiful butterfly. If it happens to be the appropriate generation in the life cycle, this newly formed creation will soon fly 3,000 miles into a totally different part of the world.

When the Monarch caterpillar forms the chrysalis and then crawls inside, it's hard to comprehend how this emulsified glob contained in the chrysalis transforms itself into a butterfly. In the same way, we can't understand what was happening with Francis during his inner transformation. However, given his outward choices, we can imagine some of what might have been happening in his heart.

As Francis went through his conversion, he certainly could never have seen or planned how it would happen or how the different parts would fit together. As the emulsified goo inside a Monarch chrysalis has the wisdom to reform itself into a butterfly, Francis had the obedience and courage to follow inner wisdom and allow himself to be led. He had an instinct and the incredible audacity to make the right decisions in critical moments.

When Francis exchanged clothes with the beggar and then begged in Rome, he experienced a triumph of compassion over pride, the death of his pride, and an increase in love for those who were poor. Even earlier in his life, during his most decadent moments, he had empathy for the poor and had been generous with them. After courageously taking on the experience of being a beggar for a day, unquestionably, he had an even greater heart for those experiencing the suffering, struggles, and humiliation of poverty. Possibly, he became more conscious of the vast gap between those who had an abundance and those who had almost nothing.

One imagines that becoming a beggar for a day also increased his discomfort with his life of privilege. For a day, he shed his father's material wealth and took on not only the beggar's clothes but shared in his suffering, disgrace, and humiliation. He started to allow himself to be pried away from his old life, making way for the new person. His pride and egotism were dying. The grip of his past life was weakening. This step toward the death of his former life opened him to greater empathy, compassion, and love.

Conversely, his attachment to his pride, social position, and vanity were diminished. Love and devotion to God were expanding. Becoming a beggar for a day reduced the artificial distance between him and the "least of these." It made room in his heart for greater love.

Francis was divesting himself of his treasure. In this particular instance, not so much material treasure but the treasure of his ego, his standing in the community, and his self-image of wealth and privilege. He instinctively knew that these things blocked him from being faithful to God but also blocked him from loving. As he let go of these ego treasures, he was making room in his heart for the treasures God was waiting to put there. He had an inner sense that he had to live this out in his life.

The leper on the road confronted Francis with a lifelong inner dread and horror. As someone who had gone to war twice and admired the knights of the time, we imagine he was ashamed of his fear. One would also guess that he intuitively knew that his rejection of these people and their suffering separated him from God and from being the person he was attempting to become. At some level, he knew his fear was driving his life as opposed to love. Forcing himself to turn around and return to the leper led to the death of that lifelong fear and rejection. The way was now open to a new life of loving even the most despised of the "least of these." Through this action, he removed an enormous impediment to his being able to love. This fear was no longer defining his life. Love blossomed in its place. As he continued to be with the lepers, he later said that what had started as a dread turned to a sweetness. There had to be an immense relief for him as he experienced this personal transformation. Confronting his dread was a continuation of saying yes to God.

Francis could never have planned the dramatic confrontation with Peter Bernardone in the town Piazza. Everything that Francis had done up until this point had been done with the father's money. The partying, the military exploits, the money that he had given to the beggars, his daily sustenance, and his colorful clothes were all provided by his father. The conflict with his father had been escalating, but his father was still paying the bills. During the time leading up to this confrontation, Francis had been steadily moving toward God and rejecting his father's values while still dependent on him.

The gap between the two continued to widen, but Francis' dependence still tied him to his father and his wealth. One imagines Francis's increasing consciousness of this, accompanied by a growing disease with this reality.

Even though Francis had been rejecting his father's values and plans for his life, he was possibly not ready to let go of the security and support. Probably, he was trying to hold on to both. One imagines that Francis was not seeking the dramatic confrontation that happened with his father. Still, once confronted with the moment in the piazza, it was clear that the break needed to be definitive. Once he emerged with clothes and money in hand and made his public statement to the gathered crowd, his biological father had no hold on him. He was now completely reliant on his spiritual father.

Probably Francis, like us, wondered, how in the world am I going to survive? Now, he had courageously chosen, leaving him with immense uncertainties. Nevertheless, he was free of all impediments in his relationship with God and fully liberated to follow the spiritual path upon which he was being led.

As with the previous experiences, this was a massive death. He was dying to all the values into which he had been born. It was a death of depending on his father and his father's money. He was letting go of clothes, security, values, and the demands of his former position. He let go of the culture in which he had been immersed and exchanged it for a completely different life. This experience was definitive for him. He was free to follow the path on which he was being led.

That this dramatic event happened publicly in front of the townspeople increased the finality of his decision and solidified his commitment. Before these experiences, he had been filled with values, attitudes, desires, and a culture that was not God. The death of these old qualities now made room for him to become a person who embodied God's love and healing. As much as it is possible for any human, he had become one with God.

Francis left the city joyful. He immediately set out for the familiar paths of Mount Subasio singing. After years of struggle and conflict, he was at peace and in harmony with himself, the world, and his God. One biographer writes,

> Amid this mysterious and bewildering harmony, the heart of Francis felt a delicious thrill; his being was calmed and uplifted; the soul of things caressed him gently and shed upon him peace. Unaccustomed happiness swept over him, and he made the forest resound with his hymns of praise.[3]

Francis had gone through a metamorphosis, which resulted in his becoming a very different person. From someone who had paid little attention to faith issues, he became someone devoted to God at every level. For those who flocked to him, he radiated God's love. Instead of being the life of the party, he became someone who radiated a life filled with God's spirit. Instead of enjoying a life of wealth, he urged those around him to sell what they had and give the proceeds to the poor. He abandoned the playboy life and, instead of wealth, embraced radical poverty.

It's tempting to look at Francis and not understand how he could live as he did. We focus on the outer parts of his life, which seem impossible. But Francis wasn't just giving up wealth and choosing radical poverty as a rule to create an alternative lifestyle. He went through a profound inner realignment that transformed his heart and inner being. At the core of his transformation was compassion. A deep, passionate love of God and of those who were poor and suffering had pushed him through to a new life. What we see in his outer life was a reflection of a profound inner transformation. The outward manifestation of his life flowed out of that.

We are never complete. Francis would face other difficult challenges requiring discernment and courage, but he persevered through a profound inner conversion and discerned a new path. He had passed through the travails that were needed for him to go forward. He, like the caterpillar and the Monarch, had gone through a complete transformation.

An Extraordinary Life Emerges

In these early years, thousands flocked to see and hear Francis like they had flocked after Jesus 1200 years earlier. People were touched by the simplicity and sincerity of Francis' life and words. Francis and those who followed him initially were a powerful and compelling presence. The people were thirsty for truth and life. They felt he was the catalyst for their finding it. They experienced God's love through this small group who were willing to give up everything.

In remembering Francis, one is reminded of John the Baptist out in the wilderness telling the people they were vipers and snakes who had to turn from the ways they were living. Francis doesn't seem to have been as harsh as John the Baptist, but he also did not give what some in later years called "cheap grace." Like John the Baptist, Francis told people they needed to change, be converted, and transformed. Conversion for Francis was not "accepting Jesus as their personal savior" or joining and attending a church. Francis insisted on a practical transformation of the way one lived. People had to return and relinquish anything they had gained through dishonesty, theft, trickery or fraudulent legal means to enrich themselves. They couldn't hold on to enmities. He told them to reconcile with those with whom they were estranged or had quarreled. He urged them to turn away from these kinds of behaviors and to love each other.

Certainly, not all who learned from and followed Francis gave up everything as those in the new community had. However, we can be confident that money was a part of what he preached. It's hard to comprehend, but Francis believed that money was evil and hated it. Francis separated himself from worldly goods. In our minds, that's impossible to understand. Perhaps his hatred of money and seeing money as evil had to do with having felt that he had found the pearl of great value (Matthew 13:45-46) and, having found it, realizing that he could lose it by holding on to material wealth. Possibly there was the sense that his love of wealth had nearly separated him from God and the joy that he had found. Probably, he felt that he was still vulnerable to its power. Francis seems to have envisioned the power of money as a mighty river with an undertow current threatening to suck under the unaware. He understood its threat and feared it could pull him back under its influence.

Francis never had a grand plan. He certainly didn't set out to establish a new religious order. He had a clear, straightforward vision. It was to live the most difficult Biblical verses as literally as possible and encourage others to do the same. For him, the parts of scripture that seemed impossible to live were a joy that he passionately shared. Francis' transforming vision was to treat the least of these as Jesus. He embraced God's vision of peace on earth and attempted to be instrumental in bringing that about. The people recognized the authenticity of his faith and his deep passion. It inspired them to turn toward and embrace God, leading to transformed lives of love.

Thank God some were faithful enough and loved God to the extent they attempted to be perfect by giving away all they had and following Jesus. Most of us are not going to do that. As the new Order of the Brothers Minor grew large, even those who had enthusiastically rushed to join with Francis rebelled against what he taught and lived. Only a handful were able to stay with what he taught. But thank God some remained on that path and are a light to the rest of us. We probably won't achieve that level of perfection, but Francis and those early followers continue to remind and challenge us to move in that direction.

A Love Relationship with God's Creation and All God's Creatures

Francis was a beacon of loving God's creation and being at one with all the creatures of creation. Unfortunately, over the centuries, Christians have venerated and remembered him but have ignored his light and wisdom concerning God's creation and how to live with our fellow creatures. In the past, when ships didn't heed the beacon of lighthouses on coastlines, disaster followed. On a global scale, the same is happening. For centuries, we have ignored Francis' light. Consequently, we are now not just wrecking a ship. We are sailing the entire planet into disaster.

Francis experienced God's creation in the same way he experienced church. It was holy and sacred. Living in God's creation with God's creatures, he felt surrounded by God. This understanding led him to a radical way of living in the world. For him, to practice the great commandment of loving God with all of one's heart, mind, and soul meant seeing the creation as God and embracing it with tenderness and care. For Francis, loving God's creation and creatures was a way of loving God.

Francis saw Jesus as his brother but also included the non-human constituents of God's creation as brothers and sisters. When he spoke of Brother Sun, Sister Moon, Brother Wind, Sister Water, Brother Fire, and sister Mother Earth he was talking about being in a loving relationship with these parts of creation. God loves this creation. Following that, Francis chose to be in an intimate, love relationship filled with respect, affection, appreciation, and tenderness with all these manifestations of God. Francis experienced God as present in every aspect of the planet's magnificent interrelated, intricate, intertwined parts. All God's creatures were loved by God and loved by Francis. They were all included in the family of God.

He saw the birds as his brothers and sister. He became friends with Brother Wolf. He invited and sang with the cricket. He would only allow the Brothers Minor to cut a tree down with his permission. For him, all of creation was sacred and to be honored. He created community not only with the creatures but with the inanimate parts of the earth as well. He experienced a kinship and connectedness with the totality of creation.

For Francis, creatures and the different aspects of the planet were not commodities valued for their usefulness and profitability. Leonardo Boff writes,

> What we observe here is another way of being in the world, quite different from that of the modernity we have criticized. The latter stands above things in order to possess and dominate them, whereas that of St Francis is together with them, to love them and live with them as brothers and sisters at home. [4]

We tend to think of the incarnation primarily as God coming to us through Jesus. Typically, we understand God was with us on earth in the flesh through Jesus. Secondarily, we believe that when we follow God's path, God can be incarnate in us human beings.

The people writing about the spirituality that grew out of Francis' life expand the idea of incarnation. They see God incarnate in God's creation. They understand that God created the planet and is present in all the different parts of creation. In short, God lives in God's creation and creatures. If we allow ourselves to be present in it, God is with us through the earth and all its infinite dimensions and manifestations. For Francis, all of life was family. The creatures and the different parts of creation were brother and sister. He truly experienced creation as the kindom of God.

For Francis, observing creation, interacting with, and seeing God in God's creatures was one way of understanding the divine. Fellow creatures were "expressions of God's overflowing love." [5] God was revealed in creation the same as through scripture, prayer, liturgy, and church.

We have glimpses of Francis coming to these understandings, but we don't have a complete picture of that process. It is clear, though, that as these insights were forming, they shaped how he lived and interacted with all dimensions of the planet. These insights were a critical part of his transformation and conversion, resulting in a far richer quality of spirituality. Other Christian theologies and understandings of the relationship with nature, especially those based on a misunderstanding of a "dominion theology," compared to Francis' beliefs concerning creation, are narrow, truncated, and reductionist.

Francis's belief system regarding God's creation was far broader and more inclusive. In that, it has the potential to enrich all of us as he lights a path to a more encompassing way of being a part of God's creation.

Meister Eckhart and Julian of Norwich lived after Francis. We don't know if Francis influenced them in understanding creation or not. But both wrote short pieces expressing sentiments consistent with Francis' intimate, personal relationship with nature.

> Apprehend God in all things, for God is in all things.
> Every single creature is full of God and is a book about God.
> Every creature is a word of God.
> If I spent enough time with the tiniest creature—
> even a caterpillar—
> I would never have to prepare a sermon. So full of God
> is every creature. (Meister Eckhart-- 1260-1328 CE)

And later, Julian of Norwich (1343-1416 CE) exclaimed: "The day of my spiritual awakening was the day I saw, and knew I saw God in all things. And all things in God."

Francis saw 'the earth and the fulness thereof" (1 Corinthians 10:26, Psalm 24:1) as God. He knew that creation was an expression of the Divine. It was then automatic for him to love this manifestation of God with his complete being.

In our modern world, Francis' ways of seeing, loving, and being in relationship with creation would be seen as beyond quaint. For many, this way of thinking is lunacy. In our culture, a more conventional way of looking at the creation is to see it as filled with natural resources that can and should be exploited to the fullest to enrich oneself. In this mindset, the value of creation is in how it can be monetized. The only challenge for those with this understanding is determining how the different parts of creation can be turned into a commodity for accumulating wealth as rapidly as possible. The parts of creation that get in the way of this drive for wealth are expendable, not valued, and reduced to waste. Francis' beliefs would not only be seen as bizarre but in any way that they interfered with the drive for wealth, would be seen as an obstacle to be bulldozed over.

> Modern-day followers of Francis articulate his very different understanding when they state, "Francis and Franciscan theologians describe the Earth and its diversity as sacramental. Life on Earth has intrinsic value because it is created by God, not merely because of its economic worth... in the Franciscan tradition, creation has integrity and intrinsic value not because of its "worth" but because it is a reflection of God." [6]

As he neared death, Francis wrote the Canticle of the Creatures, containing the core of his belief system. To our modern mind, it may seem stilted and overly pious. Perhaps if we continue to read it, our contemporary mentality may be drawn in Francis' direction, undoubtedly to our benefit.

Canticle of the Creatures

Most High, all-powerful, good Lord,
Yours are the praises, the glory,
and the honor, and all blessing.
To You alone, Most High, do they belong,
and no human is worthy to mention Your name.
Praised be You, my Lord, with all Your creatures,
especially Sir Brother Sun,
Who is the day and through whom You give us light.
And he is beautiful and radiant with great splendor;
and bears a likeness of You, Most High One.
Praised be You, my Lord, through Sister Moon and the stars,
in heaven You formed them clear and precious and beautiful.

Praised be You, my Lord, through Brother Wind,
and through the air, cloudy and serene, and every kind of weather,
through whom You give sustenance to Your creatures.
Praised be You, my Lord, through Sister Water,
who is very useful and humble and precious and chaste.
Praised be You, my Lord, through Brother Fire,
through whom You light the night,
and he is beautiful and playful and robust and strong.
Praised be You, my Lord, through our Sister Mother Earth,
who sustains and governs us,
and who produces various fruit with colored flowers and herbs.
Praised be You, my Lord, through those who give pardon for
Your
love, and bear infirmity and tribulation.
Blessed are those who endure in peace
for by You, Most High, shall they be crowned.
Praised be You, my Lord, through our Sister Bodily Death,
from whom no one living can escape.
Woe to those who die in mortal sin.
Blessed are those whom death will find in Your most holy will,
for the second death shall do them no harm.
Praise and bless my Lord and give Him thanks
and serve Him with great humility.

NOTES

[1] Most of this story is based on what we know about Francis and his father. A few parts are totally created, like the last paragraph and the section when Francis tries to explain to his father why he has chosen this life.

[2] Paul Sabatier, The Complete Francis of Assisi: His life, The Complete Writings, and The Little Flowers, ed by Jon M. Sweeney (Brewster, Massachusetts: Paraclete Press, 2015), 18.

[3] Ibid. p.52.

[4] Leonardo Boff, Cry of the Earth, Cry of the Poor (Maryknoll, New York: Orbis Books, English translation 1997), 211.

[5] Ilia Delio, et al., Care for Creation: a franciscan spirituality of the earth (Cincinnati, Ohio: Franciscan Media, 1989) 52.

[6] Ibid. p. 77.

| three |

The Quaker Miracle Worker

I'll tell you what it really means to worship the LORD. Remove the chains of prisoners who are chained unjustly. Free those who are abused! Share your food with everyone who is hungry; share your home with the poor and homeless. Give clothes to those in need; don't turn away your relatives. Then your light will shine like the dawning sun, and you will quickly be healed. Your honesty will protect you as you advance, and the glory of the LORD will defend you from behind. When you beg the LORD for help, he will answer, "Here I am!" Don't mistreat others or falsely accuse them or say something cruel. Give your food to the hungry and care for the homeless. Then your light will shine in the dark; your darkest hour will be like the noonday sun. The LORD will always guide you and provide good things to eat when you are in the desert. He will make you healthy. You will be like a garden that has plenty of water or like a stream that never runs dry. You will rebuild those houses left in ruins for years; you will be known as a builder and repairer of city walls and streets. (Isaiah 58:6-12)

Freeing the Captives

In the middle of the 19th century, this country fought an incredibly bloody war over slavery. The South was stubbornly determined to hold on to its "peculiar institution." Approximately 620,000 soldiers were killed. Combatants and non-combatants from both sides suffered many more horrors. The violence of the war did achieve its goal. The enslaved were freed.

It's important to remember, though, that roughly a century before the Civil War, slaves were also being freed -- in a very different way. In this freeing of the enslaved, not a single person was killed. No guns, cannons, explosives, or violence were used. There were no charges by thousands to be cut down by rifle and cannon fire. There was no vicious hand to hand combat in trenches with the intent of killing a fellow human being. No nightmare hospital tents were needed to saw off arms and legs without anesthesia or antibiotics. This freeing of the enslaved left no national trauma with wounds still festering to the present day.

This earlier freeing of the enslaved was carried out by a few Quakers sensitive to the immorality of slavery. They were very attuned to how their God was calling them to live related to this atrocity. Instead of using weapons of war, they freed slaves through visits, prayers, speaking in Quaker meetings, and conversations with slave owners.

Though not widely known, in our country's early history, slavery was prevalent and accepted not only in the South but also in the Northern colonies. As the country was being settled, people considered owning enslaved people to be the equivalent of owning stocks and bonds in our present day. We experience it as repugnant, but enslaved people were seen as property, the same as owning land or livestock. They were property that increased one's wealth and provided needed labor. Even for many Quakers, enslavement was largely accepted and not seen as immoral or sinful.

Surprisingly, even William Penn, the Quaker founder of Pennsylvania, owned enslaved people. By 1700, approximately one in ten Philadelphians owned enslaved people. Prominent Quaker families in Philadelphia were involved in the slave trade. Rhode Island was one of the more active colonies that imported enslaved people. Between 1709 and 1807, merchants in Rhode Island underwrote a minimum of 934 voyages to Africa that brought an estimated 106,544 enslaved human beings to the New World. By 1774, enslaved people made up 6.3 percent of the population of Rhode Island.[1] In the mid-1700s, 2.2 percent of the people in Massachusetts consisted of enslaved people, the majority of whom lived in Boston and other coastal areas.[2] The New Jersey census in 1800 found 12,422 slaves. In 1744, New Jersey's "Provincial Council declared that nothing would be permitted to interfere with the importation of Negroes." [3] There are similar examples of enslavement in all the Northern colonies.

Even though Quakers owned enslaved people and some were involved in the trade of enslaved people, there was a small contingent of Quakers who embodied a counter-cultural consciousness. Through their openness to their God, they were clear that enslavement was immoral and in opposition to their faith. They were starting to be vocal about their beliefs, particularly within the Quaker movement itself. Quakers were speaking out on both sides of the Atlantic, but around 1740, none of them were more committed and effective in combating enslavement than John Woolman. From the beginning, Woolman saw the Africans as human beings and a part of the family of God. What was hidden to the owners of enslaved people was clear to him.

Woolman was a Quaker living in New Jersey before the Revolutionary War. Sometimes fellow Quakers would come to him requesting that he write their will for them. As a young man starting out in life, his beliefs were not fully formed, but in writing these wills, he became aware that he couldn't in good conscience write the part of the will that would leave an enslaved person to a family member. He couldn't personally participate in their continued enslavement. The story is that he felt conflicted and wanted to help these older, respected people coming to him for this service but found himself uncomfortably resisting. In a deferential and respectful manner, Woolman would find a way to decline writing that part of the will.

Sometimes after gently refusing this type of request, there was the opportunity for him to voice some of his concerns about how enslavement conflicted with their shared faith. After having this kind of conversation, sometimes, the individual would return at a later time and ask him to write a will that freed the enslaved as opposed to transferring their ownership.

As Woolman kept maturing, he believed even more passionately that enslavement was inconsistent with his faith. By 1755, he concluded that for progress to be made against war, enslavement, and poverty, he would have to challenge his own church. "Freeing one slave at a time as he was doing was important work, but freeing Quakers from slavery's moral taint was the bigger job that he believed God meant for him."[4] Woolman was beginning to see and live in a different reality from the dominant society surrounding him. He was moving into his life's work, his calling.

Woolman dedicated his life to the vision of a Quaker world free of enslavement. He clung to and lived into this vision for the rest of his life. He was becoming one of the few who lived out the slogan of being in but not of the world. His faithfulness changed the world.

Woolman accepted the mission of freeing slaves and of transforming the Quaker movement. He spent large parts of his life traveling through New Jersey, Pennsylvania, Maryland, Virginia, North Carolina, and New England to convince fellow Quakers to free their enslaved people. Before setting out on one of his many journeys, he would always respectfully ask permission of the Quaker Meeting to which he belonged. Woolman traveled simply on these long trips to other colonies, at least once choosing to walk. He was remarkably successful in his mission.

We don't know which scriptures inspired Woolman to take on this mission of freeing the enslaved. It is striking, though, how strongly his life followed Jesus' words at the beginning of his ministry. In Luke, Jesus reads from Isaiah, "The Spirit of the Lord is upon me, because he has anointed me to preach good news to the poor. He has sent me to heal the brokenhearted, to proclaim liberty to the captives, recovery of sight to the blind, to deliver those who are crushed..." (Luke 4:18)

The Jubilation of Jubilee

The Jubilee protocols of Leviticus 25 are also powerful scriptures Woolman may have used. Following freedom from slavery in Egypt, the Hebrew people were led to structure who they were going to be as they established their relationship with God and determined their new identity. Many parts of the Hebrew Bible lay out laws shaping their life and culture while determining their values and identity. Some of those early mandates seem outlandish, incomprehensible, and even laughable to our modern sensibilities. However, some of these early laws were wonderful guiding principles that strengthened their faith, established a stronger community, and built relationships among them.

Laws limiting inequality of wealth were foundational in building community and justice. Some laws demanded they free all Hebrew slaves every seven years, allowing families to be reunited. Other laws called for the restoration of family land to those who had lost it when they couldn't pay their debts. These laws kept hope alive, gave fresh starts to those who would have been hopeless, and restored new life to those who felt they had lost it. It was justice and new life for those who were weaker and had gone through difficult times.

Some of these foundational verses are Exodus 21:2, Deuteronomy 15:1-18, and Jeremiah 34:8-22. These three scriptures call for the freeing of Hebrew slaves every seven years. Leviticus 25 follows the same theme but is a more expansive and comprehensive picture of the vision of how God wanted them to live together as a community of faith in which God loves all.

Leviticus 25 in the Hebrew Bible lays out an extraordinary ideal of a year when enslaved were freed, families were reunited, and land was returned to its original owners. It reads,

> "Once every forty-nine years on the tenth day of the seventh month, which is also the Great Day of Forgiveness,[5] trumpets are to be blown everywhere in the land. This fiftieth year is sacred—it is a time of freedom and celebration when everyone will receive back their original prop-

> erty, and slaves will return home to their families. This is a year of complete celebration..." (Leviticus 25:8-11a)

In the culture of Biblical times, sometimes a family-owned land, but due to any number of possible factors had become indebted and had to sell their property. In losing their property, they lost their livelihood and what sustained them and their families. Giving up their land to settle a debt, sometimes meant they had to become day laborers or beg for their living. For some, this would lead to impoverishment, forcing them to sell themselves or their children into slavery. Families lost everything, were split up, and desolate.

The year of Jubilee described in Leviticus and the other similar scriptures was a time of repairing that kind of devastation. It was a year of restoration of lost property when those who had been enslaved were set free and made whole. It was a time of grand celebration. It was a restoration not just of freedom and property but of hope for one's life, family, and future. Imagine what a celebration this would be for people who had lost their land, had become slaves, or lost sons and daughters to slavery. We can only imagine the immense relief, joy, hope, and celebration of those being set free, reuniting with their families, and reclaiming their property. The scholars say that when Jesus read the Isaiah scripture in the temple at the beginning of his ministry, that he and Isaiah before him were harkening back to these Leviticus, Exodus, and Deuteronomic verses of freedom, restoration, and celebration.

John Woolman spread this type of restoration, celebration, hope, and new life. In his travels and encounters with his fellow Quakers, he was the catalyst for these kinds of changes and celebrations. The Leviticus scripture above says the Jubilee time is sacred. Woolman was God's instrument, creating these sacred times.

Freeing the Captives: But also, the Captors

Woolman's decision-making process was different from most of us. For him, decisions were not based on whether he made more money, or whether he would be more comfortable. It was not an issue of whether people would think better of him or if he would have more status. The critical issue for him was whether an action would bring him closer to his God or if it would be an impediment in that relationship. In being closer to God, he was choosing to be God's instrument. This was the core issue for him, and he brought that mindset with him in his quest to free the captives.

Woolman was very conscious of how money, wealth, and possessions could be a "burden" in his desire to be faithful to God. As a young man, he owned a fabric store that became increasingly successful. However, he grew to believe that his business venture weakened him as a Christian. [6]

He was ill at ease selling items that he considered luxuries, which appealed to people's vanity but were not genuinely helpful. His business grew, but as it grew, he experienced it as a liability. To be true to his faith, he needed to be less "encumbered." He began downsizing his business and eventually let it go completely to focus exclusively on being a tailor with no employees. He also kept an orchard to supplement his livelihood. He felt that living a plain, simple life freed him from material attachments and strengthened his faithfulness to his God.

Given this experience, he was concerned that "superfluities" or luxuries were enticing others away from their faith. He firmly believed that living plainly supported one in the desire to follow the Christian path, and conversely, the desire to accumulate material goods and wealth was a barrier. He was clear that slave ownership was rooted in the desire to accumulate unnecessary wealth and the desire to live an extravagant life.

The above implies that Woolman was not just asking these slave owners to change but was always open to God and inviting ongoing conversion in his own life. This enabled him to be more effectively God's instrument in the transformation of others. The transformation of the Quaker enslavers and of the Quaker movement began with Woolman's own transformation.

When one becomes acquainted with Woolman, it's easy to focus on his sacrificial commitment to freeing the enslaved while remaining unaware of his insight that economic forces were powering this evil. Running parallel with his passion for abolishing enslavement was the clarity that enslavement of other human beings was fueled by a desire to accumulate wealth. For him, greed and enslavement were inextricably knotted; both separated one from God.

In asking the Quakers to free their enslaved people, Woolman was appealing to their faith and morality. He challenged the slave owners to make a moral choice, but more was at stake. He knew that in asking enslavers to free their enslaved people, he was also asking them to give away a significant part of what they had accumulated. In giving away enslaved people, the owners' wealth, income, and economic potential would be diminished. They, like people of most times and places, were concerned about how they would live as they aged. In trying to understand these enslavers and the extremely difficult ask that Woolman was making, we could ask ourselves how we would feel if someone approached us and asked us to give away a quarter, or a third, or half of whatever property we owned. How would we respond?

Woolman was challenging the slave owners to disinvest from a system that made them money and had the potential to make them wealthy. If they freed their slaves, they would have to work harder and be satisfied with less material wealth. Life at that time involved huge amounts of dirty, time-consuming, backbreaking manual labor. They would now be taking more of that on themselves. Implicit in Woolman's ask was sacrifice, a simpler lifestyle, and for some, it could mean hardship.

Slavery was a moral and spiritual issue, but for Woolman, not only owning enslaved people but the greed that undergirded slavery blocked people in their relationship with God. For him, this was paramount. In asking his fellow Quakers to free their captives, he was gently challenging them to remove the obstacles separating them from their God. He was keenly focused on being an instrument in a conversion process. In approaching these people, Woolman was appealing to their spirituality, to their faith. But in his gentle way, he was challenging them to move into their relationship with their God in a deeper, more substantive way.

The slave owners were oblivious to it, but through their enslavement of others, they were imprisoning themselves. Woolman understood that he was liberating them not only from the immorality of slavery but also from their greed. By gently encouraging them to release their slaves, he was kindly calling them away from their acquisitiveness, their idolatry, and inviting them to open their hearts to their God and their faith. By releasing their slaves, the slave owners were actualizing theirs and their descendant's liberation. Their lives and their relationship with God were being transformed. Emancipation came not only to slaves but to their captors. Even if they weren't aware of it, this was a Jubilee celebration for the captors as well as for the enslaved being released. Each time a slave owner's family responded, God's kingdom was being realized.

These transformations were far-reaching. As the changes took place, the former enslavers no longer saw other human beings as property or objects to be owned but were beginning to realize they were part of the human family. It was a step toward becoming the family of God. Concurrently, it was a movement toward a different understanding of wealth and what is really important. Those whose treasure had consisted of enslaved human beings were letting go of that kind of false wealth. They were releasing a false treasure and moving closer to the real treasure. Their hearts were becoming more fixed on eternal riches.

Encounters that Moved Mountains

We currently live in a time of profound polarization. We find ourselves on opposite sides of political and religious divides without a clue how to bridge the chasms that separate us. We find ourselves in conversations that result in raised voices, anger, frustration, impatience, and incredulity that the other person could hold such outrageous beliefs. In the wake of these encounters, instead of divisions narrowing and understanding growing, hostility surges. Families approach holiday gatherings with trepidation. To avoid unpleasant confrontations, some families set up rules about how to be together. Others, fearing hostility, decide not to be with relatives who hold such antagonistic views. We remember that in the time of slavery, the divisions around the subject of slavery were just as polarizing. The ruptures during Woolman's time were probably not as dramatic as they were closer to the Civil War. Still, just as political and religious topics are contentious now, slavery was an explosive topic during Woolman's time.

Woolman's miracle was that he could bridge the chasms of his time with his fellow Quakers. We, in our time, are largely blocked and baffled by our divisions. Woolman, however, was not stymied. Instead of hostility growing out of a potentially tense conversation, he managed to have productive encounters around a controversial issue that frequently resulted in his hosts being transformed.

He was passionate about the immorality of slavery but was able to be incredibly kind and gentle with his fellow Quakers whom he was confronting. Despite feeling great pain at the suffering and injustice of enslavement, he was not angry, condemning, or abusive with these enslavers. At least once, in a Quaker meeting, when he found himself starting to become angry, instead of speaking, he remained silent. Another time he felt that he had spoken too strongly and apologized to the meeting. Even in these times, when he was beginning to fall into more customary responses, his restraint and apology yielded positive results.

Remarkably he remained faithful to his purpose with these fellow Quakers while also continuing to be gentle and compassionate. He maintained a delicate balance in living out his mission while at the same time following the apostle Paul's admonition to speak the truth in love. By the time of the Revolutionary War, the Quakers had largely eliminated slavery by their followers. Other Quakers were devoted to this issue, but Woolman, probably more than any other single person, was most instrumental in bringing about the liberation of those enslaved by Quakers.

Being clear about the immorality of slavery, however, didn't automatically give Woolman the words or the courage to say what was in his heart. He had an ongoing inner struggle with what to say, how to say it, and when. It was difficult for him to speak in the Quaker meetings and to initiate private conversations with other Quakers who enslaved people. It was particularly problematic in that on his trips, he frequently stayed with the enslavers he was challenging. Woolman had the uncomfortable, seemingly impossible task of being the guest of his Quaker hosts and receiving their hospitality while also having to turn the conversation around to a very contentious subject. Asking these slave owners to give up their enslaved people challenged their morality and threatened their wealth.

Nevertheless, Woolman persevered. He was continually attempting to discern the right course of action and the right words in a given situation. He prayed for wisdom and the courage to speak, sometimes waiting until he felt clear from his searching.

Woolman was always humble and self-effacing. He was strategic and looked to others for guidance in unfamiliar situations. In communities where he was unknown, he looked for advice about whom to invite to a conversation and who should make the invitation for others to participate. Sometimes he would consult about the best location to have a conversation so that people would feel the most comfortable. Woolman was always careful and respectful before and during these conversations. He seemed to be able to speak in a way that allowed people to become engaged as opposed to offended.

Miraculously, Woolman was able to talk with these people and challenge their consciences in a way that frequently brought change while at the same time not creating defensiveness and anger. Given the difficulty of having conversations between people with polarized views, it seems like a miracle that Woolman could have these encounters calmly, peacefully, and respectfully. Remarkably, these encounters changed the lives of both enslavers and the enslaved.

It is easy to lose sight of, but at the core of these stories is God's power. It's easy to focus on how extraordinary these events were. It is essential, though, to remember that it wasn't Woolman precipitating these transformations. God's power was the unseen force impelling these changes. Woolman was extraordinary in being willing to be shaped into a remarkably open instrument and pliable conduit for that power to flow through.

Woolman is Following in Jesus' Footsteps

In remembering the visits Woolman had with his fellow Quakers, one is reminded of Jesus encountering Zacchaeus.

Jesus was going through Jericho, where a man named Zacchaeus lived. He was in charge of collecting taxes and was very rich. Jesus was heading his way, and Zacchaeus wanted to see what he was like. But Zacchaeus was a short man and could not see over the crowd. So, he ran ahead and climbed up into a sycamore tree. When Jesus got there, he looked up and said, "Zacchaeus, hurry down! I want to stay with you today." Zacchaeus hurried down and gladly welcomed Jesus. Everyone who saw this started grumbling, "This man Zacchaeus is a sinner! And Jesus is going home to eat with him." Later that day, Zacchaeus stood up and said to Jesus, "I will give half of my property to the poor. And I will now pay back four times as much to everyone I have ever cheated." Jesus said to Zacchaeus, "Today you and your family have been saved, because you are a true son of Abraham. The Son of Man came to look for and to save people who are lost." (Luke 19:1-10)

The following is an imagined account of Zacchaeus' retelling of his experience after being with Jesus:

> I didn't start with the idea of being someone who was hated and feared. When I was young and trying to get started in life, I wasn't planning to be

a tax collector who was a despised enemy. But when one lives in a land that is occupied by the military of another country, being able to provide for one's family is not easy. I didn't want to join the ranks of those who always lived on the edge of poverty. I didn't want to be among those who fell off that edge and lost their land. I didn't want to risk the possibility of falling into debt and having to sell my children or even being sold into slavery myself. So, when the opportunity to become a tax collector presented itself, I took it. I knew that people hated tax collectors, but I chose to live with it. My security and my family's security were more important than a few people not liking me.

At that time, the Roman army occupied Palestine. We paid taxes to the Romans, which I collected. It was common knowledge that people in my business collected more than was really owed and kept the extra for themselves. If someone didn't like that, we had the big Roman army backing us up. No one wanted the soldiers banging on their door about taxes not being paid. It's a lot easier to collect taxes if the army is your enforcer. People paid up.

I didn't begin cheating people as a tax collector. At first, I felt more for the suffering of the people. At that time, I had some feelings for how hard and precarious their life was. Two things came together to change that, though. I owed some important people money and didn't know how I was going to pay it. Also, even though I wasn't cheating people, those ingrates hated me anyway! They shunned me and said terrible things about me. Worse than that, they rejected my family. That was a mistake I wasn't going to let pass. I started adding on to what they owed. That was for my trouble and the constant grief they gave me.

Of course, they despised me! They grumbled and cursed me behind my back. They knew I collected more than they owed. I was hated, but I was not going to lose my land or children. This is the charade we go through. However, the charade is real. I ended up with their money. They ended up more impoverished and more at risk. That was the antagonistic life we shaped together.

As time passed, I cared less that they were suffering. It got so that I hardly thought about it. I stopped being aware of the pain and precariousness of their lives. I didn't think anymore that what I was doing could cause people not to have enough to eat or clothes to wear. I pushed it out of my mind that I could destroy families. I found ways to justify what I was doing. I told myself that I was more worthy than they were. I said all they had to do was work harder, and they would be alright. I was blessed; I deserved my wealth, and they deserved their poverty. Then, too, I grew to like all that extra money and what it got me.

This was my life when Jesus came to Jericho. I didn't know much about him, but he was known as a great teacher, miracle worker, healer, and maybe even rabbi. The people loved him; I didn't understand it, really, but they flocked after him like he was their savior or something. Some of them thought he was going to save them from the Romans.

He and the ones close to him have given away all their possessions. Incredibly, people rushed to see a poor man. I don't know why they were so excited by him. It's even more incomprehensible that I also wanted to see him. I had gone to great lengths to be a rich man, but was about to go to a lot of trouble to see a poor man. Still, it was the excitement in the town for the day, so why not see what was going on.

I found a perfect place to see everything up in a tree. Being up in a tree is a little undignified for a man of my status, but it's definitely better than being down in all the pushing and shoving. Besides, being down in a crowd of people who hated me might not have been safe. I had a great view, and I was not down there straining to see over those louts much taller than me. The crowds were down below, and I was above it all, just like I like it.

Then Jesus came down the street and goes to the place where I was in the tree. He looked up and called out to me. I was shocked, but he called me by name and told me to come down. He was going to my house that very day. I didn't have a clue what was going on, but I got down quickly. I was astounded that he wanted to go to my house. He's extremely popular; I'm virtually an untouchable, but it gave me status to be with him. The people hated it; they were grumbling.

Going to my house with Jesus and the crowd following and pushing all around us was dreamlike. It didn't feel like it is happening to me. Something very emotional was happening inside of me. I didn't feel in control and was confused about what was happening. People all around us were yelling out their comments and questions. They were upset, arguing, and angry, not only at me but at him now.

When we arrived at my house, I showed him all the hospitality possible. I called out the servants and had food prepared. I took care of him and his disciples, though I'm sure they were very uncomfortable being in the house of the chief tax collector. Undoubtedly, they didn't want to be associated with someone like me. I'm sure that in their thoughts, they were grumbling too.

I couldn't absorb everything the holy man was saying. I couldn't take it all in, but as we talked, everything started changing. The food came, but I wasn't hungry. The ground was shifting under my feet. I felt that as we kept going, I could see clearly, not only with my eyes but with my heart, what I had been blind to before. It wasn't pleasant! I saw with uncomfortable clarity that I had been doing terrible things to people. I knew that I had been participating in a system that was destroying my neighbors. My heart had become hard. I"d been telling myself that what I had been doing to people didn't matter. Without admitting it to myself, I had become a person spreading destruction and misery. I was profoundly wounding the whole community. I was shocked that in the conversation, I was even starting to talk about some of these things with this stranger.

I don't know what he was saying or doing that touched my heart so profoundly. What I do know is that I'd been destroying people's lives and causing them immense suffering. I'd been living a terrible life.

Certainly, when I was climbing up that tree, I never had a hint that later in the day, I would be admitting these terrible things to some holy man I had never seen before. That is what happened, though. Looking back on it, I think my part of the conversation increasingly became a confession and then conversion.

Surprisingly, I feel this man of God wasn't condemning me. I'm sure he knows these terrible things about me but, inexplicably, still accepted me, even loved me. I felt a warmth coming from him toward me. I felt guilty but strangely loved. I can't put it together. I was guilty but not condemned.

Suddenly, I was aware of the reality of God with stunning clarity. In our culture, we talk a lot about God. We have a lot of rules, holy days, sacrifices, and laws in our faith. That's our identity. Being religious, at least in the way we think about ourselves, is our culture. It's just who we are. In reality, though, for many of us, our religion is something we push over to the periphery of our lives. We give our faith a polite nod and use the words, language, and rituals enough to fit in. In truth, for many of us, our religion is more of a custom. It isn't a deeply held conviction and commitment that shapes us to the core of our beings. Before today, my life certainly was not formed by my faith. My true devotion was to wealth and to the comforts and power that came with that. In reality, that was my god.

All of that changed in a timeless instant. Suddenly, I now saw the horror I had become. I was shocked and dismayed at who I had become and the destruction I was wreaking. I knew this wasn't who I wanted to be. Before this, I felt like I had been getting what was most important in life. Being with him, I knew I was wrong. My blind eyes were opening. He has something that is far more valuable. He was calling me to be what in my deepest heart I wanted to be, even though I couldn't have said that before.

Instinctively, I knew I had to change quickly and decisively. If I was going to leave my previous life behind, I had to do it so strongly that I wouldn't go back. Intuitively, I knew that it would be easy to slide back into my old ways. I had to make changes that would commit me to the new reality I was now able to see. I knew at that moment what was demanded of me and what I needed to do. Thank God.

It's an unimaginable relief to have left behind the person who had gone around cheating people out of their livelihoods. I am shocked to feel the joy of not being captive to the greed and fears driving my life. It feels liberating to have thrown off all that grabbing for money. It's freeing to no longer be going through those terrible, angry, confrontational exchanges while cheating people.

Despite how powerful this moment was, I could glimpse the alarming peril of being pulled back into my old life. I couldn't risk sliding back into that captivity. I had to act quickly on the promise I made and start giving the money away.

This is an extraordinary moment. It's such a wonderful feeling to have started a new life. I can breathe again. I'm just so happy and grateful to be in this new place and released from a life that had been holding me captive.

This is a story of a wonderful conversion. It wasn't just that Zacchaeus left with a different belief system but that he went through a stunning transformation of behavior. Zacchaeus was no longer a person who cheated others out of their livelihood. He no longer was disseminating discord, poverty, and hate. A miracle had blossomed. Zacchaeus had amazingly been transformed into a person sowing justice, reconciliation, peace, and God's love. Inevitably, the conversion that took place in this one man began to transform the community. The reign of God that Jesus consistently taught was breaking out all around Zacchaeus. Evil lost control.

Unquestionably when Woolman visited his fellow Quakers, he had some of the same spirit of Jesus when he talked with them about enslaving other human beings, their brothers and sisters. We could wish for a video of Jesus' conversation with Zacchaeus as well as Woolman's conversations with his fellow Quakers. It would be a gift to be able to witness these encounters when something so miraculous occurred.

The apostle Paul writes that our struggle as people of faith is not against human beings but against principalities and powers. A more modern translation states, "For our struggle is not against human opponents, but against rulers, authorities, cosmic powers in the darkness around us, and evil spiritual forces in the heavenly realm." (Ephesians 6:12-13) Many of us don't often think in these terms. But if we did, we would realize that with Woolman's conversations and meetings with the enslavers and with their subsequent decisions, the powers of darkness were defeated. In those moments, the principalities and powers lost their domination. They were diminished. The world changed; evil was transformed into the kingdom of God.

It seems as if part of the reason that Woolman was able to be so effective with these slave owners was that he didn't approach these encounters with a judgmental or condemning attitude. He was deeply concerned about the immorality of slavery, but at least part of his concern was for the owners themselves. He communicated care for them and their spiritual well-being. One has to believe that the slave owners felt love coming from Woolman. We don't have the whole picture, but it is clear Woolman didn't approach these encounters as an argument to be won. He saw another level of engagement. From the start, he was looking at the encounters as a spiritual struggle; he wanted the slave owners' hearts to be changed. He wanted them to remove the obstacles that were alienating them from their God.

Woolman was laying out for these people an alternative vision of how to be on this earth. He wasn't just telling them what was morally right and how wrong they were but was reminding them of what it is to be human and to live closer to God's kingdom. Since many of these people changed, perhaps some of them had a glimpse that through enslaving others, they were turning into people they didn't want to become. Maybe there was enough light in Woolman that they could glimpse a more appealing vision of what it is to be human and how to live as a person of faith. Perhaps he was giving them an image that resonated with a hidden but more profound vision they had of themselves.

Creating Jubilee

Once, Jesus' disciples were unable to heal a boy possessed by demons. The boy's father tells Jesus that the demons have tried to kill the boy by throwing him into the fire and, at a different time, throwing him into water. (Mark 9:14-29) When the disciples ask why they failed, Jesus responds that this can only happen with prayer. In the Matthew version of this same story, Jesus emphasizes faith. In Matthew, Jesus tells the disciples they hadn't had enough faith and then teaches them that if they had faith the size of a mustard seed, they could move mountains. (Matthew 17:14-21)

Many of us are a little uncomfortable with the idea of demons and the casting out of demons. We may want to give the language of demons a wide berth. Nevertheless, is the Woolman story different from the Jesus story? If anything is evil, the way slavery was practiced in this country was evil. Whether we are comfortable using the word demonic or not, kidnapping free people from their homeland and treating them like property, including torture, breaking up families, threats, dehumanization, and rape, has to be called evil. With fellow Quakers, Woolman, again and again, eliminated that evil. How is that less an exorcism than Jesus healing the boy in the Biblical story?

As mentioned above, roughly a century after Woolman, this country fought its most divisive and bloody war over slavery. We step back from that bloodbath and remember that John Woolman was able to free slaves with visits and conversations, no war or blood. Just a miracle! These conversations and encounters moved mountains.

Seen through the eyes of faith, one believes these encounters were more than conversations between human beings. One believes these were encounters embodying God, just as Jesus' encounters with the people of his time. God is in the mix. These people are in a conversation with Woolman, but they are encountering the Divine. Woolman desired to be an instrument of God's freedom for the enslaved. He wanted to be God's instrument to eliminate slavery and reform the Quaker movement. With much prayer, discernment, commitment, sacrifice, and courage, he was remarkably successful.

Thankfully, Woolman never accepted the vision and reality of the dominant society in which he lived. He could see and cling to an atypical vision he believed God was setting before him. Woolman's vision was never of profit. It was a vision of freedom, justice, reconciliation, and God's kingdom on earth. It was a commitment to invest in real wealth that moths and rust couldn't corrupt. (Matthew 16:19-20) Miracles followed in his wake.

It may be hard for people of European descent to connect viscerally with the power and pure joy that freedom meant to people who had lost virtually everything. Woolman's journal doesn't mention what the enslaved people he helped free felt upon their liberation. However, others provide an understanding of what freedom meant to those enslaved.

Lalita Tademy, in her book *Cane River,* tells the story of several generations of her ancestors who were enslaved in Louisiana. They had no control over their own lives. Her enslaved ancestors had no power to protect themselves from physical violence, to protect their children from being sold, to shield themselves or their children from rape, or to keep a couple from being split up and sold to different owners. They always had to be extremely careful of their owners' moods, preferences, and habits so as not to offend them, which would result in physical punishment or heartbreak. If a farm or plantation was sold, it was very likely that enslaved families would be sold to different owners and separated from their loved ones.

Tademy paints a picture of enslaved people who, as the Civil War was ending, were beginning to allow themselves to hope and dream that their future might be different. It included being able to dream about preparing a future for their own children and not just the children of their owners. As the war ended, they allowed themselves to marvel at the possibility of owning land as opposed to the resignation of working someone else's land for the rest of their lives. There was the delicious experience of allowing themselves to entertain the possibility of owning property as opposed to being property.

As freedom came, this extended family, who had been split up among different owners, had the opportunity to be reunited together as a family. They began to experience, for the first time in their lives, choices that had been completely unavailable to them. For the first time, instead of their owners managing and making plans for their lives, they could entertain their own thoughts about how to go forward. Tademy imagines one of her ancestors, thinking, "There was nothing more satisfying than having plans."[7] For this same ancestor, those plans would now involve the privilege and right to have a last name, something denied to her and her family before.

Harriet Tubman, known for leading dozens of enslaved people to freedom and probably instrumental in freeing hundreds more, recounts her feelings when she crossed the Pennsylvania border into freedom. She recalled, "I looked at my hands to see if I was the same person. There was such a glory over everything; the sun came like gold through the trees and over the fields, and I felt like I was in heaven."[8]

After Tubman had freed herself, she started making underground trips back to Maryland to free others. One of those she later released was her brother Joe. At this time, the Fugitive Slave Law was in effect, meaning that she had to get him and the others completely out of the country for him to be safe. Tubman got him all the way from Maryland to the suspension bridge over the Niagara River near the falls that separated New York and Ontario. Joe was still highly anxious about being caught and would not even look at the magnificent falls. When they reached the Ontario side of the river, Tubman called to her brother that he was free. Joe was so overcome with relief he began shouting in joy, singing, and praising God. He was so enthusiastic in his celebration that he began to draw a crowd. Tubman, like

Woolman, spent her life being the catalyst for this kind of jubilation.

Though they lived a century apart, Woolman and Tubman were connected. As mentioned, Tubman was making trips back to Maryland to free more slaves. As she returned with groups of people making their way to freedom, many of the people she was hidden by on the underground railway were Quakers. The Maryland, Delaware area that she was passing through was part of one of the areas where John Woolman had been advocating for the release of slaves roughly a century earlier. It certainly appears that Woolman's impact on the Quakers aided Harriet Tubman's courageous work long after his death. Of course, Woolman would not have a hint of this later history; nevertheless, he planted the seeds for the Quakers to continue playing a substantial role in freeing enslaved people during Tubman's day.

Woolman inspired and encouraged people to free their captives. There is no evidence that he used the Leviticus Jubilee verses, the Isaiah scriptures, or those at the beginning of Luke in his conversations with his fellow Quakers. Nevertheless, he was an incarnation of these scriptures as he dedicated his life to creating Jubilee freedom for enslaved people.

Woolman would never have seen himself as having power. He appears to have been an incredibly humble man, merely paying attention to and acting on his conscience while daily trying to be guided by his God. Nevertheless, looking back at the impact of his life, one sees that he had enormous power. We could phrase it differently and say that God was able to exercise God's power through him. Woolman probably would never have seen his work as creating a year of Jubilee and celebration. He wouldn't have thought of himself as having power, but guided by his faith, he was able to be the catalyst for enormous transformations in individuals, the Quaker faith, and in the culture of the time.

Pointing Toward the Kingdom—of God

In Woolman's life, thinking small materially allowed him to grow large spiritually. If Woolman had taken the expected, conventional route in life and continued to develop his business, we would never have heard of him. Undoubtedly, he would have lived an exemplary life, but, in all likelihood, he would never have traveled so extensively, challenged many slave owners in multiple colonies, and given his message of deliverance and freedom for the captives at countless Quaker meetings. Had he not done all these things, all those lives would not have been transformed, and the world would have been far poorer. Woolman chose to be poorer materially, which resulted in many being blessed with freedom and others being enriched with real wealth spiritually.

Had Woolman chosen the more conventional life path and developed his business, then the impact of his life would not have happened or would have taken place on a much smaller scale. There would have been no Jubilee celebration by the many freed slaves. Woolman was a catalyst for these Jubilee scriptures becoming incarnate.

Woolman's openness to a countercultural scriptural message about money and wealth freed many and opened the door for the Jubilee celebration for slaves. Initially, the slave owners who freed their slaves probably had mixed feelings about losing their property and the loss of needed labor. They were materially poorer and had to work harder themselves. One can imagine that in the beginning, they didn't feel celebratory. However, the freedom of Jubilee was just as important in their lives as it was for the freed slaves.

The Quakers believe that every person has something of the light of God within them. Woolman would have been confident that each of the slave owners he was meeting with carried that light of God within. However, their light was becoming covered with ashes, and the embers holding that light were gradually diminishing. In his visits with these people, Woolman was brushing the ashes off those embers and gently blowing a little oxygen on those ebbing coals, giving new spiritual life to what had been fading.

The former slave owners had been participating in and profiting from a system based on kidnapping, breaking up families, torture, beatings, rape, intimidation, and murder. They were committing terrible crimes. With the release of their slaves, they were no longer captive to enforcing that evil system. Being free from this structure was a huge event in their lives. One imagines that over time, they began to experience their own liberation as they freed other human beings. Maybe they weren't celebrating, but it is not hard to imagine them being relieved that they were no longer enforcing that evil system.

We imagine their inner light growing and the God within being liberated in ways that had been impossible when they had been captive to the belief that human beings were just another form of property. Woolman and the enslavers were living out Jesus' words at the beginning of his ministry. The captives were free, and the blind were able to see. It was not the beloved community of which Dr. King was to speak later, but it was a strong step in that direction.

The scriptures from Leviticus, Isaiah, and Luke mentioned above come from different periods of history, but all proclaim the theme of liberation. The writer(s) of the Jubilee verses, Isaiah's call to release the captives, Jesus holding up the Isaiah verses, and John Woolman's life all point toward some of the qualities that make up the kingdom of God.

The earlier Jubilee verses point toward a vision of a more just society. They move toward a community wherein all are free, none are owned, no one is treated as property, and all are valued and loved by God. The Jubilee verses set out a formula for the economic leveling of society. Those who are richer don't keep amassing wealth, property, and power, while those who are poorer have less, lose status, lose their families, and are trapped in a downward spiral. These verses help maintain equality of wealth. More than that, they are steps in creating a society where all are of value, have hope, have the opportunity to support their family, and are seen as included and loved by God.

In Jesus' first words in the temple in Nazareth, he doesn't use the language of "kingdom," but when the words he read are lived, the written word becomes the living word. God's kingdom breaks through on earth.

In Woolman's embodiment of these scriptures, a part of the world is repaired and healed. The lives he touches become more whole. The kingdom breaks through in the captives' release and the transformed lives of former slaveholders. "Thy kingdom come on earth as it is in heaven" becomes far more than a few words prayed in a worship service. All along the paths that Woolman travels, elements of the kingdom break out. The good news of the gospel emerges as freedom, transformation, and celebration replace evil, captivity, and suffering.

As the kingdom comes into the lives of the people Woolman touched, love is enacted. Leviticus 25 doesn't use the word love, but when captives are freed, people have the opportunity to stay on their land, and families are not separated; they experience it as being valued and loved. When Jesus uses Isaiah's words at the beginning of his ministry of freeing the captives, restoring sight to the blind, and relieving suffering, it's not a rule or law or just a good thing. Jesus is saying that the reign of God is starting and being made incarnate. Some will experience the joy of being delivered from evil. Leviticus exults that this is a time of restoration and calls for trumpets to be blown everywhere in the land. Indeed, it is a sacred time of freedom and celebration. It is a kingdom of love.

War: Impotent in Changing Hearts and Minds

This chapter began by acknowledging that enslaved people were freed through the Civil War's violence while also remembering that roughly a hundred years before the war, Woolman had been freeing them in a very different way. It's enlightening to compare the long-term effects of both methods. The evidence is that Woolman's practice in following Jesus's path was more powerful in changing the hearts of those captivated by the ideology undergirding slavery.

The Civil War ended slavery, but the attitudes of white supremacy underpinning the fight for slavery remained intact. The racism and hate that sustained slavery remain entrenched in our culture and have played out in many forms of injustice continuing to this day. Multiple methods have been employed since the Civil War to maintain white privilege and supremacy.

Horrific violence toward Blacks has been a primary method for maintaining white power and subjugating people of color. Our history books have failed to educate us about massacres of Blacks and, occasionally, the Whites who supported them. In 1866, there was a massacre of at least 200 Blacks and Whites in New Orleans who had met to guarantee Blacks the right to vote in the new state constitution. In 1898, Whites in Wilmington, North Carolina, planned and organized a massacre, killing between 60 and 300 Blacks. The mob destroyed Black businesses and burned their neighborhoods. In 1921, Whites attacked the Black area of Greenwood, part of Tulsa, Oklahoma. The mobs killed 100-300 people and set fire to 35-40 city blocks. The flames leveled 1,256 homes, left 8,000 homeless, and destroyed 150 businesses. There were other terrible massacres of people of color. These three massacres are a sampling of what is not included in what we learn about the history of our country.

Shockingly, lynching, both public and hidden, was another form of violence used to maintain white supremacy. The Equal Justice Initiative has documented over 6,000 racial lynchings of Blacks in America between 1865 and 1950. They believe white lynch mobs killed thousands more African American people whose deaths may never be uncovered.[9]

Whites lynched Black people for such insignificant things as suing a white man for killing his cow, insisting that a white co-worker return a shovel, addressing a police officer without using the title "mister," drinking from a white man's well, and striking to protest low wages.

Communities sometimes advertised these lynchings as entertainment events for people to come to as they would to a fair or a community picnic. Parents brought their children to witness these killings, passing hate from one generation to the next. Those attending sometimes made pictures of the hangings, which they made into memorabilia like postcards. The lynchings were acts of terror to keep Blacks "in their place." It's hard to comprehend such evil and equally challenging to understand celebrating it.

After the Civil War, plantation owners unjustly imprisoned African Americans to have forced labor to take care of their crops. The sharecropping system that developed in the South after the war was similar to slavery. It involves too much detail to state here, but many economic policies dating from the Civil War until now have repeatedly put people of color at a disadvantage.

We use the language of racism, prejudice, white supremacy, and white power to describe this history. Yet, it is hard to look at this account and to call it anything other than hatred.

With the election of a Black president, some of us hoped we were taking a huge leap toward putting our racist history behind us. We were quickly disabused of that notion when the man who followed him campaigned, saying that people coming from Mexico were rapists. As president, he followed that up by talking about Haiti and African nations as shit-hole countries. After the riots in Charlottesville, where white supremacists had a strong presence, he said there were "good people on both sides." Later, the president retweeted a tweet of a Florida man shouting for white power. There are numerous other examples of the president's racism.

It's not just what the president says, but the evidence is that his statements have unleashed racism and hatred throughout the country. The president's racist comments have encouraged people to be much more overt in their racism. Many stories document people calling the police on people of color who were doing nothing wrong or illegal. Sometimes, these people were simply on or going to their own property. There have been multiple stories of police violence and killings of black people under very questionable circumstances.

The worst of these, of course, was the horrific killing of George Floyd. It's hard not to think of that as a modern-day lynching.

The country is now embroiled in what to do about Confederate memorials, statues, and military bases named for Confederate war heroes. The use of the Confederate flag is a significant source of conflict. A strong contingent of the country wants to protect and embrace these symbols of slavery. Their attachment gives a chilling picture that a century and a half after the Civil War, the mindset of slavery is still intact, influential, and a part of our national identity.

There are many more examples of the racist and slavery mindset. Other sources illustrate those examples in much greater detail and more eloquently. The above is a very abbreviated section to encourage reflection on the impotence of the Civil War in changing people's hearts positively.

The war resulted in the release of enslaved people. However, as is apparent, hearts, minds, and attitudes were not changed. This history contrasts profoundly with the changes Woolman and his fellow Quakers initiated following Jesus' nonviolent way. The Quakers peacefully ended slavery among their followers before the Civil War. After the Revolutionary War, Quakers contributed to the successful effort to abolish slavery in Pennsylvania. They petitioned the United States Congress to abolish slavery in the entire country, but that effort was unsuccessful. After the Revolutionary War, they joined with other religious denominations in the Upper South in persuading enslavers to release those enslaved by them. They had some success with this. As noted above, Quakers not only ended slavery among their followers but were an active part of the Underground Railroad. To this day, Quakers continue to be a strong voice for equality and justice.

The evidence is that the Quakers not only freed their enslaved people but that their hearts, attitudes, and minds were also profoundly transformed by Woolman's nonviolent approach. Reflecting on it from a historical perspective, not only was the path of Jesus effective and peaceful, it was more powerful than war. Almost two and a half centuries after Woolman's death, we still benefit from his vision and commitment.

'The Seeds of War and Slavery Are Identical

When wars are being cranked up, most of us believe or are led to believe that we go to war because we are threatened, our security is endangered, or some other country is about to attack us. We are led to believe that it is always another country that is at fault, and we, whatever country or time we are in, are logically protecting ourselves from the evil of an aggressor. That can be true. However, many times, it's false, and Woolman had the insight to think more deeply about the other reasons we go to war. He challenged, "May we look upon our treasure, our furniture and our garments, and try to discover whether the seeds of war are nourished by these, our possessions."[10] In recent years, this quote has been hauntingly sung by Paulette Meier.[11]

Few of us are in the habit of thinking that we go to war to enrich ourselves. We want to believe that we are fighting for liberty, democracy, freedom, country, and security. We are easily seduced into believing that some country is threatening us. The people in power who led us into war are far more aware of the hoped-for plunder and treasure of war. The average person doesn't usually think that our desire for more possessions nourishes the seeds of war. However, Woolman cuts through the din of the war drums and the demonizing of the enemy. He asks if the seeds of war originate in our desire for more wealth. He was extraordinarily insightful about how the economic forces that made slavery so entrenched are the same as those that lure us into war.

Woolman could see through the fog that frequently masks the real intent of cranking up the killing machine. Shedding material gain in his own life, choosing simplicity, and his undivided devotion to God gave him extraordinary clarity. He could pierce through the sometimes intentionally created haze of fear and false patriotism intended to stampede us into war. He was clear that at its core, war is often about wealth and possessions—in short, plunder.

Roughly a century after Woolman's death, the nation was overwhelmed by the massive violence and destruction of the Civil War. This catastrophe was brought on by people determined to maintain their plunder. There was a lot more wealth to hold onto than we usually realize. When the Civil War started, there were more millionaires in the Mississippi Valley than in any other part of the United States. The country's nearly 4 million enslaved people would have been valued at $3.5 billion. That would have made them worth more than all railroads and manufacturing combined, more than any other single asset in the economy at that time. [12] Many in the South had become dependent on enslaving people to satisfy their greed. They had become trapped in the same web that Woolman had devoted his life to eliminating. Even in the face of death and destruction, they never loosened their grip.

Jesus taught us that our hearts are where our treasure is. (Luke 12:34) Thinking about those who went to war to protect slavery, it's shocking to realize that their treasure was rooted in the enslavement of other human beings and the wealth that enslaved labor brought them. There is the verse stating that "... the love of money is a root of all sorts of evil, and some by longing for it have wandered away from the faith and pierced themselves with many griefs." (I Timothy 6:10) Certainly, by the end of the Civil War, these people had pierced themselves with many griefs resulting from their love of money.

In retrospect, it is easy to look back and to be very judgmental of the enslavers. It seems incomprehensible that they could develop and cling to such a cruel and vicious system. However, it may be that we are not as pure as we think. Probably, we are all on a continuum, with John Woolman at one end and the enslavers on the other. If we examine our values, including what we invest in and the fruits of those investments, we might find ourselves further from Woolman and uncomfortably closer to the enslavers than we originally imagined.

As mentioned earlier, many scriptures about money, property, and wealth seem impractical and extreme. However, God gives them to us in love to guide us away from the terrible things we human beings do to one another and the planet in our pursuit of wealth. At first glance, these verses may appear daunting and impossible to follow, but they exist to save us and transform the world. They lead us away from false values and behaviors that deaden our souls and separate us from our Creator. These scriptures are given in love to protect us.

NOTES

[1] History of American Women: Slavery in America: Slavery in Rhode Island, Accessed 3/18/2025, https://www.womenhistoryblog.com/2008/01/slavery-in-rhode-island.html.

[2] Rebecca Beatrice Brooks, "Slavery in Massachusetts," December 20, 2012. https://historyofmassachusetts.org/slavery-in-massachusetts/.

[3] *Douglas Harper,* "Slavery in New Jersey," *Slavery in the North,* 2003, http://slavenorth.com/newjersey.htm.

[4] Thomas P. Slaughter, *The Beautiful Soul of John Woolman: Apostle of Abolition,* (New York: Hill and Wang 2008), 173.

[5] In these verses, some translations use the language of Jubilee and some use Great Day of Forgiveness. It is confusing because other scripture designates the tenth day of the seventh month the Great Day of Forgiveness.

[6] John Woolman, *Quaker Spirituality: Selected Writings,* ed. Douglas V. Steere (New York, Ramsey, Toronto: Paulist Press, 1984) 176-9.

[7] Lalita Tademy, *Cane Rive*r (New York and Boston: Warner Books, 2001), 237.

[8] Kate Clifford Larson, *Bound for the Promised Land: Harriet Tubman, Portrait of an American Hero* (New York: Ballantine Books, 2004), 84.

[9] "Reconstruction in America: Racial Violence after the Civil War," *Equal Justice Initiative,* 2020, https://eji.org/reports/reconstruction-in-america-overview/.

[10] Phillips P. Moulton, *The Journal and Major Essays of John Woolman,* (Richmond, Indiana: Friends United Press, 1971) 255.

[11] Phillips P. Moulton, *The Journal and Major Essays of John Woolman,* 255. Also, Paulette Meier, Wellsprings of Life: Quaker Wisdom in Chant, released April 4, 2020.

[12] Coates, Ta-Nehisi. "Slavery Made America." *The Atlantic,* June 24, 2014, https://www.theatlantic.com/business/archive/2014/06/slavery-made-america/373288/.

| four |

Dorothy Day

When Jesus heard what had happened, he withdrew by boat privately to a solitary place. Hearing of this, the crowds followed him on foot from the towns. When Jesus landed and saw a large crowd, he had compassion on them and healed their sick. As evening approached, the disciples came to him and said, "This is a remote place, and it's already getting late. Send the crowds away, so they can go to the villages and buy themselves some food." Jesus replied, "They do not need to go away. You give them something to eat." "We have here only five loaves of bread and two fish," they answered. "Bring them here to me," he said. And he directed the people to sit down on the grass. Taking the five loaves and the two fish and looking up to heaven, he gave thanks and broke the loaves. Then he gave them to the disciples, and the disciples gave them to the people. They all ate and were satisfied, and the disciples picked up twelve basketfuls of broken pieces that were left over. The number of those who ate was about five thousand men, besides women and children. Matthew 14:13-21

Loaves and Fishes: A Story Inspired by Matthew 14:13-21, Mark 6:30-44, Luke: 9:10-17 and John 6:1-14

It's chaos, but we love it. In this little small town that I live in, we've all heard that the holy man, Jesus, is near here and moving toward the far shore of Galilee. We all want to see what he will do and what will happen. We never have excitement like this. Occasionally, the Roman soldiers come through; that's excitement we don't want. But this is different. We're all bustling around, getting ready to join the crowd.

We've all heard about Jesus, but we don't really know who he is and don't clearly understand what he is about, but that doesn't matter. He is famous, and we don't want to miss this once-in-a-lifetime happening. Some think he's a prophet, some have heard he heals, and they want to be healed. Some even believe that he might be the Messiah. The faithful think he is truly a once-in-a-lifetime man of God, and others believe he is just a fake holy man. Others don't know and don't care; they just want to be part of the excitement. I'm one of the latter. I don't know what or who he is, but I definitely want to be a part of whatever is going to happen.

We live in these little villages out in the countryside with our crops, sheep, goats, and chickens. It's all pretty quiet and routine; frankly, it's dull as a donkey braying. But for once, something exciting is happening, and I'm scrambling to get out the door so it doesn't leave me behind.

As I'm happily rushing out, I'm jolted by my wife declaring, "We're also going."

"No. It's your job to care for the house and the boys."

"This holy man is for all of us. I'm going and taking the boys," she insists.

"Absolutely not."

"This Jesus talks with women. He heals women. Women help support him. The boys may never have an opportunity like this again. We're coming."

I'm totally opposed. I'm the man; I'm supposed to be in charge. But if I stay here arguing all day, asserting my authority, I might miss everything. Besides, in the end, she might not obey me. So, to save face and exercise my role as the head of the household, I magnanimously grant it.

"Alright, alright, get ready quickly. We have to get moving."

She hurriedly throws a few things to eat in a bag, and we all rush out. At last, after all the family uproar, we are finally bubbling along with the crowd.

It's exhilarating. Some people are following behind Jesus, and others have figured out where they think he and the disciples are going and are racing ahead. The road and the countryside are full of people. It's like a big festival or holy day. We enjoy being with neighbors and friends and speculating about who this extraordinary man is, what they have heard about him, what he might do, and what will happen. It's great fun, and we all are enjoying being with our neighbors and others who are new to us.

We keep following for hours and steadily move further away from the villages and deeper into the countryside. We are all starting to get tired. Our excitement has drained away, and the boys are beginning to be a little impatient and wonder what we are doing and when we will stop and rest. I started to get angry with my wife. I knew they shouldn't have come.

Finally, we are stopping. The crowd is gathering around Jesus. Somehow, as we started gathering together, my family was upfront and close to Jesus and his disciples.

We settle in, but after walking for a long day, I'm aware people are murmuring about food. Maybe grumbling is more accurate. I can even hear the disciples anxiously talking among themselves about food; I think they are worried. People had wanted to hear Jesus teach and possibly see a miracle, but their hunger is overshadowing all that early energy and excitement. We've got a little bit that my wife packed, but it is hardly enough for the four of us. Many people haven't brought food or didn't have anything to bring.

As I'm becoming more aware of what is going on around us, all of a sudden, I realize that my oldest son has gotten up and is heading toward the disciples. Not only that, but he also has the bag of food my wife had hastily thrown together. I'm incredulous as he hands the bag to one of the disciples. I'm shocked! We needed that food, and now we've got nothing. We had taught him to share, but this level of sharing is way beyond what we meant. You have to do these things in moderation! I wanted to yell at him to come back, but that would have been too embarrassing. There's nothing I can do now.

The disciples take the food to Jesus as my son returns to sit with us; I sit watching in disbelief. Then Jesus takes the loaves and fishes from the bag, blesses them, and starts distributing them to the people.

As I watched our food being shared, I was changing. I was starting to be moved that the food we had brought was being blessed by the holy man and shared with the crowd. I was even beginning to be glad about that.

Then, an unexpected thing happens. Others around us see what is going on. I watch as some of them who have been hiding food start pulling it out and handing it to Jesus, determined their food will also be blessed and shared. Fear and self-protection lose their power as the holy man transforms them into generosity.

I know from the stories that at other times, people trying to get close to Jesus have been unruly, pushing, and shoving. But this time, it is different. I watch as the people quietly settle in, sit down, and wait for Jesus to get to them. Jesus, with a slight smile, walks contentedly among those gathered. He seems happy to be out among us. I watch him warmly greet people and bless the food people are giving him. I sense that it is not just the food but that we also are being blessed. My heart is peaceful, and it appears that is happening with the others there.

Those further back in the crowd see what is happening. I watch and realize that a few cagier types have seen and been in these crowds before. It was apparent they weren't interested in the holy man. They had known this was an opportunity to make money and had scrambled around buying extra food from the villages and farmers as we passed through following Jesus. They hadn't bought just for themselves but had purchased a lot and loaded up their donkeys. They intended to sell it for a profit when people were hungrier.

But I watch with astonishment as they abandon profit, unload their donkeys, and urge Jesus to share it all. It appears even these people are moved as they sense the magnitude of the moment and don't want to miss being a part of it. They are also captivated by this experience as they feel a spirit of community and love spreading among us. Maybe none of us understand it, but I sense a feeling growing among us that we all want to be a part of it.

It's obvious those who had brought nothing are relieved and touched that they are unexpectedly being cared for. It appears that whether we started with food or no food, we are at peace.

I start to be aware that it is more than the food we are receiving. I sense our spirits are being fed. Most of us were probably not aware that this was what we hungered for the most. I started this day for a lark but now realize I was desperate for spiritual food and for my life to be closer to what this man embodies. I have the unusual feeling of being valued, included, embraced, and loved even, not only by Jesus but by all these people around us.

Some of us know Jesus teaches about the kingdom of God, and we know some of the stories he told about that. I'm startled to become aware that those teachings have become alive, miraculously, in us. We are participating in a moment of God's kingdom. Our hearts are changing, and we sense this is the treasure we have been seeking.

I'm aware of an unusual feeling of caring not just for myself and my family but for all of us. I can't know, but I believe that is happening with others. We are no longer separate, striving individuals but are connected and want for others what we want for ourselves. We experience a spirit of oneness with those around us and with God. We want the well-being of all.

We see food left over and are startled to realize that we live amid abundance. When we care for others, there is more than enough for all. It starts to break into our consciousness that along with the material abundance, there is an abundance of love and spiritual food. As there is more than enough to fill our stomachs, spiritual food is abundant, more than enough to fill our hearts and souls.

Some want Jesus to start a violent revolution against the Romans. He has a different goal. He is creating a revolution in our hearts.

Loaves and Fishes: A Twentieth Century Version

In John 14:12, Jesus tells the disciples that if they have faith in him, they will not only do the same kinds of things he is doing but will do even greater things. Of course, that is hard to accept. One doesn't have to get into a comparison with Jesus about what is greater, but there was a twentieth-century version of feeding the five thousand.

In 1933, in the depths of the depression, Dorothy Day and Peter Maurin followed in Jesus' footsteps by launching the Catholic Worker Movement. They began by publishing The Catholic Worker paper. Jesus started with five loaves and two fishes. Dorothy began with two checks totaling $57.00 that covered the publishing costs of 2,500 copies for the paper's first edition. Instead of paying the rent, gas, and electricity for her apartment, she used the two checks to print the first edition. What grew out of that $57.00 probably exceeded their wildest expectations. In three years, they were printing 150,000 copies that they shipped out of New York all over the country. Almost spontaneously, they began starting houses of hospitality for those without homes and providing meals for the destitute.

The Catholic Worker wasn't just information. It was a paper that touched people's hearts and changed their lives. Some responded by coming to New York and volunteering. As other readers around the country resonated with the paper, they incorporated its values by also establishing houses of hospitality and providing food for homeless people in the cities where they lived. Others sent money or provided buildings.

Countrywide, tens of thousands of destitute people were fed, and thousands of homeless people were provided housing. Millions were challenged and fed spiritually by the witness of this community. The loaves and fishes were again multiplied.

She Hardly Appeared a Saint in the Making

From childhood through young adulthood, Dorothy Day gave few hints that she would eventually be considered for sainthood in the Catholic Church. She wasn't a hellion, but much of her life would not have been seen as a model of the saintly type.

Her family was nominally Christian but was actually mildly hostile to Christianity. [1] The family didn't attend church and didn't teach Christianity in the home. Dorothy would sometimes go to church services with various neighbors and friends, but her parents were passively opposed and relieved when she stopped going.

When Dorothy was eight, she attended a Methodist church with her best friend from a neighboring family. However, one day, the mother of that friend witnessed Dorothy in an argument with her brother. When the mother heard some of Dorothy's colorful language in this disagreement, she terminated the friendship and stopped taking Dorothy to church. Finding that she was not allowed to play with her friend, Dorothy was content to play with the "tough gang" of adolescent boys in the neighborhood.

Dorothy and her family lived in Oakland, CA, but moved to Chicago soon after the San Francisco earthquake in 1906. At sixteen, Dorothy would attend the University of Illinois for two years. Following this, she moved to New York. As a young adult, she was usually employed in some type of writing work for publications that were considered radical.

Her friends frequently came from the literary world. They were reporters, playwrights, editors, and theater critics. They were often very talented and well-known in that world, and some would become famous, Eugene O'Neil being the most prominent. Dorothy also constantly attempted to write novels but had minimal success.

Dorothy and her writer friends were also well known for working hard and drinking hard. Sometimes, during bar hopping, they would frequent some of the seediest dives in New York. Dorothy had a reputation for being able to drink with the best of them. During these occasions, she was outgoing, gregarious, and an enthusiastic raconteur of bawdy stories. She had a reputation for carousing in the bars well into the morning hours but still arriving ready to put in a solid day's work the next day.

Certainly, these literary friends were not known for their religious beliefs nor committed to a spiritual life. More commonly, many of them were contemptuous of Christianity and the religious world.

During this part of her life, when she was partying and working with these other writers, Day had a strong personality and was very independent and self-assured. She was the picture of a strong woman with her own thoughts, which she wasn't hesitant about expressing. She was competing in a man's world and was holding her own. That ended when she became sexually involved in a destructive relationship with another writer.

In this particular relationship, Dorothy was emotionally bullied and abused. She seemed to have had an inner vulnerability to this specific man and lost her sense of self while involved with him. He determined what she should read and what she could write, once even throwing the book she was reading out a train window because he disapproved. Her friends were concerned that he might also be physically abusing her. Given how independent, assertive, and forceful she had been, it's surprising she allowed this to happen.

During this relationship, she became pregnant. The man made it clear that he wanted no part of a child and that she was totally on her own. She chose to have an abortion. There was some off-again, on-again in this relationship, which he eventually terminated.

In the months following this relationship and these experiences, she was unraveling and probably reached the lowest point of her life. She became depressed and attempted suicide at least once and probably twice.

On the rebound from the relationship and recovering from the emotional drain of the abortion, Dorothy embarked on a marriage to an affluent older man. They spent a year in Europe. Upon returning to the States, she admitted that the marriage had been a mistake and promptly divorced.

Her friends were not known for their puritanical beliefs, but following the divorce, a few of them became concerned that she was becoming promiscuous. A couple she was living with were troubled that she was becoming "more libidinous than ever"

Following this period of her life, in 1924, Dorothy became involved in a far healthier love relationship than she had previously experienced. Forster Batterham was the brother of one of her friends. With him, she left some of the chaos of her former life. She had passed through years of stressful, painful relationships, causing her sadness and despair. With Forster, she felt safe and surrounded by happiness and quiet beauty. She thought of Forster as her common-law husband. Out of this relationship, Dorothy was delighted that she could give birth to a daughter.

In looking at these vignettes of her early life, one might think that Dorothy would not be a likely candidate for possible sainthood. However, it appears that God saw that beginning differently.

For many of us who are familiar with Dorothy, the picture above is probably not the image we have of her in our minds. We are more likely to remember the photograph of a much older woman sitting on her combination cane and three-legged stool during the United Farm Workers strike in 1973. That picture is of a very calm, resolute, elderly woman on the picket line facing two armed officers from the sheriff's department. She appears to be more than holding her own with these officers. At seventy-six years of age, she appears to be a serene bastion of integrity and strength in a potentially explosive moment.

Attracted to the "Sweetness of Faith"

During these early years, there was another side of Dorothy Day present. She was drawn to faith, or, as she says, haunted by God. [2] Despite having a minimum of encouragement toward a life of faith from her parents as a child and discouragement from her companions as a young adult, a part of her seems to have always been searching for God and a sense of God searching for her. She was powerfully touched when, in the back room of a saloon, Eugene O'Neil recited to her Francis Thompson's "The Hound of Heaven," a poem about fleeing from God. The poem became imprinted on her life, giving her a sense of being followed and longed for while simultaneously filling her with hope and expectation.

Day remembers that as children, they were taught to say their prayers and to have a sense of right and wrong. When she started school, she remembers praying the Our Father. As a child, she didn't hear much of religion, but when she heard God's name, her heart leaped. When she was eight, the family lived in Oakland, CA. A friend who lived in the neighborhood took her to a Methodist church. She recalls experiencing the "sweetness of faith." [3]

The family was living in Oakland when the great earthquake of 1906 hit the West Coast. She remembers that her family and her neighbors did everything possible to help the people of San Francisco, where the quake had been most devastating. They opened their doors and gave away their clothes to those who were being ferried across the bay. She loved the joy of being able to do good.

After the earthquake, the family immediately left Oakland for Chicago, where she had a neighborhood friend who told her about the saints. Day was profoundly moved during one of these conversations. She says,

> "I only remember my feeling of lofty enthusiasm, and how my heart almost burst with desire to take part in such high endeavor...This was one of those occasions when my small heart was enlarged and I could feel it swelling in love and gratitude to such a good God, for a friend like Mary, for conversation such as ours; I was filled with a natural striving, a thrilling recognition of the possibilities of spiritual adventure."**[4]**

Another neighbor, the mother of some friends, became an example when Day was twelve. Day was looking for her friends. Not seeing them outside, she spontaneously ran into their house, searching for them. She didn't find her friends, but when she went through the house, she encountered her friend's mother in the back bedroom, on her knees, praying. Witnessing this, she says, "I felt a burst of love toward Mrs. Barrett that I have never forgotten, a feeling of gratitude and happiness that warmed my heart. It was she who taught me what to do."[5]

While still in this neighborhood in Chicago, an Episcopalian priest visited the home. On learning that Day's mother had been brought up in the Episcopal Church, he convinced her to send the children to the church where he was pastor. During this time, as Day attended worship, she grew to love the Psalms and the prayers of the Collect. They filled her with joy. She was particularly enthralled with the *Benedicite* and the *Te Deum,* experiencing them as more beautiful than anything she had known. All forms of beauty, whether in song, story, nature, or human love, prompted her to want to cry out with joy.[6]

The family moved to the north side of Chicago, where she attended a different Episcopal church. Here, she studied the catechism, moving her toward baptism and confirmation. It didn't hinder her that neither parent was supportive. Her mother acquiesced to her following through with baptism and confirmation at the urging of the minister. Her father gave in, fearful that his unusual daughter might turn toward the Catholic Church if blocked from this route. For him, this option was not only worse but totally intolerable.[7]

As an adolescent, Day experienced the very human struggle with sexual feelings, her budding faith, and her attempt to understand that part of her life. She acknowledges that this struggle went on for years.

It's remarkable that with no support from her parents, Day had such a strong attraction to the church. Some of her friends were receiving substantial encouragement from their parents as Day was being mildly discouraged. Nevertheless, she followed through on her own, and what she received from the church had a significant impact.

In her adolescent church experience, it's striking that Day experienced the Psalms and the liturgical parts of the church so powerfully. Some people participate in these parts of a worship service feeling little or nothing. Others might be bored, and some (possibly her parents) would experience them with hostility. In contrast, Day was profoundly moved. They touched something deep in her and elicited a strong emotional response. For her, they were joy and beauty. It appears that for the young Day, they were a religious experience.

Later as a young adult, when in most ways Day was not outwardly religious, she found it meaningful to spend time in cathedrals. While living in New Orleans, she was drawn to the St. Louis Cathedral. She purchased a book instructing one how to use the rosary. A friend had given her a rosary, so she would take the book and rosary to the cathedral, one assumes, experimenting with that form of prayer. She also sometimes came for Mass and was moved by different parts of the service and impressed by the devotion of the people around her. Later in life, she felt that the time she spent in St. Louis Cathedral was the start of her conversion as an adult.

In Day's early adult life and later with the Catholic Worker, she was not hesitant to be arrested when standing for her beliefs. At the age of twenty-two, though, she was arrested under very different circumstances. The police arrested her, believing her to be a prostitute. In reality, she was befriending an acquaintance, Mae, who had attempted suicide, been hospitalized, and then demanded to be released from the hospital.

After being released, Mae called Day from the headquarters of the Industrial Workers for the World, commonly called the Wobblies. The Wobblies had a flophouse where visiting union members stayed when they were in New York. Mae had called Day from there, needing food, something to wear, and support. Day unhesitatingly went to her aid. When she saw that her friend was sick, she decided to stay with her during the night.

As it happened, the police raided the house that night, and since only men were supposed to be there, the police assumed that the two women were prostitutes. Both were arrested and packed in a cell for several days with others who were, in fact, prostitutes. While there, they suffered many of the usual indignities that accompany imprisonment.

At first glance, it may seem that this account might belong in the previous section with the other stories depicting how Day didn't appear to be a saint in the making. However, Day's response to this woman and her attitude toward this experience are remarkable and outside of the norm. An intriguing part of this story is that the woman Day befriended and suffered for was not a close friend. Day knew Mae because they were in love with the same man, yet Day didn't hesitate to go to her aid when asked. Then, Day was incarcerated because she went out of her way to care for her.

Since they were both competing for the same man, it's surprising that Day would be the person Mae would choose to call for help. That she would reach out to and trust a rival under these desperate circumstances says a lot about how she experienced Day. Under the circumstances, it took an extraordinary quality for Day to respond with such empathy and care. Moreover, if most of us were subjected to a humiliating incarceration for several days under these conditions, the more common reaction would be resentment and blaming Mae. There is no evidence that Day ever fell into these kinds of incriminations.

From the incarceration, Day had some of the normal feelings most of us would have from such an ordeal. She had the common feelings of shame, regret, self-contempt, and humiliation. Uncommonly, though, a part of her didn't want to be spared what she was going through. Part of her intuitively knew that she wanted to share the suffering of the poor, the guilty, and the dispossessed, which she was experiencing in this jail. Few of us would have the insight that imprisonment on a false charge could be a valuable growth experience, but Day did.

Even when young and during a time in her life when she didn't consider herself to be a person of faith, Day had extraordinary spiritual qualities setting her apart.

The Inner Conflict

Day's life was complicated, in that she was strongly attracted to a life of faith while at the same time having an intense conflict with the church. Even as a child, she had the insight that something was wrong with the way Christianity was practiced.

> Children look at things very directly and simply. I did not see anyone taking off his coat and giving it to the poor. I didn't see anyone having a banquet and calling in the lame, the halt, and the blind...I wanted, though I did not know it then, a synthesis. I wanted life and I wanted an abundant life. I wanted it for others too. I did not want just the few, the missionary-minded people like the Salvation Army, to be kind to the poor. I wanted everyone to be kind. I wanted every home to be open to the lame, the halt, and the blind, the way it had been after the San Francisco earthquake. Only then did people really live, really love their brothers. In such love was the abundant life and I did not have the slightest idea how to find it.**[8]**

At this point in her life, Day had not experienced a great deal of poverty firsthand, but she was a voracious reader and had been reading Prince Kropotkin and Upton Sinclair. Kropotkin was a Russian nobleman who renounced his aristocratic title. He was known for being an anarchist and scientist, but he also identified with the suffering of the serfs in Russia and wanted a form of government that created justice for them. Upton Sinclair wrote *The Jungle* about the horrific conditions of the people who worked in Chicago's meatpacking plants near where she lived. Dorothy resonated with the stories of immense suffering by underpaid poor people trying to survive while working in these plants.

She says that since "...*The Jungle* was about Chicago where I lived, whose streets I walked, made me feel that from then on, my life was to be linked to theirs, their interests were to be mine; I had received a call, a vocation, a direction to my life."[9] She understood this was what she was asked to do, but the church seemed to have an entirely different value system and direction. She was baffled, and for a good part of her life, immobilized by this difference.

Day continued reading religious works, including the New Testament. She was inspired by the words but not by the lives of those who understood themselves to be Christians. An affinity, empathy, and commitment to the poor were built into her spiritual DNA. She was drawn toward God and equally committed to the poor.

Beginning college at age 16, she started an intentional process of separating from the church. As she continued reading books that intensified her feelings about poverty, the chasm with the church widened. She had a great deal of clarity about the suffering of the poor and the injustice at the root of their distress.

During this period, she talked about religion while at the same time rejecting it. She felt critical of religious people who seemed happy and comfortable despite the injustices in the world. She began to feel isolated from the Christian community in because it appeared that the way she experienced her faith had nothing to do with the way other Christians experienced theirs. She chose to cut it out of her life. She made a conscious and deliberate decision to harden her heart. She made this decision not out of lack of belief but out of disillusionment with the church.

Not finding a commitment to the poor in the church, Day turned to those in whom she did find that commitment. In the 1920s, a broad and diverse group of people in large cities was concerned precisely with the issues that were critical to her. Dorothy found what she was looking for in various left-wing political movements and publications. She was drawn to the exciting mix of anarchists, labor unionists, communists, socialists, Suffragettes, Wobblies, and the publications supporting these causes. All of these organizations shared her sensitivity to the plight of the poor and working people. Most of the people in these groups that she aligned herself with were either indifferent or hostile to religion. She had a hugely inquiring mind and read widely in class struggle, philosophers, the labor movement, and sometimes religion.

As a young adult in the 1920's, Day led a life immersed in these causes and groups. She frequently worked and wrote for various radical publications that supported them. She didn't hesitate to be arrested while standing for the values in which she believed.

Day constantly lived on the edge financially. She was very assertive and creative in seeking jobs and was usually successful. When money was scarce, she would make arrangements to share living accommodations with friends or would sometimes couch surf. She was courageous, decisive, bold, adventuresome, and indefatigable. On the surface, she did not appear religious.

Turning Toward God

In the mid-nineteen twenties, Dorothy entered into a time of happiness and joy. She had received $5,000 for the screen rights to a novel she had written. Her friend Peggy Cowley persuaded her to buy a small rustic cottage on the beach of Staten Island. The purchase of the house coincided with Dorothy meeting Forster Batterham. Dorothy and Forster created a life together on the island and grew to love each other deeply. It was a special time she always treasured.

They took pleasure in being on the beach and collecting driftwood for the stove, their only source of heat. Forster enjoyed going out in his boat, fishing, tending his lobster traps, and gardening. Dorothy delighted in decorating their home with the small gifts from the sea she found washed up on the beach. For meals, they frequently savored the bounty from the sea. They appreciated the wonderful, eccentric, colorful community of people who lived in their simple homes nearby. Dorothy particularly enjoyed and felt nurtured by this community of friends as they shared with and received hospitality from each other. Dorothy describes their life there as joyous and lovely.

During this time, the faith that sometimes bubbled to the surface throughout Dorothy's life began to develop. She began to pray more, mainly when walking. She sometimes used the rosary with which she had been gifted, not knowing if she was saying it correctly but not caring because it made her happy. Sometimes, she felt sluggish or dull in starting these walks, but as she walked, that changed. By the time she returned, she felt filled with exultation. Prayer became a delight, and she began to attend Mass regularly on Sundays.

Since Forster was an atheist, it is ironic that the relationship with Forster nurtured and supported Dorothy on her faith journey. It was not intentional, but his passionate love of nature helped to connect her to the Creator of all things. She says that "...it was life with him that brought natural happiness, that brought me to God."[10] Given that, it is ironic that her maturing faith was to become a threat to their idyllic life.

Dorothy was blissful at becoming pregnant. She felt "...so much in love, so settled, so secure that now I had found what I was looking for."[11] When her baby, Tamar, was born, she was so joyful that while still in the hospital bed she wrote a widely read article sharing her joy with the world. She felt she could hardly contain the flood of gratitude and joy she was feeling. She was alive in a way she had never experienced.

While pregnant, Dorothy was resolute that she would have the baby baptized. She didn't want her daughter to repeat the mistakes of her own early years. She felt she had floundered through years of doubt and lack of discipline while leading an amoral life. She wanted to avoid that for her daughter and believed that she was protecting her daughter from following that path by having her baptized. Even though she was unwavering in her commitment to Tamar's baptism, she knew that it could be disastrous for her relationship with Forster.

Forster was deeply committed to an opposing belief system. He was an anarchist and atheist and felt the church was a lot of superstition, mumbo jumbo, and morbid escapism. It conflicted with how he saw himself, his life, and the world. He had never wanted to bring a baby into the world, though he would later grow to love and enjoy their daughter. However, her baptism and Dorothy's steady progress toward her own baptism were daunting threats for the couple.

Given Forster's beliefs about the church and government, he was adamantly opposed to any type of marriage ceremony. In being true to his own beliefs, he felt that submitting to a marriage ceremony by either of these institutions would be hypocritical.

As Day feared, the relationship started to founder as the clash around their two opposing belief systems escalated and began driving the couple apart. The process of the two lovers separating was excruciating, stretching over months. They repeatedly separated but also were irresistibly drawn back together in sweet but heartbreaking reunions.

With apprehension and foreboding, Dorothy nevertheless moved steadily toward her baptism. A major fight with Forster was the catalyst prompting her to follow through with the decision. There was no joy in the baptism for her, and it effectively ended the relationship with Forster. It also tended to isolate her from other longtime friends. They were not as hostile to the church as Forster, but they weren't supportive and couldn't understand why she wanted to do such a bizarre thing as committing to the Catholic Church.

The Herald of Synthesis Arrives

In December 1932, when Dorothy was living in New York, there was a march by poor people on Washington. Dorothy didn't go as a participant but did obtain a contract to cover the event as a reporter. She was hugely sympathetic to the people and their cause. She described standing on the street watching the "ragged horde" with participants from all over the country. She was filled with pride and joy in celebrating their courage. At the same time, she detested her role as only an observer.

Since becoming a Catholic, she had not participated in this kind of direct action, and she missed the community that grew out of it. In the early years after her baptism, the political activism she had been involved with before didn't seem to be part of Catholicism. She deeply missed being involved in this type of advocacy and felt she had become ingrown and self-centered. The Communist Party had organized this march, and she resented that Catholic leadership was not supporting and organizing actions like this.

After the march, Dorothy sent off the article she had been hired to write but remained distressed about the people she had seen and their pain. She felt great compassion and tenderness for them and believed she had been unfaithful and unsupportive to them as a new Catholic. Probably, these feelings had existed for the five years since she had become a Catholic but were most troubling at this moment. After the march, she found her way to a church. While sitting there, she offered a painful prayer that a path would open for her to align her life on their side and that she could use her gifts for the poor and the workers.[12]

Dorothy returned to New York. After an intense few days in Washington and an eight-hour bus ride back, she was ready for some quiet and anxious to see her daughter. Understandably, she wanted to sit down and have a cup of coffee while visiting with her brother and his wife, who shared the apartment. However, a stranger was waiting, insistent on seeing her.

The stranger, Peter Maurin, was convinced that Dorothy was meant to work with him. He had read several of her articles and believed that she was destined to be influential in both the temporal and spiritual worlds and that the two of them were meant to work together in doing this. He had been there looking for her before and was uncommonly persistent in seeking her out.

Peter was an odd guy. Maybe he was a saint. He had no formal education but was extraordinarily bright and well-read. Much of the time, he had only one change of clothes and lived a life of voluntary poverty. He was twenty years older than Dorothy and a devout Christian who liked to think of himself as a troubadour of God.

In his troubadour role, he condensed some of his knowledge into verses incorporating repetition that he would sing out on corners and in the streets to whoever would listen, and would sing out even if they didn't listen. Sometimes, the verses would have an antiphonal quality such that people listening would join in and chant at appropriate intervals.

Neither Peter nor Dorothy used the word, but Peter was constantly attempting to evangelize and, in doing so, was sometimes annoying. He frequently talked nonstop, and others had difficulty getting him into a back-and-forth conversation. But he was convinced that he had a message that others needed to hear, and he persevered in delivering that message. Sometimes, he would engage street people, and sometimes, he would work his way into the offices of significant, influential people; it made no difference to him. Later, after the Catholic Worker community had been established, some community members dismissed him or paid little attention to him.

Dorothy didn't dismiss him. There were times when he wanted to talk to her, or at her, and she was busy and couldn't be present to him. But she seemed to have intuited that what he was communicating was essential, and she needed to hear it. Maybe she felt his message was particularly relevant to her. She was at a time in her life when something was missing. She was searching. Peter was a peculiar guy, but he was the person who had the message Dorothy needed to hear, and he arrived at the perfect time in her life when she was able to hear and respond. She later came to believe that Peter was God's answer to her prayer that God would open a path for her to align herself with the workers and poor.

Dorothy said that since she was a child, she hadn't seen Christians taking off their coat and giving it to the poor nor throwing a banquet and calling in the lame, the halt, and the blind. She had experienced what she wanted after the San Francisco earthquake when people had taken in those who had lost everything and shared whatever they had with them. This had been her model for how to love and for what Christianity should be. She wanted a joining of Christianity and her passion for loving the poor, but she didn't see that synthesis being lived out by the church.

It may seem strange to some, but in Dorothy's mind, the work of caring for and fighting for the rights of the poor, homeless, hungry, immigrants, refugees, farmworkers, Blacks, sharecroppers, and workers was not the role of the church but was the natural domain of the communists, socialists, anarchists, and other radicals. In her mind, this was their mission and not the church's role. Not only in her mind but in the culture, the church was not associated with being on the side of these people and their struggles. The popular perception was that the church hierarchy and structure were linked with corporations and wealth, and the radical groups were on the side of the poor. She was struggling to hold on to both the church and her love for the poor but didn't understand how to do that.

The strange guy waiting for Dorothy when she returned from Washington was the person to help her bridge this chasm. Peter was the catalyst who helped her see that the works of mercy, love, social justice, peacemaking, and political activism were a true expression of the Christian faith. This work was a manifestation of divine love and an indispensable mission of the Christian church. Until Peter came, she had not heard the biblical teachings on social justice. But as she heard and grasped this, she could see that living the Christian faith in this way was what she had always wanted since she was a little girl. From observing the rest of her life, it's clear this was a profoundly liberating and energizing realization for her.

The Catholic Worker Movement is Born

Peter talked a lot after meeting Dorothy. She couldn't absorb it all at once, but she understood three things he was advocating: (1) There should be a newspaper for clarification of thought. (2) They should start houses of hospitality. (3) Farming communes needed to be established. Dorothy didn't see the houses of hospitality or the farming communes as having anything to do with her, but she resonated strongly with starting a newspaper. Her father and three brothers worked on newspapers, and she had spent most of her adult life writing. She had strong ideas about what she wanted to write. However, there was no money for any of this.

Peter brushed off the concern about money. He believed that in the church money was not the critical ingredient to start a good work. He contended that the essential component needed was that the right people be present and willing to commit. If the people were generous with their work, God would not be outdone in His generosity of providing the funds. Peter was confident the money would come in.[13]

During this time, Dorothy had been reading about Rose Hawthorne Lathrop, who started a cancer hospital for the poor toward the end of the 1900s. Rose had also started with practically nothing, but her work resulted in establishing half a dozen hospitals around the country. Reading about Lathrop and listening to Peter inspired Dorothy so that she was ready to launch out. She had a typewriter, a kitchen table, and plenty of paper. Six months later, when it came time to print the first Catholic Worker, she came up with $57.00. In time, that $57.00 was returned thousands of times through donations by people inspired by their work. The loaves and fishes were being multiplied.

The first edition of the Catholic Worker went out in May 1933. It contained stories of racism in the South, the difficulty of being a sharecropper, child labor near where they lived, rental evictions, a strike over wages, and more. These are the types of stories that Dorothy covered and wrote about in her journalistic career. She was passionate about writing this kind of story, and one senses that she reveled in having a paper in which she could pour them out.

The paper rapidly became a huge success. They printed 2,500 copies for the first edition. Four months later, it was 25,000; by the end of the year, 100,000. By 1936, they were sending out 150,000 copies. Frederick Buechner wrote, "Your vocation in life is where your greatest joy meets the world's greatest need." Dorothy's passion and joy had landed on a great need, resulting in a huge response.

As the paper gained fame, people came to help. There was a need for these people to eat, so they set up a kitchen. One young woman, soon to have a baby, appointed herself to prepare meals. More came to help but had nowhere to live. The first house for people to live in was for the women helping put out the paper.

The first house of hospitality started not from a plan but from filling a need. Dorothy reports that a woman came to her with her belongings in bags and told her that she understood they had houses of hospitality. Dorothy explained that they didn't. The woman exclaimed, "You write about houses of hospitality; why don't you have them?"[14] Evidently, Dorothy felt challenged by this woman. One would guess that she felt discomfort in writing about houses of hospitality without having any established. Dorothy reports that in response to this challenge, they went out and bought a building for their first house of hospitality. From that point on, the movement accumulated buildings as they needed them for both workers and those with no place to live.

As well as being homeless, people on the streets were hungry, so the kitchen expanded. In the early days of the movement, one volunteer recalled arriving early to cut a mountain of bread and was aware that another volunteer had gotten the first 100 gallons of coffee ready to be served at about 6:15 AM. The line waiting outside extended for 200 feet on the street.

The third part of Peter's vision was to establish communitarian farms that were intended to be agronomic universities to solve numerous problems. He believed that farms like this could alleviate the issues of homelessness, hunger, and unemployment. Peter always yearned for opportunities to promote what he called "clarity of thought."[15] He envisioned these farms being a place to do that. The farms would be locations for bringing speakers, including himself. Both Peter and Dorothy thought that the farms would be ideal places to hold retreats. Peter envisioned that communitarian farms would bring about physical, spiritual, and emotional health for the community.

In practice, the farms weren't idyllic. It appears there was a minimum of direction, leadership, and structure resulting in a pretty chaotic atmosphere. The people there were extraordinarily diverse, including some quite difficult individuals. They had very different visions of what the community should be and what they wanted to do there. Some of those visions conflicted with the goals of the movement. The members often worked at cross purposes with each other, both deliberately and accidentally.

Some who came were more scholarly, but others felt they were there to work the land and build the farm. Both sides felt the other was not doing their share. One group liked collecting clay near the shore to make dishes and bowls. This was fine except that when washing up in the kitchen sink, they repeatedly stopped up the plumbing. People who appreciated the Catholic Worker would send alcoholics and patients being released from mental hospitals to the farm but wouldn't send money to help with their upkeep. One college student unwittingly rooted up much of an established asparagus patch in order to plant other vegetables. Another did the same to a sweet potato patch, thinking they were a weed. One long-time guest built a cabin for himself near the entrance to the farm. He would tell guests coming to the farm that the others who lived there were thieves, drunkards, and loafers. When retreatants came, he would tell them that the community never gave him anything to eat or wear. Packages of clothes started arriving for him, which he promptly hoarded. Dorothy struggled with these challenges and constantly attempted to discern how to live out her faith amid these tests. She was remarkably successful in accepting the sometimes cranky, eccentric people living on these farms.

In their work with those who were poor and homeless in the city and on the farms, there was the ongoing question of how and whether to set limits with their guests. Dorothy challenged volunteers, national leaders, and church leaders with abandon. However, she was reticent about challenging and setting limits on their guests. Part of it was that she saw their guests as Jesus. In her mind, serving poor folk who came to their ministries was the same as serving Jesus. She also believed that their own faith and love grew as they served these people whose behavior was sometimes unacceptable by all usual standards. "The greatest challenge of the day is how to bring about a revolution of the heart, a revolution which has to start with each one of us," she stated.[16] Seeing these people as guests and treating them as Jesus was helping in bringing about her goal of creating a revolution in the hearts of those working within the Catholic Worker movement.

In writing about one extraordinarily difficult individual, she said "that he was an instrument chosen by God to make us grow in wisdom and faith and love." [17] Another time, she said, "We could not put people out on the street... because they acted irrationally and hatefully...It was a practice in loving, a learning to love, a paying of the cost of love."[18] She understood that loving some of the hardest to love meant sacrifice, but in the practice of attempting to do it, they moved closer to who they were called to be.

Nevertheless, amid unruliness and disarray, some of what Dorothy and Peter hoped for did happen. They held retreats that were not popular among some but very appreciated by others. Peter and Dorothy brought in speakers who helped with the goal of clarification of thought and how to go forward with their spiritual journey. On the practical side they were successful in growing vegetables that helped feed themselves and also provided food for the houses of hospitality in the city. Of course, the farms provided a place for some people to live.

The Different Pieces Came Together to Birth a Movement

Once the first Catholic Worker paper was published and out on the streets, the transformation that had been taking place in Dorothy was solidified. It was a defining moment similar to when Francis returned his clothes to his father and declared his allegiance to his Father God. Dorothy had taken many decisive steps, but once she and Peter put out the paper's first edition, she was on a new path that never changed. The first publication of the Catholic Worker opened the door to the life for which she had been searching. Strikingly, it was a life of voluntary poverty but abundant in spiritual riches.

After much floundering and searching, Dorothy was living out her vision for herself and the church. She had found the synthesis for which her heart had been yearning. She had always empathized with and fought for the least of these. Now she was doing that through her faith. This was her treasure. The pieces of her life now fit together; her whole being went into her call.

A synthesis took place in Dorothy, but there was also a synthesis in how Peter and Dorothy fit together. Peter was the idea person; the person with the vision. He had read extensively and not only filled Dorothy with his thoughts, theology, and Biblical knowledge but was constantly recommending books for her to read. He had been living many of these concepts he was teaching long before meeting Dorothy.

Dorothy felt that they were living out Peter's vision and that she was the one constantly learning from him. She had been struggling with how to fit these concepts together all her life, and Peter gave guidance in that. She deeply resonated with his thoughts. However, she was the one who became the driving force implementing the vision. She was the one with the ability to make these beliefs become flesh. She was the leader, decision-maker, and executive of the Catholic Worker movement. She was the face and point of the organization. When decisions were made, both before and after Peter's death, hers was the prevailing voice. The synthesis of these two coming together with their different gifts birthed the Catholic Worker movement.

A Prophetic Voice for Justice

The movement was a prophetic voice not only for alleviating poverty but for social justice across the board. From the beginning, they were leaders in opposing racism and segregation. They understood themselves as pacifists but were not passive in their opposition to war, resisting the draft, and working for peace. They were steadfast in opposing the development of nuclear weapons. As Dorothy had always wanted, they were a strong voice for immigrant rights and particularly supported Cesar Chavez and the farmworkers movement. Anti-Semitism was shockingly prevalent in the U.S. as they were getting started, and they were unwavering in combating that hatred.

Being controversial was a way of life for The Catholic Worker; it was impossible to agree with all of their positions. They were frequently not in agreement among themselves on controversial issues. The Catholic Church hierarchy was often displeased at the stands the Catholic Worker took as the paper consistently challenged the institutional church. On the other hand, many of those working with Dorothy were unhappy that she occasionally took conservative positions consistent with Church policy. The movement lost support from both the left and the right for not taking a stand on the Spanish Civil War. The single most unpopular position they took was not supporting the entry of the United States into World War II.

Not only Catholics but Protestants and others from different faith communities were drawn to them because of their work with poor people and their prophetic voice and witness. It was harder for some to see that their witness grew out of a profound spirituality that Dorothy and Peter faithfully nurtured in their own lives. Others who joined with them were on a broad spectrum in their respective spiritual journeys. But just as Dorothy and Peter were models of leadership in their prophetic endeavors, for those who were open and searching, they were consummate guides in being faithful to a deeply spiritual path.

Dorothy says in one of her autobiographies, *Loaves and Fishes,* that beginnings are always exciting. That's often true. But it can be so difficult to stay true to the vision over time when beset by the swarm of challenges that daily threaten to derail a mission like the one on which Dorothy and Peter had embarked. As they became players on the national stage, these challenges quickly compounded. Over decades, they, but mainly Dorothy, had to make thousands of choices, all with the inherent danger of losing sight of the goal. Unquestionably, Dorothy and Peter made mistakes, but it appears that, in being so profoundly rooted in their spiritual disciplines, they were able to follow their faith closely enough to stay true to their goals. In doing so, they became beacons to be followed for generations.

A Different Vision of the Church: A Different Vision about Money

Dorothy Day found parts of the history and political stances of the Catholic church appalling. At the same time, she was extremely loyal to the church. Before her baptism, Day was fully aware of the many sins and crimes throughout the church's history. She knew that people had been slaughtered, terrible wars fought, torture practiced, sexual sins committed, racism practiced, and that violent oppression was a part of church history. Despite this, she maintained a strong devotion to the institution of the church while committing her life to stand against many of its past and present abuses.

Despite ongoing tension with the institution, Day loved the church's sacramental life. She went to mass daily. She went to confession and frequently mentioned how it had been helpful for her in her spiritual practice. She reached out to and depended on certain priests to teach and lead retreats. She thought of the church as her spiritual home and was thankful it was there for her.

In coming to terms with a very flawed church, Peter was helpful to Dorothy by insisting that their role was to fight for the true spirit of the Catholic church. He believed it was the responsibility of every Catholic to fight for what the church is supposed to be. Peter strongly advocated they not abandon the institutional church to those who believed and practiced what he and Dorothy felt was the opposite of the true church. Peter insisted they were following a long-honored tradition of Catholic dissent that many had practiced by obeying the church while at the same time challenging it. Day, who had always been a citizen reformer of the country, embraced being a reformer of the church.

One of the places she adamantly disagreed with the church was about money. Toward the end of her life, in reflecting on this, she stated:

> *There are days when I want to stop all those poor people giving their coins to the church, and tell them to march on the offices of the archdiocese—tell all the people inside those offices to move out of their plush rooms and share the lives of the hungry and the hurt. Would Jesus sit in some big, fancy, air-conditioned room near the banks and the department stores where the rich store their millions and spend their millions? Would he let Himself be driven in big black limousines, while thousands and thousands of people who believe in Him and His church are at the edge of starvation? Would he tolerate big mansions and fancy estates and luxurious traveling, while people come to church barefooted and ragged and hungry and sick, children all over the world? In my mind, there is only one answer to questions like those: no!* [19]

At one point, she said, "I am sickened—when I see Catholics using their religion as a social ornament. Peter used to tell me that a good Catholic should pray for the church as if it is a terrible sinner, in bad need of lots of prayers."[20]

They lived in what they called voluntary poverty. They shared the same living arrangements as the people to whom they gave hospitality, which was primitive and sometimes frankly revolting. Both Peter and Dorothy dressed in used clothing. In pictures, Peter looks pretty dapper with a coat and tie, but much of the time, it was his only change of clothing.

Those who were a part of the Catholic Worker certainly didn't want to be homeless and on the streets. However, to visitors, those who volunteered to be helpers merged with those who needed help. It was their goal that homeless guests and the workers at the houses of hospitality be indistinguishable.

Some volunteers would stay for extended periods, and others would leave pretty quickly. When it came time to go, many left feeling guilty that they could not live this extremely difficult life. Dorothy was constantly attempting to reassure these people that it was alright to leave and that not everyone was called to the life that they had taken on. For those who felt they didn't have the courage or thought of themselves as too selfish, she took care to let them know that the Catholic Worker life was not for everyone. Dorothy would admit to these people that there were times when even she thought of leaving.

Day acknowledged that their guests could sometimes be foul-mouthed, mean, nasty, and difficult to deal with. In conceding this, she was also clear that she and the volunteers were not always able to handle these situations with equanimity.

Working at the houses of hospitality and on the soup line was challenging. Part of what kept them on course with even the most difficult of their guests was remembering Jesus' words "...whatever you did for one of the least of these brothers and sisters of mine, you did for me." (Matthew 25:40)

When they could remember and act on this vision, love happened. All the work these people did of feeding people who were hungry, providing housing for those without homes, advocating for the oppressed, and getting arrested for peace were acts of love. Obviously, it's very different from how love is seen and understood in our culture. However, they were clear that it is love as portrayed in the scriptures and Christian faith.

Stretching to love difficult, seemingly unlovable people demanded a lot. In accepting this challenge, these people were in the process of moving forward in their own ongoing conversions. As they extended themselves beyond their comfort zones, they were being transformed. In some of the difficult moments, when they could get through the guest and the volunteer exterior, mercifully, they encountered joy. Not all were aware, but Dorothy and Peter knew that they were constantly dependent on God to stay on this path.

Christianity and Capitalism – According to the Catholic Worker

A primary source of tension between the Catholic Worker and the church hierarchy centered around capitalism. The church hierarchy was allied with the wealthy and those in power. Those leading the Catholic Worker believed that Christianity was incompatible with capitalism. It was apparent to them that capitalism was a system that funneled money to those with capital. In contrast, those without homes, immigrants, Blacks, workers, the vulnerable, and the marginalized were funneled toward impoverishment and destitution. They strongly maintained that the people they were supporting and advocating for were victims of capitalism.

Day didn't tend to write and speak in theoretical terms about capitalism, and most of the time, she didn't even use the word. In her extensive travels around the country, she frequently visited those who were oppressed and suffering. In telling the story of these people and the injustices they faced, she was also telling the story of the dark underbelly of capitalism.

An example would be, in the early years of the Catholic worker, she visited the Tenant Farmers' Union in Memphis and Arkansas. She went at a time when large insurance companies were purchasing vast tracts of land that local tenant farmers had formerly farmed. The insurance companies were now systematically dispossessing and evicting the families who had been living on these lands. These families were being pushed out of their homes into tents sometimes in the winter, with nowhere to go and their household goods piled around them. She witnessed mothers who were hungry and cold being moved out of their homes in winter. In one house she visited, an older man who was dead but still in bed. She visited churches where strikebreakers had smashed benches, pulpits, and broken windows and riddled the walls with bullet holes. She listened to stories of men being beaten and kidnapped and others shot and wounded. Another was killed by those determined to break the Tenant Farmers' Union.

This was just one of the countless stories that Dorothy and The Catholic Worker told over the decades about people who were oppressed by a capitalistic system valuing wealth accumulation over the well-being of people. Over decades, they told stories of immigrants, farmworkers, factory workers, child laborers, homeless people, and people of color oppressed by an economic system designed to enrich the wealthy. They were a Christian presence unequivocally, stating that capitalism is an unjust, oppressive system in direct opposition to our faith.

Those at the Catholic Worker recognized capitalism as a system in which people on both ends of the economic spectrum were diminished. The lords of capital were losing their conscience, humanity, and spirituality. Those on the bottom of the economic scale were deprived not only of the material goods needed for survival but also of their sense of dignity. They were forced into destitution, accompanied by the physical, emotional, and spiritual toll that took on them.

This was part of the logic undergirding the life of poverty those at the Catholic Worker committed themselves to. For them, the voluntary poverty they had chosen was very different from the destitution of the people they were serving. They felt that seeing and empathizing with poverty was not enough. Dorothy wrote, "To help the organizing, to give what you have for relief, to pledge yourself to voluntary poverty for life so that you can share with your brothers is not enough. One must live with them and share in their suffering. Give up one's privacy, and mental and spiritual comfort as well as physical."[21] It's hard to understand, but Peter believed that the voluntary poverty they practiced was a gift of God. By living such a sacrificial life and by consistently choosing the side of the impoverished as opposed to those in power, the movement was automatically a challenge to those in positions of authority in the Catholic Church (and, of course, to us).

The Movement Mushroomed

The handful of people putting out the first 2,500 copies of The Catholic Worker in 1933 sold it on the streets of New York but also enthusiastically sent it out all over the country. In three to four months, circulation was 25,000. By 1936 it had climbed to 150,000 and was finding its way to other parts of the world. In 1937 it rose to its peak distribution of 190,000.

It was as though people had been waiting for the message the paper was putting out. Young people responded by coming to New York to help during summer vacation. Others who graduated from college in the middle of the Depression weren't able to find jobs and came as volunteers. As these people gained experience with the Catholic Worker in New York, some felt called to return to their own cities and began opening Catholic Worker houses of hospitality and farms in other parts of the country. Today there are estimated to be over 200 Catholic Worker houses of hospitality worldwide.

Of course, when they were starting, there was no money. But as Peter had counseled, God was not to be outdone in generosity. Just as people volunteered, others wanted to be a part of their mission and contributed buildings and money. The loaves and fishes continued to be multiplied. One could not say that they lived comfortably, but the resources came in to buy and run the houses of hospitality, to provide food for the soup kitchens, to purchase and support the farms, and of course, to keep the paper going.

Almost instantly, Dorothy became a celebrity. She was constantly called to be a speaker around the country at strikes, union meetings, student organizations, political actions, antinuclear and peace activities, actions supporting immigrant rights, and to other houses of hospitality. At times she was on the road for up to four months being a spokesperson for the oppressed and suffering while inspiring those who had accepted the call she and Peter had put out. Notably, she was also a model of how to practice Christianity more faithfully. In a sense, Dorothy and Peter were calling the church back to its true identity. The Catholic Worker movement became a religious and political force.

In an article printed in 2015 or after, Dorothy's granddaughter, Martha Hennessy, poignantly sums up her grandmother's life.

> Dorothy has been mentioned as a Catholic who really helped the Catholic Church here stay true to its mission. She kept reminding the Church what it truly means to be Catholic, and I think it's just an ongoing struggle. But the world is a very seductive place. Wealth and power and influence are very potent drugs, and so the Catholic Worker must stand in contrast, and as a witness, to be with the poor. As Dorothy would say, you must grow in your spirituality in a way that you can see Christ in the most disenfranchised. That's got to be a reminder, because it goes in direct contrast with America's culture of ambition, and accumulation of material well-being. I think the more affluent materially, the more destitute we are spiritually. And so the CW is there, just to remind us that we cannot have a war economy without great human cost. It (the Catholic Worker lifestyle and message) carries the solutions to our militaristic, racist culture.[22]

NOTES

[1]Unless otherwise noted, the material in this subsection is taken from the recent biography, John Loughery and Blythe Randolph, *Dorothy Day: Dissenting Voice of the American Century* (New York: Simon & Schuster, 2020).

[2]Dorothy Day, *The Long Loneliness: The Autobiography of Dorothy Day*, (San Francisco: Harper and Row, 1952) 11.

[3]Ibid. p. 20.

[4]Ibid. p. 24.

[5]Ibid. p. 25.

[6]Ibid. p. 28

[7]John Loughery and Blythe Randolph, *Dorothy Day: Dissenting Voice of the American Century*, 19.

[8]Dorothy Day, *The Long Loneliness: The Autobiography of Dorothy Day,* (San Francisco: Harper and Row, 1952) 37.

[9]Ibid. p. 38.

[10]Ibid. p.134.

[11]Ibid. p. 136.

[12]Dorothy Day, *Loaves and Fishes* (Maryknoll, New York: Orbis Books, 1963), 13.

[13] bid. p. 11.

[14]"Revolution of the Heart: The Dorothy Day Story," *American Public Television,* https://www.pbs.org/show/revolution-heart-dorothy-day-story/.

[15]There doesn't seem to be a clear, concise statement of what "clarity of thought" meant for Peter. One would have to assume that he was talking about how to be as clear as possible about living and practicing a life of following Jesus. Certainly, Peter believed that much of the information available about doing this was neither clear nor helpful.

[16]"Revolution of the Heart: The Dorothy Day Story," *American Public Television.* https://www.pbs.org/show/revolution-heart-dorothy-day-story.

[17]Day, *Loaves and Fishes,* 62.

[18]Day, *Loaves and Fishes,* 50.

[19]Robert Coles, *Dorothy Day: A Radical Devotion* (United States and Canada: Da Capo Press 1987) 76-.

[20]Coles, *Dorothy Day: A Radical Devotion,* 59. I am running a few minutes late; my previous meeting is running over.

[21]Dorothy Day, *Little by Little: The Selected Writings of Dorothy Day,* Edited by Robert Ellsberg (New York: Alfred A. Knopf 1983), 239.

[22]John Surico, "What Makes A Catholic Worker?" Accessed March 20, 2025, http://www.newestyork.co/14-what-makes-a-catholic-worker.

PART TWO: THE WAY OF THE WORLD

In 1815, a group of men, including one of my ancestors from Riceville, Virginia, traveled to Lincoln County, Kentucky, to buy cattle. It was a successful trip in that they found a seller who had cattle and five horses he wanted to sell. Instead of leaving immediately after purchasing the livestock, the group stayed in the area for several months. During that time, a romance developed between my ancestor and the daughter of the couple who owned the plantation. They fell in love and decided to marry. There was a quiet home wedding, and soon afterward, the new couple and the others in the group made plans to return to Virginia. Before leaving, the bride's parents insisted that their daughter accept the gift of a fourteen-year-old enslaved girl as her maid to take with them.

Around sixty years ago, my aunt, who discovered and wrote this history, was delighted to tell it as a wonderful love story. These men went to buy cattle and came back not only with livestock but a bride. How romantic! And wasn't it sweet that the bride's parents gave their daughter, the fourteen-year-old enslaved girl, as a wedding present? Part of this account is a love story. The other part is a horrific story of a family being ripped apart. An adolescent girl is involuntarily torn away from her parents and family, never to see them again. It's an illustration of one of the terrible evils of enslavement.

In contrast to the path of Jesus, this is the path of the world. The story is a microcosm of how the world frequently works, sometimes in small ways and sometimes on an enormous scale. In our humanity, we become so immersed in the daily parade of the terrible that we, like my aunt, fail to recognize we have already fallen into the abyss. Our human way of seeing the world becomes so distorted that we celebrate the horrific as wonderful. In honoring the horrendous as wonderful, we teach it to our children. The terrible continues as an accepted, even celebrated part of culture, worldview, and values. When the terrible becomes the accepted norm, decisions - national, corporate, and individual - are inevitably based on those distorted beliefs, perpetuating crimes through generations. Sometimes, these crimes are on an enormous scale. Those of us of the Christian faith should recognize them as sins.

The people and entities you will be introduced to in this part of the book have chosen a completely different ideology, value system, and life path from Francis, John Woolman, and Dorothy Day. For these countries, corporations, and people, the Biblical verses about money, wealth, and property would seem ridiculous. They chose to accumulate as much wealth as fast as possible, regardless of the human cost. Inevitably, their greed caused others unimaginable suffering. Many of these people would have understood themselves to be Christian, but regrettably, those scriptures about money, wealth, and property had failed to penetrate their hearts.

| five |

The "Late Victorian Holocausts"

The LORD sent me to the palace of the king of Judah to speak to the king, his officials, and everyone else who was there. The LORD told me to say: I am the LORD, so pay attention! You have been allowing people to cheat, rob, and take advantage of widows, orphans, and foreigners who live here. Innocent people have become victims of violence, and some of them have even been killed. But now I command you to do what is right and see that justice is done. Rescue everyone who has suffered from injustice. (Jeremiah 22:1-3)

The European Powers: Honoring the Horrific

If someone enters a store or a house with a gun and robs the inhabitants of their belongings, we know that is theft. If the thief beats or kills the inhabitants in the process, that is a heinous offense, and we call the perpetrator a criminal and want to lock them up.

However, if a country does to another country the equivalent of what the criminal does, that has often been praised and celebrated by the citizens of the perpetrating country. In the past, when a country used its power, influence, and military to occupy a less powerful country, instead of being called a crime, it's been called colonialism. Colonialism is actually worse than a criminal robbing a store and killing someone in that not only does the perpetrator country beat, rob, dominate, and kill inhabitants of the occupied country, they continue doing it for decades. Instead of calling this a crime, the colonizing powers have celebrated their colonization of weaker countries. Even the word colonization is a euphemism; if we are truthful, we would call it a military occupation sometimes resulting in genocide

The European Powers ignored the horrors of colonialism. They told themselves that they were involved in wonderful, patriotic endeavors that brought wealth and honor to their country. From the history coming to prominence in more recent times, it seems those writing of colonialism were looking at reality like my aunt was looking at slavery in my family's past.

Great Britain became one of the foremost colonial leaders. It took pride that the sun never set on its empire and boasted that Britannia ruled the waves. When Britain was at the peak of its power, influence, and wealth, it was the largest empire in history. The country reveled in its reputation and still looks on that period with pride. However, if more contemporary understandings of history are correct, Great Britain's wealth and glory were based on unimaginable suffering and millions of deaths in its colonies.

India was undoubtedly Britain's largest and most profitable colony, to the extent that it was referred to as "the jewel in the imperial crown." In India and other parts of the southern hemisphere, life depends on the nourishing rains of the monsoons. However, the monsoons failed to appear three times during the period of 1876 through 1908. When this happened, there were terrible droughts and millions died of starvation. Various online accounts put the number of deaths during the famine of 1876-78 between 5 and 10 million. *The Lancet*, the foremost medical journal of the time, reported 19 million people in India died from the famine in 1896-1902. Other sources stated that the famine in 1907-08 resulted in another 2.1 to 3.2 million deaths. By 1914, eight million more whose immune systems had been severely compromised by debilitating hunger had succumbed to malaria, tuberculosis, and the plague.[1]

The droughts afflicting India were present in much of the Southern Hemisphere and famine was widespread. However, Mike Davis, author of the *Late Victorian Holocausts: El Nino Famines and the Making of the Third World,* maintains that in India most of that suffering and death could have been alleviated. Davis acknowledges that the droughts were terrible and would have caused severe hardship by themselves. He insists though, that the primary cause of the millions of deaths in India was not drought; it was how Britain used its power to control and manipulate India's economy that was lethal to India's inhabitants. Put bluntly, Britain's goal as a colonial power was to enrich itself to the fullest extent possible. When the monsoon rains didn't come and were replaced by the threat of famine, the British policy didn't change. They continued using their power to accumulate India's wealth, not to save millions from starving.

In an earlier famine in 1873-74, the British had acted responsibly and imported rice from Bengal and Bihar. Britain had also provided relief works and a "gratuitous dole." This earlier program had limited the deaths in this particular famine to only 23 deaths. This program could have provided a model for the famines that were to follow in the next 32 years. However, this concern for human life and the accompanying loss of profit came under withering fire. The Economist wrote that this program encouraged lazy Indians to believe that it was the responsibility of the British government to keep them alive. Some senior British civil servants claimed it was a "mistake to spend so much money to save a lot of black fellows."[2] The humane response received such harsh criticism that when the subsequent famines started in 1876, the British way of dealing with it was deadly.

Davis argues that even in the midst of the famine, there was a surplus of food in India. The problem wasn't a lack of food, but that Britain forced India to export massive quantities of wheat in the midst of severe starvation. While the famine was raging, Britain's policies forced India's wheat exports to rise dramatically from 3 million tons in 1875 to 10 million tons in 1900. This diminished by more than three times the amount of wheat available to the millions starving in India during that period.

A contributing factor was that the world operates within a capitalist/free-market system. This means that if more money were available in other parts of the world to buy wheat, the grain automatically follows the money and sells at the higher price. In India, people were dying beside grain silos and by railroad cars filled with wheat. However, since those in other parts of the world had more wealth to purchase it, that grain automatically followed the money--out of India and away from those dying of starvation.

Repeatedly the British rejected the possibility of modifying their free-market policies during the famines. They had committed themselves to the teachings of Adam Smith, author of *The Wealth of Nations.* Smith had adamantly taught that the natural law of supply and demand should not be interrupted during a famine. Following that doctrine, the British viceroy ordered that the government not interfere in the free market to reduce the price of food for the masses.[3]

Multiple times in the last quarter of the nineteenth century the suggestion surfaced that Britain reduce its taxes on Indians so they would have more money to buy food. Every time this was raised as a possibility, it was rejected. Once when it was proposed that taxes on cotton could be reduced, Lord Salisbury, secretary of state for India at that time, put forth the belief that reducing taxes on cotton, which would have made more money available for those suffering to buy food, was out of the question. He was adamant that to make this kind of policy change was communism, and wealthy Britain should never sacrifice their profits in order to benefit a poor India.[4] Whenever similar ideas of reducing taxes surfaced, the British found reasons to quash that possibility.

The British established work camps for the Indians. However, if they lived within ten miles of these camps, they weren't allowed to work there. They set up the sites so that people who worked there had to live at least ten miles from the camp so that they would have to walk ten miles to and from the camp each day. The food rations given at these camps provided less sustenance for the manual labor than was later supplied to the inmates at the Buchenwald concentration camp under the Nazis. This whole plan was so impossible that one British district official suggested that "it would be better to shoot down the wretches than to prolong their misery in the way proposed." Another British official believed the tiny ration would result in a slow but sure death.[5]

Even gifts to relieve the suffering were repeatedly rejected. To enforce this, the plenipotentiary Famine Delegate, Sir Richard Temple, initiated the Anti-Charitable Contributions Act of 1877, making it illegal to make relief donations that might interfere with the market determining the price of grain. The British House of Commons agreed that the "...supreme principle was that India was to be governed as a revenue plantation, not an almshouse."[6]

Many of us think of the Nazi Holocaust as the supreme example of evil on a national scale and of course it was dreadful. However, by the title of his book, Davis is challenging us to consider that there are other holocausts equal to or greater than that terrible crime.

The British had become so immersed in the terrible that they failed to recognize the abyss. Their way of seeing the world had become so distorted that they celebrated the horrific as wonderful. They had developed a belief system that no matter if it cost millions of human lives, the market economy should dominate all other values and concerns. At times, Davis calls this rigid belief their theology, and indeed it was, helping them justify their greed. Some saw Temple as using free market economics to mask what was, in reality, colonial genocide.[7]

Underpinning this belief system was the conviction that British lives were more important than Indian lives. Of course, the British never articulated it this way; they said the opposite. Nevertheless, the way the British imposed their policies on India made clear that Indian lives had no real value other than enriching Britain. Contributing to this belief system was the British desire to be the dominant country in the world and the hubris accompanying that. These terrible convictions had become the accepted norm for Britain. Decisions, national, corporate, and individual, were based on these distorted beliefs and values, perpetuating crimes through generations. In our modern world, we hesitate to use the term sin and rarely use the term with issues related to money and wealth. But those of us who understand ourselves to be Christian need to be straightforward in stating that this is the path of the world, and we should recognize it as sin.

For people of faith, Christian and those of other religions, who hold beliefs about the perils of money, we need to recognize that the Indian holocaust and other lesser-known colonial holocausts were motivated out of greed. It is an example of money being the root of all evil. (I Timothy 6:10)

If we are to learn from these crimes, we need to recognize that in a practical sense, for the actors on the colonial stage, God was not God, regardless of what they may have thought was their god. In the operational sense, wealth, property, and profit had become the god of the colonial powers. Britain claimed to rule the waves, but Britain itself was ruled by profit, at a terrible cost. This was their god.

The pictures of the people in these famines are horrendous. About the time these atrocities were occurring, Kodak had developed a small camera that missionaries were carrying all over India. Davis says that the cameras turned missionaries into documentarians. The missionaries tried to alert India's administrators to alleviate the horror of what was happening but were ignored. These photos, many of which Davis includes in his book, are appalling. Some of them are on the internet. One site where some can be found is: https://www.gettyimages.in/photos/famine-india?family=editorial&assettype=image&phrase=famine%20india

Colonialism 101

Most of us living in the US probably don't think much about the colonial system of earlier times. We know that this country fought the Revolutionary War to free us from Britain's rule, but possibly, we don't think much about our being a colony of Britain and what that meant. We may remember that a primary cause of the war for our independence was British taxation. We may not remember that from Britain's perspective, the primary purpose of the thirteen colonies was to enrich themselves.

Colonizing countries didn't want their colonies to develop. For the British, the rationale for the American colonies was to provide raw materials to be exported to the parent country, where they would be turned into finished goods. To the American colonies' exasperation, they were not allowed to manufacture items made out of iron or to make woolen goods or hats under British rule. Only the colonizing country was allowed to profit from this kind of manufacturing.

The colonizing powers enriched themselves with the wealth of the occupied countries. However, the opposite was also true. The countries being colonized were impoverished through this process. The colonies were always required to pay taxes. Beyond this, the way the transfer of wealth took place depended on the natural resources of the country being colonized. However, the purpose of colonization was always to steal as much wealth from the occupied country as possible.

The story Britain has told itself and the world about its colonization of India is that maintaining its rule in India was costly for Britain. Two-thirds of British citizens are still proud of their colonizing history and believe that their colonies were better off for having been under British rule. They have claimed that Britain didn't gain any economic benefit from India and only stayed there out of pure benevolence and desire to be helpful to the country.

In recent years, this perspective has been strongly challenged. Utsa Patnaik, an Indian economist, after extensive research published by the Columbia University Press, calculates that over almost two centuries, Britain drained an eye-popping $44 trillion out of the Indian economy during the period in which it ruled India.[8]

Shashi Tharoor, a former member of the Indian Parliament, asserts that when Britain first came to India, the Indian economy was 23 percent of the world economy. When the British left, India's share of the world economy had fallen to 4 percent. Tharoor maintains that the reason for this plunge is that for well over a century, Britain had been enriching and developing itself by draining India's wealth.[9]

Since this information confronts the story that has been told for over a century, there will certainly be questions and pushback to this recent research. But if we stop to reflect on the traditional story that the British clung with the full force of their empire to maintain India as a colony out of goodwill and benevolence, we realize that is absurd. Britain has always been an example of a country functioning out of self-interest through cold, hard "realpolitik."

A part of this realpolitik was that the fortune Britain looted from India financed Britain's imperialist goals. The British were very conscious that to expand their empire, they needed the wealth they were robbing from India to finance their wars in China, Afghanistan, and South Africa.

Britain was operating out of capitalist principles motivated by profit and doing everything possible to further its empire and national interests. There may be some revision of Patnaik's numbers, but Britain maintained its grasp of India to rob as much wealth as possible for as long as possible. Davis asserts, with extensive documentation, that Britain's single-minded determination to enrich itself through its colonization of India caused the deaths of millions of human beings.

This chapter begins with the prophet Jeremiah's strong statement telling the king that he had been "allowing people to cheat, rob, and take advantage of widows, orphans, and foreigners who live here. Innocent people have become victims of violence, and some of them have even been killed. But now I command you to do what is right and see that justice is done. Rescue everyone who has suffered from injustice." (Jeremiah 22:3) Surely, Jeremiah was trembling as he knew he was risking his life in confronting the king, but the prophet followed through with what he had been commanded to say.

As far as we know, Jeremiah went to speak to the king alone. In India, God needed masses of truth-tellers to take up his mantle in confronting the British Empire. Certainly, high-level officials speaking truth and values to Queen Victoria were required to make her aware of the crime Great Britain was inflicting on the Indian people. Others were needed to publicize to the British people the horror that was taking place in India. Some in the British Parliament ought to have confronted the acceptance that India was a revenue plantation and certainly should have argued that shipping the grain out of India during a famine was murder. Military members ought to have refused to carry out the orders that were causing people to starve to death. British administrators should have refused to cooperate with the forced starvation they were mandating. This atrocity called for thousands, if not millions, of Jeremiah's.

When we take the scriptures about money, wealth, and property that initially seem so impossible and put them in this context, perhaps their purpose and importance start to take on a different meaning when we see the crimes that are committed when they are totally ignored.

NOTES

[1]Mike Davis, *Late Victorian Holocausts: El Nino Famines and the Making of the Third World* (London – New York: Verso, 2001), 174.

[2]Ibid. pp. 36-37.

[3]Ibid. p. 31.

[4]Ibid. p. 38.

[5]Ibid. p. 38.

[6]Ibid. p.33.

[7]Ibid. p. 37.

[8] Ajai Sreevatsan, "British Raj siphoned out $45 trillion from India: Utsa Patnaik." *Mint,* Updated November 21, 2018,

https://www.livemint.com/Companies/HNZA71LNVN-NVXQ1eaIKu6M/British-Raj-siphoned-out-45-trillion-from-India-Utsa-Patna.html.

[9] Rupert Taylor, "The Alleged $45 Trillion Theft from India. *Owlcation*, Updated January 24, 2025, https://owlcation.com/humanities/The-Alleged-45-Trillion-Theft.

| six |

The King's Colony

Israel's officials are like ferocious wolves, ripping their victims apart. They make a dishonest living by injuring and killing people. And then the prophets in Israel cover up these sins by giving false visions. I have never spoken to them, but they lie and say they have a message from me. The people themselves cheat and rob; they abuse the poor and take advantage of foreigners. I looked for someone to defend the city and to protect it from my anger, as well as to stop me from destroying it. But I found no one. So in my fierce anger, I will punish the Israelites for what they have done, and they will know that I am furious. I, the LORD, have spoken. Ezekiel 22:27-31

The Belgian King's "Officials Are Like Ferocious Wolves, Ripping Their Victims Apart"

King Leopold II of Belgium was single-mindedly determined to own a colony and devoted his life to achieving that goal. He planned, schemed, lied, misled, flattered, charmed, threatened, manipulated, and awarded medals to achieve his ambition. In 1885, after working a couple of decades to achieve this end, he succeeded in becoming the sole owner of what was named the État Ind´ependent du Congo, or the Congo Free State.

Leopold's colony was larger than France, England, Germany, Italy, and Spain combined. It was seventy-six times the size of Belgium and almost one-quarter the size of the United States. Under the laws and in the eyes of the Western world, Leopold now owned these vast lands and promptly made himself "King Sovereign" of it all. Obviously, Africans never had a choice in this decision.

This was a huge personal coup for Leopold but an enormous tragedy for the African people of this enormous territory. In the process of looting the Congo, Leopold and the people working under his rule caused the death of approximately ten million Africans and wreaked massive suffering on millions more. The culture, way of life, family structure, and communal traditions were all devastated for millions of people. It's hard to imagine the scope of the brutality, cruelty, and depravity King Leopold's regime inflicted on the African people. The human cost was staggering.

For all colonizing powers the goal was to extract as much wealth as possible from their colonies. At first, ivory from elephant tusks was the primary monetary product of the Congo. As Leopold consolidated his grip on the territory, worldwide demand for rubber exploded. It was evident enormous fortunes could be made. Since the Congo contained wild vines that produced rubber, that became a massive bonanza for Leopold and his investors. However, for the Africans, the rubber craze had the impact of a deadly plague resulting in the death of millions.

In the early days of Leopold's invasion of the Congo, he sent Henry Morton Stanley to lead a huge expedition through an unexplored (by Europeans) part of the Congo. While on this expedition, they ran out of supplies bringing some of his porters and soldiers close to starvation. In order to obtain food and supplies, they would capture and hold native women prisoner until the village chiefs would supply them with food. Fearing they would be attacked for this behavior; Stanley ordered his men to burn all the villages in the area.

A European working under Stanley describes one of the massacres that took place as a result of the order. This slaughter was before the rubber rush, but is a glimpse of the massive devastation that engulfed the entire Congo in the following years. The European tells the story below.

> *It was most interesting lying in the bush watching the natives quietly at their day's work. Some women... were making banana flour by pounding up dried bananas. Men we could see building huts and engaged in other work, boys, and girls running about, singing... I open the game by shooting one chap through the chest. He fell like a stone... Immediately a volley was poured into the village.*[1]

To accomplish his goals, Leopold knew that he would need an army trained and willing to do this same kind of violence to innocent people. It was called the Force Publique. The core of this army was made up of Europeans frequently looking to break out of dead-end jobs in Europe. To create a much larger army, Leopold started what were euphemistically called "schools," in which young Africans from the Congo were forcibly relocated to populate the schools. These schools were spread throughout the Congo; each had a priest and a soldier as instructors.

The purpose of these schools was not to educate in the usual sense of the term but to indoctrinate the young people into sadistic violence. As "students," they were subject to this violence, delivered through a hippopotamus hide whip with corrugated edges called a *chicotte*. Chains and iron collars frequently used to subjugate the Africans were also used on these young people. As they grew older, the schools funneled the young people into the Force Publique army, where they were ordered to inflict terrible carnage on their fellow Africans, frequently using the same methods that had been used on them.

One of the army's primary responsibilities was capturing and forcing the African men to harvest the rubber. The army occupied the African villages and kept the women, children, and chiefs hostage until the men returned with the rubber they had been ordered to gather.

Upon returning to Britain, Baptist missionaries told the following story testifying to the terror they had witnessed being inflicted on the Africans as they were forced to harvest rubber.

> Lined up...are 40 emaciated sons of an African village, each carrying his little basket of rubber. The toll of rubber is weighed and accepted, but...four baskets are short of the demand. The order is brutally short and sharp---Quickly the first defaulter is seized by four lusty "executioners," thrown on the bare ground, pinioned hands and feet, whilst a fifth steps forward carrying a long whip of twisted hippo hide. Swiftly and without cessation the whip falls, and the sharp corrugated edges cut deep into the flesh—on back, shoulders and buttocks blood spurts from a dozen places. In vain the victim twists in the grip of the executioners and the whip cuts other parts of the quivering body –and in the case of one of the four, upon the most sensitive part of the human frame. The "hundred lashes each" left four inert bodies bloody and quivering on the shimmering sand of the rubber collecting post.
>
> Following hard upon this decisive incident was another. Breakfast was just finished when an African father rushed up the veranda steps of our mud house and laid upon the ground the hand and foot of his little daughter, whose age could not have been more than 5 years.[2]

Cutting off the hands of Africans was a part of the modus operandi for the occupation. Sometimes the European occupiers cut off hands as punishment like in the case above, and sometimes, they cut off the hands of Africans to prove to their superiors that they had killed the number of people they said they had.

These kinds of grotesque atrocities were multiplied thousands of times. The Congo was huge, and many thousands of workers were conscripted for the rubber collection. In 1906, one company responsible for harvesting only a small fraction of the rubber had forty-seven thousand rubber workers on their books. This forty-seven thousand would need to be multiplied many times over to encompass those gathering rubber throughout the Congo. [3] The story quoted above is a picture of the typical working conditions for the entire area.

Massacres, kidnappings, mutilations, whippings, hostage-taking, and executions were simply the business model. It's hard to comprehend the amount of violence and inhumanity that Europeans inflicted on the African people of the Congo.

There are numerous photographs on the internet documenting the brutality. At first glance, it's sometimes difficult to understand what is happening in some of the pictures. One may see a photo in which a well-dressed white man is standing with several Africans dressed in loincloths. However, the caption lets us know the Africans are holding severed hands that have been cut off from a family member or a loved one. Another is a picture of an African sitting on a low platform looking at something. Then one learns that he is looking at the hand and foot of his five-year-old daughter, who had been dismembered because the village had not harvested enough rubber.

When seen through the European colonialists' eyes, African lives had no value other than to make money for the colonizers. Leopold and the Europeans needed African bodies to be porters, build railroads, make up a military force, provide food, be servants, and, critically, to harvest rubber. For Leopold and the Europeans working under him, the violence they inflicted on Africans was unimportant to the extent of being a non-issue. The extent to which that was true is shocking.

The colonial system in the Congo was even worse than chattel slavery because enslaved people were considered property with value. Therefore, even when owners were brutal, they were also concerned about protecting the value of their investment. Europeans had no monetary investment in the people of the Congo, so human life meant nothing to them. In fact, Africans were not considered human. In some situations, the colonizers would simply massacre the people if it helped them get more rubber. Sometimes they would massacre one village or group so that others in the area would realize that this would be their fate if they didn't cooperate.

Many made fortunes on the rubber. Obviously, Leopold was at the top of the pyramid concerning that. Before his death, he deliberately made it difficult to trace how much he had profited from the Congo, so it's impossible to know exactly how much he stole from the Africans. Nevertheless, after his death, one Belgian scholar made a conservative estimate of $1.1 billion in today's dollars. In relating this, Adam Hochschild notes that after Leopold's death, in the legal wrangling about who was to inherit parts of his fortune, no one was present to represent the Congolese people.[4]

Dishearteningly, the Congo was not an exception in colonial behavior. On the contrary, it became the model. Other countries, envying the profits being extracted from the Congo, followed Leopold's example in their colonies which contained wild rubber vines. France's African colonies were smaller than the Congo, but their occupation was just as brutal. "Forced labor, hostages, slave chains, starving porters, burned villages, paramilitary company "sentries," and the chicotte (hippo hide whip) were the order of the day."[5] The area occupied by the French lost roughly 50 percent of its population in the same way the Congo had due to these atrocities.

Leopold had attempted to hide his carnages. The Germans didn't even bother to try. In what is today's Namibia, they simply announced genocide against the Hereros population. The Hereros rebelled against the Germans, and in 1904, Germany responded by sending in a heavily armed force. The orders were that they were to shoot every Herero. To make this even clearer, the command ordered their troops not to take any male prisoners. In 1903 the Hereros population numbered about eighty thousand. After the German war against them, in 1906, there were less than twenty thousand.[6]

The treatment of native populations in other parts of the world was similar. At the same time the Germans were seeking out Hereros to exterminate, the United States was waging a brutal counter guerrilla war in the Philippines against the natives fighting for their independence. Following the pattern, the U.S. tortured Filipinos and burned their villages. 200,000 Filipinos were killed or died of disease and hunger related to the war. Of course, before and after this war, the U.S. had decimated the American Indians for their property. The aborigines in Australia fared no better as Britain massacred them, similar to how the Germans slaughtered the Hereros.[7]

It's hard to comprehend that out of their drive for wealth, Europeans and those of European descent were so completely unfeeling and lacking in conscience about their own cruelty. For people to collectively commit crimes of this magnitude, they must have been living under a distorted belief system. As enslavers had been captured by lies undergirding their brutality, so were these colonists. These lies had been justifying the same kind of cruelty for centuries. Ironically the Europeans were coming from supposedly Christian nations who were even sending missionaries to convert the Africans.

Thankfully there were some heroes amid the carnage. Initially, most of Europe didn't know what was happening in the Congo. Leopold had planned to cover it up as long as possible. He created propaganda to make it appear that he was a benevolent dictator/king ruling in ways that benefited the native people. Gradually the horror of what was happening there began to surface.

Edmund Dene Morel was one of the most prominent people crusading to end the carnage. Hochschild writes,

> Brought face to face with evil, Morel does not turn away. Instead, what he sees determines the course of his life and the course of an extraordinary movement, the first great international human rights movement of the twentieth century. Seldom has one human being –impassioned, eloquent,

> blessed with brilliant organizing skills and nearly superhuman energy—managed to put one subject (Leopold) on the world's front pages for more than a decade.[8]

One would guess that Hochschild reached hundreds of thousands of people with his message. Many joined him in his efforts. Some of those supporting him were missionaries who had served in the Congo and came back horrified at what they had witnessed. They brought the pictures they had taken and spoke to people throughout Britain and Europe.

It's hard to comprehend but the Western European countries and people perpetuating these crimes understood themselves to be Christian. The subsection below partially explains how they could profess to be Christian and still commit these crimes.

Theological Underpinnings of the Horrific

Most people have never heard of the Doctrine of Discovery and have no interest in some archaic church doctrine written centuries ago by popes we could care less about. However, this doctrine has been a major force shaping the minds of people, so they were willing to commit the types of atrocities cited above. The ideas, thoughts, and beliefs contained in this doctrine have been undergirding, guiding, inciting, and condoning some of the worst human behavior and crimes stretching back at least from the 15th century to the present.

In 1452, Pope Nicholas V wrote a letter, called a papal bull, to King Alfonso of Portugal. This letter, combined with a couple of other subsequent papal bulls, became known as the Doctrine of Discovery.

When the papal bulls that made up the Doctrine of Discovery were written, popes and monarchs were seen as being above all other creatures, and exercised enormous power. The popes' authority was not limited to the spiritual realm but was decisive in political and legal decisions determining the course of the world. Popes had the ability to govern monarchs' actions and shape the thought, culture, and geography of the Western world.

In the phrase, "Doctrine of Discovery," the essential word is discovery. In the fifteenth century, Europeans were sailing, exploring, and adventuring in parts of the world that were relatively unknown to them. From their perspective, they believed they were discovering and exploring new lands. As they encountered people in these lands, the Indigenous people didn't see their land as being discovered. In some cases, their ancestors had been there for millennia. However, from a European standpoint, these lands and people were being discovered. As the Europeans believed they were discovering and exploring new lands, the church saw a need to establish instructions about how this was to be done with regard to church doctrine.[9]

In 1452, Pope Nicholas V wrote to King Alfonso of Portugal, giving him the authority to "...invade, capture, vanquish, and subdue all Saracens and pagans...to reduce their persons to perpetual slavery and to take away all their possessions and property."[10] This papal bull was based on "... various theological and legal doctrines formulated during, and after the Crusades, non-Christians were considered enemies of the Catholic faith and, as such, less than human."[11] It's hard to realize how dramatic and far-reaching this mandate was. At this time, Portugal was a major world power and had begun exploring and establishing bases on the coast of Africa. The indigenous people in these lands were not Christian. Therefore, they were seen as pagan by the pope.

In this papal bull, Nicholas was telling Alfonso he not only had permission but was being encouraged to invade, wage war, kill, capture, and enslave Native people on the grounds they were not Christian. Furthermore, Alfonso was given the right to steal their land and property. In reading this papal bull, some understand that Alfonso and subsequent kings not only had the right but were mandated to commit these crimes.

Over time, the precepts in the Doctrine of Discovery were adopted by large parts of the European world and by people of European descent. Sometimes, they were used consciously with the pope's authority, and sometimes, they were adopted by people who had never heard of the Doctrine of Discovery and would have utterly rejected the authority of popes. After the protestant church was formed, the edicts of the doctrine penetrated protestant thought as well as the beliefs of people who had no religion at all. It originated with the Vatican, but it was a legal document and provided the foundation for laws and practices worldwide.

Whether people were consciously using the pope's authority or whether the ideas had just permeated Western culture, the doctrine was used to justify brutality, murder, and theft of Native people for centuries. It was used to provide the rationale and legal arguments essential in justifying slavery and the slave trade worldwide. The doctrine gave license and encouraged Hernan Cotes, the Spanish conquistador, in 1525 to march his army through Mexico, killing 100,000 indigenous people on his way to destroying the Aztec capital of Tenochtitlan.[12]

The U.S. Supreme Court used the Doctrine of Discovery to justify the removal of natives from their tribal lands. "Writing in 1823 for the Supreme Court ruling in Johnson v. McIntosh, Chief Justice John Marshall said the doctrine meant that "unoccupied lands" were those "lands occupied by Indians but unoccupied by Christians."[13] Continuing, he wrote, "that the principle of discovery gave European nations an absolute right to New World lands." [14] Native peoples were given certain rights of occupancy. Obviously, those were minimal rights, given that this and subsequent court decisions were used to move Native tribes off their lands.

Even as late as 2005, in the United States, the Doctrine of Discovery was used in the Sherrill v. Oneida Indian Nation case to deny the Oneida Indian Nation the right to regain its territory. Notably, the progressive justice Ruth Bader Ginsburg wrote the decision. The American Indian Law Alliance asserts that the doctrine is the cornerstone for Indian land law in the U.S. and Canada. It has been used in

Australia, New Zealand, Africa, Latin America, and the Caribbean to deny native peoples their rights.[15]

The papal bull of 1452 was strengthened in 1493 after Columbus sailed to what became known as the "New World." Under the tradition of "discovery," he sailed with the understanding that he had the authority to take possession of any lands "discovered" for Ferdinand and Isabella, the sovereigns of Aragon and Castile. This set up a conflict between Portugal and Spain about which country had the right to invade and colonize which parts of the world. Pope Alexander, who was then pope, mediated this dispute with another papal bull stating that Spain had no right to lands already in "possession of any Christian lords." Then, to further clarify, the pope made a line of demarcation, giving Portugal the right to conquer and dominate lands on one side of the globe and Spain on the other. These two papal bulls were the primary documents making up the Doctrine of Discovery. Use of the doctrine started with Portugal and Spain, but over the next several centuries, the doctrine was also used by Britain, France, Holland, and later after it was founded, the United States.[16]

In the papal bull of 1493, Pope Alexander decreed that by "subjugating" the people who would be "discovered," the "Christian Empire" would be spread. Embarrassingly, the leader of the Christian world is proclaiming that the monarchs under his authority should spread Christianity by invasion, war, enslavement, military occupation, and theft. [17] In Alexander's papal bull, he mentions that the monarchs would propagate the faith by conquering these lands, but the real goal was domination, plunder, land, and empire.

Given the way Christianity began, it's sadly ironic that Nicholas, Alexander, and the sovereigns were in the process of establishing an empire. Jesus was born a lowly subject of an empire and was executed by that empire. For the first three hundred years of its existence, the Roman Empire persecuted the church. In its early years, the Christian Church lived under an empire but didn't succumb to it. The church was like a tenacious weed that, despite attempts to eradicate it, was determined to persevere and offer an alternative vision of what is important and how to live.

Unfortunately, in 313, the Roman Emperor, Constantine accepted Christianity, and ten years later, Christianity became the Roman Empire's official religion. This was a giant step toward the church losing its identity. By the fifteenth century, with these papal bulls, the church had totally lost its way. With the Doctrine of Discovery, instead of being persecuted, the church was creating an empire that, like all empires, would be the persecutor.

At different times in history, both Nicholas and Alexander had the title of pope. However, it's misleading to think of these men as spiritual leaders or as worthy to carry the title of pope. It would be more appropriate for them to have been given titles like Nicholas the Enslaver, Nicholas the Murderer of Innocents, Alexander the Brutal, or Alexander, Emperor of Holocausts. Their papal bulls flung the door open to greed, conquest, torture, mass murder, slavery, and other forms of inhumanity. They promoted precisely the opposite of what Jesus lived and taught.

For centuries, the Doctrine of Discovery's tenets and beliefs indoctrinated the Western world's mindset, culture, and values. The message to white Europeans and those who came to the new world was that Indigenous people, who were nearly always people of color, had no value or rights. The Native people had no right to their property and were not even considered human. For centuries, the church propagated these lies.

Concurrent with this was the belief that the wealth obtained from these new lands was the real prize and what was truly of value. As this belief system invaded the Western world, countless violent invasions followed. Over the centuries, millions were murdered, millions were enslaved, and millions had their lands and wealth stolen.

The Congo was invaded over 400 years after the papal bull of 1452 was written. Still, the principles in the Doctrine of Discovery were a primary source of the European mindset that they were morally free to invade the Congo, pillage its wealth, and enslave its people. Moreover, many obviously believed there was no problem in massacring and brutally beating people they found there. The people doing this had so completely incorporated the ideas from the doctrine that an African worker's deficit of a few pounds of rubber justified cutting off the hand and foot of a five-year-old because her father, who was essentially enslaved, had been unable to harvest the amount of rubber demanded.

Nicholas and Alexander's papal bulls, in effect, said that Black lives didn't count as human. They could be invaded, killed, enslaved, and their property stolen as though they didn't exist. They were seen as of no consequence. Today, people of color clearly sense that they have been and still are being treated as though their lives don't matter. Though most may not be aware of it, the slogan of "Black Lives Matter" strikes at a core belief handed down centuries ago in the Doctrine of Discovery.

Typically, we think that battles and wars determine the course of the world. It is hard to take in, but the concepts embodied in the Doctrine of Discovery have been shaping the development of our world for centuries as much as any battle or war.

What if the Doctrine had followed Scripture?

Imagine if the Doctrine of Discovery had said that the people in these unknown lands were fully human, loved and cherished by God, and were to be treated as such. What if the doctrine had said that the land and possessions of people being discovered belonged to those who lived there, and their ownership of these properties was to be recognized under church law and morality? What if the church had reminded people of what the scripture said about money, property, and wealth? If this had been the way the doctrine was written, the world would have developed very differently.

The atrocities would not have automatically disappeared. People would still have had the desire to steal the lands and property of native peoples. The desire to enslave vulnerable people to enrich oneself would have still been present in human hearts. Greed would always have been ready to corrupt humanity in terrible ways. Europeans and those of European descent would still have had the human frailties that we all have and would still have committed atrocities given their organization and superior weaponry.

However, they would not have had the permission and mandate from the highest moral authority in the Western world for these crimes. As Europeans were discovering and exploring lands unfamiliar to them, there would have been resistance to brutalizing the Natives of those lands rather than automatically believing the people there were less than human and of no consequence.

In the U.S., the laws promoting westward expansion without regard for Native land and lives would not have had the legal underpinning of the Doctrine of Discovery. Some settlers would have still robbed Native people of their land and possessions, but there would have been far more resistance.

Europeans would have realized that the Native people they were encountering around the world were fully human, loved by God, and to be treated as such. The church would never have assured those exploring unfamiliar lands that they were being good Christians while actually being barbaric. Atrocities would have happened, but Western culture would have shifted so that no one would be so utterly hard-hearted as to wantonly without conscience go around cutting off the hands and feet of small children in order to frighten a village into harvesting a few more pounds of rubber.

If the Doctrine of Discovery had said that the people being discovered were fully human, loved, and cherished by God and that they and their lands were to be treated as such, the church would never have become an empire. If the church had taken this stand, many would have been unhappy and angry with the church. Powerful people would have rebelled against the church, and many would have abandoned it. But the atrocities would have been slowed. Instead of the doctrine injecting evil with steroids, there would have been resistance to these kinds of terror. Those who were the least of these would have had the Christian Church standing with them, protecting them instead of a ruthless conqueror attacking, robbing, and enslaving them.

NOTES

[1] Adam Hochschild, *King Leopold's Ghost: A Story of Greed, Terror, and Heroism in Colonial Africa* (Boston and New York: Houghton Mifflin Company, 1998), 99.

[2] Hochschild, *King Leopold's Ghost,* 216-17.

[3] Hochschild, *King Leopold's Ghost*, 163.

[4] Hochschild, *King Leopold's Ghost*, 277.

[5] Hochschild, *King Leopold's Ghost*, 280.

[6] Hochschild, *King Leopold's Ghost*, 282.

[7] Hochschild, *King Leopold's Ghost*, 282.

[8] Hochschild, *King Leopold's Ghost*, 2.

[9] "Doctrine of Discovery: in the name of Christ," *Indigenous Values Initiative,* 2025, https://indigenousvalues.org/decolonization/doctrine-discovery/.

[10] "Doctrine of Discovery: in the name of Christ, *Indigenous Values Initiative,* 2025, https://indigenousvalues.org/decolonization/doctrine-discovery/.

[11] Steve Newcomb, "Five Hundred Years of Injustice: The Legacy of Fifteenth Century Religious Prejudice," Taken from *Shaman's Drum.* 1992, p. 18-20. http://ili.nativeweb.org/sdrm_art.html.

[12] Jason Hickel, *Less is More: How Degrowth Will Save the World* (London: William Heinemann, 2020), 51.

[13] "Doctrine of Discovery: in the name of Christ, *Indigenous Values Initiative,* 2025, https://indigenousvalues.org/decolonization/doctrine-discovery/.

[14] "Doctrine of Discovery," *Upstander Project,* Accessed March 20, 2025. https://upstanderproject.org/learn/guides-and-resources/first-light/doctrine-of-discovery.

[15] "Doctrine of Discovery," *American Indian Law Alliance,* Accessed March 20, 2025, https://aila.ngo/issues/doctrine-of-discovery/.

[16] Steve Newcomb, "Five Hundred Years of Injustice: The Legacy of Fifteenth Century Religious Prejudice" Taken from *Shaman's Drum.* 1992, p. 18-20, http://ili.nativeweb.org/sdrm_art.html.

[17] Steve Newcomb, "Five Hundred Years of Injustice: The Legacy of Fifteenth Century Religious Prejudice." Taken from *Shaman's Drum.* 1992, p. 18-20. http://ili.nativeweb.org/sdrm_art.html.

| seven |

Defeating Regulation While Creating Death

Don't take advantage of widows, orphans, visitors, and the poor. Don't plot and scheme against one another—that's evil. Speak out for those who cannot speak, for the rights of all the destitute. Speak out, judge righteously, defend the rights of the poor and needy. Zechariah 7:9-10

The Human Wreckage

If one set out to design an industry to be as destructive as possible, it would be hard to design one more devastating than the tobacco industry.

Former FDA Commissioner Scott Gottlieb, M.D. stated that tobacco is "the only legal consumer product that, when used as intended, will kill half of all long-term users." [1] The World Bank states that the use of tobacco kills more people yearly than COVID-19. Smoking tobacco is estimated to have killed 100 million people in the 20th century, and projections for the future suggest an astounding one billion people could die from smoking this century if no action is taken. [2]According to the CDC, in the U.S., 480,000 die annually from the effects of tobacco, including more than 41,000 from secondhand smoke.[3]

Smoking cigarettes is responsible for 90% of lung cancer, which more people die from than any other form of cancer. Chronic obstructive pulmonary disease (COPD) is the country's fourth leading cause of death, with 85 to 90 % of these cases caused by tobacco use. Smoking is a major contributing factor to heart disease, strokes, asthma, reproductive problems in women, premature birth, diabetes, blindness, and other types of cancer. [4] Monetarily, tobacco use costs the global economy an estimated US$ 1.85 trillion annually in health care costs, lost productivity, fire damage, destructive farming practices, and litter.

What's wrong with this picture? A so-called legitimate business causes 480,000 U.S. deaths a year, killed an estimated 100 million worldwide in the last century, and is projected to kill an astounding one billion human beings worldwide this century.[5]

We shouldn't be shocked. This industry exists because it has been and continues to be highly lucrative for its executives and stockholders. A Credit Suisse report states that a measly one dollar invested in tobacco stocks in 1900 would have grown to an investment worth $6.3 million by 2010. This increase is 165 times more than the average industry.[6] To maintain that high profitability, the industry doesn't let anything distract from its goal of selling the maximum number of cigarettes possible.

It raises the question of how an industry that inflicts such massive health and economic costs can be legal. One would think that a business doing this kind of carnage would automatically be shut down and the people running it locked up. Why is an industry wreaking this kind of devastation allowed to do business?

The Battle for Profit Over Life

In the early 1950s, led by the scientific community and the media, there was a growing awareness that smoking cigarettes caused disease and death. The public became alarmed, resulting in an outcry for local and national governments to take action against the tobacco industry.

As knowledge about the danger grew, the tobacco industry became concerned. As this information became more widespread, the industry never attempted to use authentic scientific research to protect the public's health. From the beginning, their goal was not to protect human life but to preserve profits. As the concern about the danger of tobacco continued to grow, the companies knew they needed to combat it with a united front. Even though they were competitors, they colluded to mobilize their enormous resources and jointly fought against the threat of regulation and higher taxes. The companies organized to crush any opposition that would cut into their immense wealth. The result is that for decades, the companies have denied the harm (which they knew to be true) caused by tobacco and joined in a determined unified effort to suppress critics, manipulate public opinion, falsify science, dominate public policy, and synchronize their strategy on litigation.

Since smoking kills half of their long-term customer base, tobacco companies were fighting for new customers. To make that situation even more problematic, only five percent of their customers start smoking after the age of 18. Therefore, the executives of these companies know that the industry is dependent on addicting young smokers to replace the smokers who are dying to maintain their high profitability. Consequently, one of their prime advertising targets is youth. Professor Chris Whitty of the United Kingdom poignantly states that tobacco companies make a large percentage of their profits from people they have addicted when young and then keep them addicted to a product they know will kill them.[7]

Laws have been passed to stop the industry from targeting teens and to prohibit them from making products designed to attract teens. However, the tobacco industry knows it depends on addicting younger users, so it looks for opportunities to sneak around these prohibitions.

The tobacco industry has done this by marketing candy and fruit-flavored cigarettes using vanilla, cherry, chocolate, and blueberry flavors, among others. Except for menthol, the sale of flavored cigarettes was prohibited in 2009. To avoid the prohibition, the companies still flavor cigars and e-cigarettes. Tobacco companies know celebrities influence youth, so they use celebrity endorsements to attract them. The industry claimed they were selling "low harm" products. The courts didn't agree and found that they lied about the health claims of these types of cigarettes, resulting in the companies being convicted of racketeering for the way they promoted the health benefits of the light, low-tar, filtered cigarettes. The companies created games to attract younger buyers, like raffling off a car. Buy one pack, get one free was another hook that enticed younger buyers. They also targeted youth by advertising in magazines that young people read. They even inserted pictures of tobacco products in Saturday morning cartoons. The Joe Camel cartoon character was one of the most effective ads targeting children and teens. One study found that as many 3–6-year-old children knew Joe Camel as knew Mickey Mouse. Joe Camel was so effective in addicting kids that the character was banned in 1998.

Whitty also emphasizes that a large percentage of the tobacco industry's profits are made from people with mental health issues, the unemployed, and those in difficult financial situations. The young and the most vulnerable members of society are the ones targeted by the industry.[8]

The people running the tobacco industry chose to lie to the public in order to confuse them about the health effects of tobacco. One of the primary ways they did this was articulated by a Phillip Morris executive who wrote a paper stating that the goal of their advertising was to create doubt. The paper stated, "Doubt is our product." [11]The goal was to deliberately confuse the public about the risks of smoking. The executives made the decision to use pseudo-science, in effect lies, to conflict with scientific evidence so that the public wouldn't know what to believe.[10]

The companies used every tactic at their disposal to fight regulations and restrictions. They monitored those arrayed against them in order to anticipate what their actions would be; developed a robust media campaign to shape public opinion in favor of the industry; utilized their economic power for campaign contributions to gain votes and favors from politicians; developed a powerful lobby; recruited experts who were supposed to be independent; tapped smoker's rights groups to create an impression of spontaneous support; formed alliances with farmers, retailers, and advertising agencies to influence legislation; intimidated opponents with their legal and economic power; utilized their economic power to buy respectability; and used their economic and political power to force their way to be included in trade agreements.

The industry became so successful in fighting back against regulation that it became a model for other industries in how to resist when the public and government attempted to reduce the use of or regulate their product.

"We Have Met the Enemy"

The executives and investors connected to the tobacco industry continue to make themselves wealthy as they destroy people's health and well-being. They are putting their energy, brainpower, and monetary resources into developing a product that causes death. An appropriate reaction to this account is to wonder how people could agree to invest in and work for an industry that wreaks such havoc on their fellow human beings solely for profit. The more one becomes aware of the magnitude of the devastation to people's lives, the greater the understandable temptation to be outraged and judgmental. It prompts the question of what happened to their moral compass.

Specifically, it prompts the question: Since the tobacco industry is primarily located in the South of the country and the South is thought of as being the Bible belt of the country, where was/is the church in this controversy?

And where are we? If we continue to reflect on this, some of us will uncomfortably remember the Pogo comic strip character stating, "We have met the enemy, and he is us." If we own mutual funds, annuities, or other forms of investments in which money is invested in multiple companies, there is a strong possibility that we are among those investing in, earning from, and supporting the tobacco industry.

NOTES

[1] Scott Gottlieb, "Statement from FDA Commissioner Scott Gottlieb, M.D., on pivotal public health step to dramatically reduce smoking rates by lowering nicotine in combustible cigarettes to minimally or non-addictive levels," *Food and Drug Administration,* March 14, 2018, https://www.fda.gov/news-events/press-announcements/statement-fda-commissioner-scott-gottlieb-md-pivotal-public-health-step-dramatically-reduce-smoking.

[2] "U.N.: Smoking could kill 1 billion by 2100," *NBC News,* February 7, 2008, https://www.nbcnews.com/health/health-news/u-n-smoking-could-kill-1-billion-2100-flna1c9449574.

[3] "Burden of Cigarette Use in the U.S," *Centers for Disease Control and Prevention,* Last Reviewed: October 8, 2024, https://www.cdc.gov/tobacco/campaign/tips/resources/data/cigarette-smoking-in-united-states.html.

[4] "Cigarette Smoking," *Centers for Disease Control and Prevention.* September 17, 2024, https://www.cdc.gov/tobacco/about/index.html.

[5] "Economic Costs of Tobacco Use," *Tobacconomics,* April 2019, https://tobacconomics.org/files/research/523/UIC_Economic-Costs-of-Tobacco-Use-Policy-Brief_v1.3.pdf.

[6] James Hickman, "A super safe stock fell 19% last Friday...And you should be worried," *Schiff Sovereign,* August 1, 2017, https://www.schiffsovereign.com/stocks/a-super-safe-stock-fell-19-last-friday-and-you-should-be-worried-22215/.

[7] Eleanor Hayward Heath, "Professor Chris Whitty attacks 'kill for profit' tobacco companies and warns smoking killed 90,000 Brits last year - more than Covid, *Daily Mail.com.* May 19, 2021, https://www.dailymail.co.uk/health/article-9596473/Chris-

Whitty-attacks-tobacco-companies-people-die-smoking-Covid.html.

[8] Aine Fo, "Dishonest to say smoking debate is about health versus freedom, says Whitty," *Yahoo! News,* June 9, 2022, https://uk.movies.yahoo.com/dishonest-smoking-debate-health-versus-134803334.html.

[9] Max Rohr, "Doubt is our product." *PHCPPROS,* May 13, 2015, https://www.phcppros.com/articles/367-doubt-is-our-product.

[10] David Michaels, "Doubt is their product," *Oxford University Press,* https://global.oup.com/academic/product/doubt-is-their-product-9780195300673?cc=us&lang=en&.

| eight |

Poison

I looked again and saw people being mistreated everywhere on earth. They were crying, but no one was there to offer comfort, and those who mistreated them were powerful. (Ecclesiastes 4:1)

Heroes in the Midst of Death

When some have lost conscience and succumbed to the pressures and powers of this world, when lies and greed seem insurmountable, thankfully and encouragingly, sometimes heroes arise amid the darkness. There are moments when we are blessed with people who have enormous courage, integrity, love, strength, and inspiring tenacity who stand against the powers of evil and become a saving force for good. At least two such heroes rose up in Parkersburg, WV, in the late 1900s and early 2000s.

The first of these heroes was Wilbur Tennant. Tennant was a rough-hewn farmer who had been happily raising cattle on his farm in Parkersburg until they started dying. Some cattle were throwing up blood, going blind, and developing tumors. Moreover, very gentle cows began acting strangely and sometimes violently charged him. Tennant knew that something was poisoning his cattle, so he set out to do everything possible to stop it. He went to everyone around Parkersburg that he thought could possibly be helpful, starting with the West Virginia Division of Natural Resources and the West Virginia Department of Environmental Protection. They ignored him, so he turned to doctors, journalists, and veterinarians, but also to no avail. As far as we can tell from the written accounts, it appears that no one wanted anything to do with him and what was causing the death of his cattle.

He began dissecting his cattle that had died despite the terrible smells when he opened them up, removed discolored, oddly shaped, and unhealthy-appearing body parts, and stored them in his freezer. His idea was that, eventually, he would convince someone to examine them and tell him what was killing his cattle. He received no encouragement or support but was fiercely determined not to be deterred.

An enormous DuPont plant owned land that abutted Tennant's farm. A stream that ran through the Dupont property and onto Tennant's farm had become discolored. Tennant suspected the stream was carrying chemical waste onto his property and poisoning his cattle.

In 1999, discouraged, frustrated, and angry, Tennant fortuitously contacted Rob Bilott, a corporate lawyer in environmental law who worked in a blue-ribbon law practice in Cincinnati, Ohio. Bilott and the law firm that he was in nearly always defended large corporate clients instead of going up against them.

Ironically, as a small boy, Bilott had visited his grandmother in Parkersburg, where he had enjoyed some of his fondest boyhood memories. When Tennant first called Bilott, almost as an afterthought, he fortuitously mentioned Bilott's grandmother. If Tennant hadn't dropped this small but critical piece of information into the conversation, some familiar with this story suggest that Bilott may never have consented to see him. However, he did mention it, and Bilott agreed to meet with him. Through this unlikely, tenuous connection, history in this part of the world started to turn. The moral arc of the universe that Dr. King liked to point us toward had begun a momentous turn toward truth and justice.

Bilott visited Tennant and witnessed the environmental degradation Tennant had been telling people about for years. It appears that personally seeing the degradation, his grandmother having lived there, and his own cherished childhood memories of the area motivated Bilott to take the case. Despite obstacle after obstacle, he began heroically taking the case from one level to the next for the following twenty years. He is still working on it.

The Beginning

The story began decades earlier, in 1951, when DuPont started buying PFOA, short for perfluorooctanoic acid, known inside Dupont as C8. The corporation purchased the substance from 3M and used it to manufacture Teflon. From the beginning, there were questions about the product's safety.

During WWII, many plastics began to be developed for the war effort. When the war ended, companies began finding non-military uses for them and immediately began marketing these products to the public. By 1951, congress started to be concerned about the possible health hazards of the products. It formed a committee to investigate them to see if legislation was needed to protect the public's health.

It was a watershed moment. Immediately, not just DuPont but the chemical industry as a whole chose to go to war against not only possible regulation but also against safety, health, and the environment. Instead of wanting to know if there were health hazards from these new products, the chemical industry immediately acted to protect earnings rather than genuinely attempting to discern if some of their recent inventions were toxic and unsafe. Without knowing whether their inventions were dangerous or not, the industry hired a public relations firm to discredit any emerging information that might indicate a product could be hazardous. To protect the chemical industry from regulation, the PR firm Hill & Knowlton implemented many of the same methods they later used to stifle tobacco industry regulation. Immediately, the chemical industry's thirst for profits had become the dominant factor in their decision-making process.

The industry didn't know many of its products would poison the planet, but even in those early days, it had indications that some of its products were dangerous and potentially harmful. What was it about the mindsets of the people making the decisions for DuPont that made them automatically oriented toward choosing profit instead of safety?

Like the tobacco industry, the chemical industry was also successful in minimizing the regulation of its products. In 1958, Congress did manage to pass a regulatory bill, but chemicals already in use were grandfathered in as safe to use. Internal documents uncovered later showed that as early as 1954, DuPont had held PFOA off the market out of concern that it might not be safe.[1]

In 1961, a French company began marketing a frying pan coated with Teflon. This seems to have precipitated Dupont to disregard possible dangers that PFOA might not be safe as they began selling their own Teflon-coated "Happy Pan". Production and marketing went forward despite DuPont's chief toxicologist warning executives that Teflon should be 'handled with extreme care." She alerted the company that rats and rabbits had enlarged livers when exposed to PFOA, which suggested toxicity. However, sales of the product expanded rapidly, so soon, it was making the company $1 billion a year.[2 It seems that was too much profit for the company to pass up, regardless of the possible danger to their workers, the public, and the environment.

Warning Signs Were Abundant

Over the decades, tests, studies, and severe worker health problems consistently indicated that PFOA was toxic. One of those workers was Ken Walmsley, who had been working at the DuPont plant since 1962 when he was nineteen. Walmsley had several different jobs at the plant, but in 1976, he was transferred and began working in the chemical analysis laboratory, where part of his job was testing different kinds of Teflon products. Unknowingly, Walmsley was being exposed to PFOA in two different ways. He was drinking the water the plant had contaminated with PFOA, and he was testing Teflon products.

In 1976, he started having severe cramps that would send him racing for the bathroom. The pain was so intense that the doctor instructed his wife to get him to the hospital immediately. After a series of tests, the surgeon recommended they operate. During the surgery, they discovered ulcerative colitis in which his small intestines were covered with scar tissue, which was wrecking his digestive system. The surgeon removed the scar tissue or adhesions, and the short-term prognosis was good. However, the surgeon warned that he was concerned about Walmsley's future. It had been a serious surgery, and the recovery was difficult and prolonged. Still, after three months, Walmsley returned to work in the Teflon lab, where he continued to drink the water and test Teflon products.

For about 15 years after the surgery, Walmsley enjoyed relatively good health, was active, and played sports despite some stomach issues. In 2001, that respite period of good health ended. The pain returned with increased intensity. Again, he sometimes had to race to the bathroom, but at this point, sometimes he didn't make it. The doctors performed tests but initially weren't finding anything to clarify the situation or give him relief.

Eventually, subsequent tests showed that he had aggressive rectal carcinoma. He had known that ulcerative colitis put him at a higher risk for rectal cancer, but now that threat had materialized. The physical losses disrupted the normality of his life; emotionally, he was devastated. Disheartened, he felt he could no longer continue working and resigned from DuPont.

Walmsley lost the life he had known. His spleen was removed, and his teeth turned black and rotted out. Surgery closed his rectum and made an opening for his waste to empty into a pouch. He lost his independence and his confidence. He had been an outgoing person who enjoyed people but now was fearful of leaving the house. In imagining his retirement, he had dreamed of teaching math, coaching a baseball team, and traveling. Simple daily pleasures of chewing a steak, sipping a beer, or even sitting on a toilet were gone. He felt that these things were stolen from him by the company he had trusted and devoted his life to.[3]

Another employee at the company, Sue Bailey, gave birth in 1981 to a baby with only half a nose and an eyelid that fell to the middle of his cheek. He wasn't expected to live. At his birth, Bailey was hesitant to hold the baby, fearful that he would die in her arms. Bailey worked at the Dupont plant pumping PFOA into onsite pits at the plant. Dupont doctors said there was no connection between congenital disabilities and PFOA. Another woman at the plant had a baby with similar defects.

Over the decades, there had been multiple studies and tests to determine if it was safe to be exposed to Teflon. About the same time Sue Bailey had given birth to her baby, DuPont was getting data from two secret studies showing that PFOA caused eye defects in lab animals. DuPont kept this information secret while moving female workers to parts of the plant where they wouldn't have contact with the chemical.

In 1982, after further testing of employees, DuPont's medical director cautioned the company that employees were being subjected to levels of PFOA that could be dangerous. He strongly urged that all possible steps to reduce exposure be taken.

DuPont monitored 50 female employees who had been exposed to PFOA to determine if the product caused abnormal children. The result from the study indicated that it did. However, DuPont terminated the pregnancy study and did not inform the regulators.

Bilott learned that by the 1990s, DuPont knew a laboratory study implied that PFOA caused DNA damage. Another study indicated PFOA was linked to prostate cancer.

3M manufactured PFOA and supplied the material to DuPont. They also suspected that PFOA was toxic and were particularly concerned that the chemical could be more dangerous because there was evidence that PFOA collected in the body rather than breaking down. One 3M study determined that workers exposed to PFOA were three times more likely to die of prostate cancer than those not exposed. 3M also tested the substance on monkeys and discovered that even monkeys in the group receiving the lowest dose of PFOA had weight loss and liver swelling. One monkey in the same low-dose group collapsed in a catatonic stupor and died. The company notified the EPA of its findings in April of 2000 and began phasing out production of the product. DuPont knew of these findings as 3M and DuPont shared what they had learned about the toxicity of PFOA with each other.

The above is but a sampling of the red flags indicating potential PFOA health hazards that DuPont learned about over several decades. However, they did not use this knowledge to make the necessary changes to protect their employees' lives, the surrounding communities, and ultimately the world.

A pattern had developed. DuPont kept doing tests and checking to see if PFOA was dangerous. Unfailingly, the evidence came back that, in all probability, it was. For decades, Dupont consistently covered up, minimized, and denied the indications of toxicity they themselves were amassing.[4] But the time of successfully covering up and denying was ending. They were about to be exposed.

The Tennant Suit, EPA Fine, and Two Class Action Suits

In 1999, Rob Bilott came on as attorney for the Tennants, filed a suit against DuPont, and began the tedious process of uncovering all that DuPont had been hiding since the 1960s. The case started slowly with a minimum of success. The pace began to pick up when Bilott discovered a reference in a DuPont document referring to a chemical called PFOA. Over DuPont's objection, Bilott requested a court order for DuPont to turn over all documentation related to PFOA.

The court granted Bilott's request, and boxes containing 110,000 documents arrived. Bilott spent months organizing the material. It contained evidence of how DuPont had covered up the story of how they had been spreading the poisonous material to continue manufacturing and profiting from it. Bilott was shocked at the vast amount of incriminating material DuPont had sent him.

When DuPont realized that Bilott had the incriminating information, they settled the suit with Wilbur Tennant and his family. Usually, this would have been the end of the story. However, given what he now knew, Bilott was angry that DuPont had known that PFOA was extremely poisonous yet had been dumping tremendous quantities of it into the earth, waterways, and the air for decades. They had not only been exposing their workers but anyone who came into contact with the substance.

Bilott spent months writing a brief 972 pages long with 136 attached exhibits stating that DuPont was releasing chemicals that may present a significant threat to health and the environment. He sent the letter to every relevant regulatory agency. Bilott was not just informing these agencies; he claimed fraud and wrongdoing. At this point, he was not only a threat to DuPont but to the whole fluoropolymers industry.[5]

Due to Bilott's initiative, in 2005, DuPont reached a settlement with the EPA for a $16.5 million payment. At the time, the EPA had never settled for such a hefty penalty. However, it was less than 2 percent of DuPont's profits on PFOA that year.

As mentioned above, patterns developed in the way DuPont resisted dealing with the PFOA problem. Now, a pattern was developing with how Bilott and his team pursued this issue. The pattern was that as Bilott would win one suit and there would be a settlement, new avenues would open up for the team to pursue a more significant legal issue. The Tennant case and DuPont's settlement with the EPA exposed that DuPont had contaminated the water supply for the towns in the surrounding area.

Bilott and the team working with him had established in the previous cases that DuPont had dumped hundreds of thousands of pounds of PFOA powder into the Ohio River. They also knew that the company had flushed 7,100 tons of PFOA-contaminated sludge into unlined digestion ponds. From there, it had been seeping into the ground and drinking water not only of Parkersburg but Vienna and Lubeck, West Virginia, and Little Hocking, Ohio. This meant that 70,000 people in both West Virginia and Ohio had been drinking water contaminated by PFOA for decades. Bilott suspected that not only DuPont employees but also many people drinking the water developed diseases from ingesting the toxic substance.[6]

This belief led Bilott to bring a class-action suit against DuPont for the towns whose water supply had been contaminated by PFOA. In September of 2007, Dupont settled. They agreed to pay for new water filtration facilities for the six water districts that had been contaminated if the communities wanted them. They also agreed to pay a cash award of $70 million that could be used to capitalize a scientific study of the people who had been drinking the water to see if there were probable links between PFOA and disease.

For three years, Bilott had been working for nothing, but he and his legal team received $21.7 million out of the settlement. Some might have expected that Bilott would breathe a sigh of relief, declare victory, and move on. There were strong reasons for him to do that. Bilott, however, was angry that DuPont had not done anything to make this situation right. Moreover, he had developed relationships with people in these communities who were suffering from illnesses and financial hardship. Bilott believed that these illnesses were due to being poisoned by the company. He began to consider bringing a class-action lawsuit against DuPont to force the company to pay for any harm they may have caused by exposing their employees and surrounding communities to PFOA.

To take on this lawsuit would be an enormous undertaking with colossal risk and pressure. Taking on DuPont in this type of class-action suit would put Bilott's law firm at significant financial risk and Bilott himself under substantial pressure. Bilott and his law firm could lose big.

By this time, it appears that Bilott had become more and more connected with the people in the community. He was more personally aware of their illnesses and suffering. He was increasingly aware of the destructiveness of PFOA and angry that DuPont continued to take no responsibility. All this motivated him to take the chance and push on with the new class-action suit.

At first, the legal team designed the lawsuit only for DuPont employees. However, they decided to expand the suit to include people in the surrounding water districts who had been drinking the water and could also have been poisoned. The problem was, if they wanted to do this, how could they motivate the thousands of people in these communities to sign up to become suit members?

Fortunately for the legal team, West Virginia law was written so that if they chose to proceed with a class-action suit, DuPont would have to pay for all the people in the case to be tested for possible health issues related to PFOA. The idea surfaced that they could use the money they had received in the first-class action settlement with DuPont to pay people to become a part of the subsequent class-action suit. The suit members voted to do this, and thousands came forward to receive $400 and signed up to be part of the suit.

The class-action suit went forward; the study was to determine if PFOA was harmful and, if so, how dangerous. The team designed a system to test 70,000 people to see if they had PFOA in their blood and, if they did, how that might correlate with their health problems.

As the case progressed, the DuPont lawyers took every opportunity to obstruct the process by attempting to delay, postpone, and relitigate what had already been decided. Their goal was not to prove they weren't guilty but to do everything possible to block the case from moving forward.

The scientific panel launched into their work, but testing 70,000 people was such an enormous project that getting the results was painfully prolonged. The legal team waited a long seven years for the panel results. That extended time period was highly stressful for the members of the suit and for Bilott.

Even though the trial had taken place, Bilott and his team continued to work on the case with significant ongoing expenses. However, no income from the case was coming in to sustain their work. Bilott's law firm continued to pay substantial costs related to the case.

As the study stretched out year after year with no conclusion, people who were a part of the evaluation were being diagnosed with cancer and other health problems were calling him, anxious to know why they hadn't heard anything about the results of the scientific panel. Some of the plaintiffs were desperate for settlement money to help with medical expenses. Others were dying and anxious to get settlement money before their death. Bilott constantly needed to travel to Washington to meet with the EPA. The years passed, the costs mounted, and the pressure intensified.

Probably due to the stress, Bilott began to have his own health problems. He had attacks of blurry vision, speech difficulty, problems moving part of his body, and his arms would become numb. The symptoms would last days. The added pressure was that if the case were unsuccessful, the firm would have to eat all the expenses they had been paying over the years while waiting for the results.

After a long seven-year wait, relief arrived. In December 2011, the results from the scientists started coming in. They stated there was a "probable link" between PFOA and ulcerative colitis, pre-eclampsia, high cholesterol, testicular cancer, thyroid disease, and kidney cancer. Due to DuPont's continued resistance to taking responsibility for the destructiveness of their actions, there was still a lot of legal work to be done before the people would start receiving compensation.

Following this decision, there were several test cases. DuPont lost all of these cases. As several test cases were settled in the plaintiffs' favor, the punitive amounts of the awards kept rising. At this point, "DuPont agreed to pay $670.7 million to the people represented in 3,500 lawsuits pending in Ohio and West Virginia." Determining who would get what portion of the settlement monies would be a complex process. Lawsuits and legal maneuvering related to PFOA are continuing, not only in West Virginia but worldwide.

The Worldwide Costs Continue

DuPont's decisions and actions contaminated the entire planet. "Where scientists have tested for the presence of PFOA in the world, they have found it. PFOA is in the blood or vital organs of Atlantic salmon, swordfish, striped mullet, gray seals, common cormorants, Alaskan polar bears, brown pelicans, sea turtles, sea eagles, Midwestern bald eagles, California sea lions and Laysan albatrosses on Sand Island, a wildlife refuge on Midway Atoll, in the middle of the North Pacific Ocean, about halfway between North America and Asia."[7] And of course, PFOA is present in virtually all of us.

This story has not ended. 3M decided to quit making Teflon, so obviously, they could no longer sell to DuPont. Even after all the information about the disease and environmental degradation PFOA causes, instead of making the choice 3M made, DuPont opened its own factory to produce Teflon in NC. Legal actions are now swirling around this plant and how it may be contaminating communities downstream from it. At one point, DuPont declared it no longer used PFOA or C-8. However, they were reportedly preparing to use C-6, which has a similar structure and may be toxic in exactly the same way.[8] Regrettably, for them, for of us, and the planet, DuPont is still captive to profit.

The Power of the Spiritual Path

This story could have had a different, happier ending. Even before DuPont began to use PFOA, there were indications that the chemical was dangerous. As DuPont continued to use it, multiple tests indicating toxicity and warnings from their own medical people, combined with the illnesses of their employees, were an opportunity for DuPont's management to reassess the safety of PFOA. The red flags were screaming for the people who knew this information to take action.

From a spiritual perspective, there were multiple opportunities for DuPont to have a conversion moment–conversion in the sense of turning from going in one direction to going in another and turning from greed toward responsibility. It would have also been turning from danger and destructiveness to care. There was an opportunity for them to allow the scriptures about wealth to pull them back from the abyss.

Dupont desperately needed someone to help surface the looming disasters they were hurling toward. They didn't know it, but they urgently needed a modern-day John Woolman with his skills, temperament, depth of spirituality, and care for their souls to call the executives and board members back to who they were created to be. It would have been hard for these executives and board members to recognize they had become captives and subservient to the $one billion yearly profits.

Rob Bilott continued to confront DuPont legally after Tennant's death. He was hugely courageous, tenacious, took risks, and sacrificed. He was prophetic from a legal stance and remarkably successful. Thank God for him.

Bilott and John Woolman were attempting to carry out a similar mission. They both were confronting people about their greed, immorality, and destructiveness. Both men were successful, with Woolman relieving the enslavers of some of their wealth and Bilott doing the same with DuPont. Both brought about relief and partial justice for those who were oppressed or suffering. But there were significant differences.

Bilott had the power of the legal system to confront DuPont. On the other hand, Woolman had no power to force his fellow Quakers to do anything. He attempted to avoid confronting enslavers harshly but tried in every way to relate in a way so that they would feel that he was on their side. He would use other Quakers as intermediaries if he thought it would be helpful. He didn't compromise his message but would remain respectful, strove not to antagonize, and appealed to the best side of the people he was addressing. He had no legal power or monetary power. One would have to say that Woolman depended on God's power.

There was another difference. Woolman was successful in being a catalyst for enslaved people to be freed, but more than that, he facilitated a change of heart in the enslavers. Through Woolman's intervention, they chose to change and release their enslaved people. They became freer through doing that. Woolman was following Jesus' path of freeing the captives.

Thank God Bilott had the ethics, courage, tenacity, and willingness to sacrifice. Thankfully, he hung on like a bulldog as, again and again, he confronted DuPont in the legal arena and won. We are indebted to him, those working with him, and others like him. Regrettably, it appears from the accounts that there has been no real change in DuPont's stance even after being confronted with the suffering their greed had caused and losing repeatedly in the courts. On January 22, 2021, the legal system, through Bilott's commitment, forced DuPont and its spinoffs to give up $4 billion in a settlement. They had already given up $tens of millions in previous court cases. Still, Bilott's commitment and the legal arena were powerless to change the hearts of people determined to maximize profit regardless of the human and environmental costs.

We admire and are thankful for Bilott and people like him who fight for justice in the legal arena. May there be many more like him. However, Woolman's life is both challenging and mystifying. Is it possible for other people of faith to follow him in becoming God's instrument in inspiring others to sacrifice wealth to be truer in their faith? How do we grow into becoming a conduit for God to change people's hearts in that way?

NOTES

[1] Mariah Blake, "Welcome to Beautiful Parkersburg, West Virginia: Home to one of the most brazen, deadly corporate gambits in U.S. history," *Huffington Post*. https://highline.huffingtonpost.com/articles/en/welcome-to-beautiful-parkersburg/.

[2] Ibid..

[3] Robert Bilott and Tom Shroder, *Exposure: Poisoned Water, Corporate Greed, and One Lawyer's Twenty-Year Battle against DuPont* (New York: Atria Books, 2019), 365.

[4] Mariah Blake, "Welcome to Beautiful Parkersburg, West Virginia: Home to one of the most brazen, deadly corporate gambits in U.S. history," *Huffington Post*, https://highline.huffingtonpost.com/articles/en/welcome-to-beautiful-parkersburg/.

[5] Nathaniel Rich, The Lawyer Who Became DuPont's Worst Nightmare, *New York Times*, January 6, 2016, https://www.nytimes.com/2016/01/10/magazine/the-lawyer-who-became-duponts-worst-nightmare.html.

[6] Ibid.

[7] Ibid.

[8] Mariah Blake, "Welcome to Beautiful Parkersburg, West Virginia: Home to one of the most brazen, deadly corporate gambits in U.S. history," *Huffington Post*. https://highline.huffingtonpost.com/articles/en/welcome-to-beautiful-parkersburg/.

| nine |

Addiction

This is what the Lord says: Judge fairly, and do what is right. Rescue those who have been robbed from those who oppress them. Don't mistreat foreigners, orphans, or widows, and don't oppress them. Don't kill innocent people in this place. Give justice to the weak and the orphan; maintain the right of the lowly and the destitute. (Jeremiah 22:3-4)

The Rise of a Philanthropic Dynasty

In the last part of the twentieth century and the first part of this century, the Sackler family became one of the wealthiest extended families in the world. They weren't as famous or as well-known as some, but those seeking enormous donations for their universities, art galleries, museums, and similar projects knew them well.

The Sacklers have been referred to as a philanthropic dynasty. There is The Sackler Wing at New York's Metropolitan Museum of Art. Tufts University has a Sackler graduate school. Columbia University has a Sackler Institute. At Oxford, there is a Sackler Library. The Louvre in Paris boasts the famous Sackler Wing of Oriental Antiquities. The popular Temple of Dendur at the Metropolitan Museum of Art is housed in the glass-walled Sackler Wing. Harvard has the Arthur M. Sackler Museum, and the Arthur M. Sackler Museum of Art and Archaeology is at Peking University in China. The Tate Museums in London have benefitted from the Sacklers, as has the Solomon Guggenheim in New York and the Metropolitan Opera.

The Sacklers, like Francis' father, Peter Bernardone, wanted to be influential with their wealth.[1]

The family dynasty began with Arthur, Mortimer, and Raymond Sackler. All were educated as physicians, but their careers focused on the business world in ways that intersected with the medical field. The brothers bought and developed multiple businesses, sometimes those selling similar types of products. They particularly profited from aggressively marketing and promoting pharmaceuticals. Early in their careers, there were suspicions about the ethics and sometimes the legality of their creative but questionable business practices. The brothers' adeptness at keeping their business ventures hidden made uncovering the questionable practices extremely difficult.

In 1952, the Sackler brothers bought a little-known business called the Purdue Frederick Company. When they bought it, the company had annual revenues of around $22,000. It had been selling tonics and elixirs since 1892, with the primary product being Gray's Glycerine Tonic Compound. It was amply fortified with sherry and advertised to make people feel better. In the early years after the brothers purchased the business, it also sold such mundane products as an ear wax remover and a laxative.

Purdue Frederick continued adding products to its sales inventory, and by the 1970s, it had become an extremely profitable enterprise. Mortimer and Raymond had become wealthy from Purdue Frederick. In 1987, when Arthur Sackler died, the two remaining brothers bought out Arthur's share for $22,353,750.

The company increasingly began to focus on pharmaceuticals designed to treat pain. In 1984, the company released MS Contin, a morphine-based sustained-release pain killer. Following that emphasis, in 1991, it was incorporated as Purdue Pharma LP. In 1996, they released what was to become their flagship product, OxyContin. At the launch party for OxyContin, Richard Sackler, anticipating huge profits, enthusiastically stated that the drug "will be followed by a blizzard of prescriptions that will bury the competition."[2] Unfortunately, more than the competition was to be buried as a result of OxyContin being introduced.

By this time, the Sacklers and Purdue Pharma, with their extensive experience, had become masters at marketing pharmaceuticals, particularly pain medications. Using their marketing expertise, they initiated a very aggressive campaign to promote OxyContin as safer than alternative painkillers. It was promoted as less likely for users to become addicted than from pain medications such as Percocet and Vicodin.

In promoting the product, opioid manufacturers made gifts and payments to doctors to prescribe their opioids. One study reported that "... the industry spent about $40 million promoting opioid medications to nearly 68,000 doctors from 2013 through 2015, including by paying for meals, trips, and consulting fees... Even as the opioid epidemic was killing more and more Americans, such marketing practices remained widespread."[3]

Coinciding with the release of OxyContin, Raymond Sackler was interviewing a newly hired sales representative. During the conversation, he was enthusiastic about how OxyContin would turn Purdue Pharma into a pharmaceutical powerhouse. "OxyContin," he declared, "is our ticket to the moon."[4] It was indeed their ticket to the moon. In 2016, Forbes magazine estimated the value of Purdue Pharma to be around $13 billion. The company the brothers had bought in 1952 with total annual sales of $22,000, had rocketed into a company that in 2017 had sales of $31 billion in OxyContin alone.

The extended Sackler family had been spectacularly successful in amassing colossal wealth and prominence. They were at the top of the social ladder and were courted by major museums, universities, and nonprofit organizations throughout the world that hoped to benefit from their wealth. They had achieved the financial success billions around the world only dream of accomplishing.

Purdue wasn't the only company doing this. Once Purdue led the way with opioids and its innovative marketing, other pharmaceutical companies, pharmaceutical distributors, and pharmacies quickly followed suit to grab their share of the profits. Purdue was the one blazing the way with their highly aggressive promotion, but the other major players in the pharmaceutical industry wasted no time in following suit.

Shattered Lives–Shattered Dreams

However, what had seemed to be a dream life for some began to careen toward a nightmare for others. People who were prescribed OxyContin were frequently becoming addicted with alarming consequences. Many were crushing the drug and then snorting it. Others found ways to inject it. Some were becoming dependent even when using the opioids as prescribed.

Users were stealing from their families and breaking into their neighbors' homes to obtain drugs. Families were investing their life savings in treatment for their loved ones. Parents searched in pawnshops for family heirlooms that had been taken there by an addicted child. Jails in hard-hit areas were filling up with drug-related crime perpetrators. In some places, the number of children placed in foster care doubled as their addicted parents could no longer care for their young children. Grandparents found it necessary to take over the care of their grandchildren. Many using the drugs were dying of overdoses. Opioids were shattering lives, families, and communities.

For approximately 20 years, Purdue Pharma denied that OxyContin was a significant factor in causing the opioid catastrophe. In his book *Pain Killer,* Barry Meier reports that a group in Southwest Virginia made repeated attempts to warn Purdue about the disastrous impact OxyContin was having in western Virginia. The Virginia people knew that other areas in different parts of the country were facing the same types of crises their communities were experiencing. Individuals and groups began informing Purdue what was happening in their localities, hoping the company would alter its marketing practices. These communities were persistent and made multiple attempts but were unsuccessful. They concluded that Purdue would go through the motions of listening and offering reassurance. However, it became increasingly clear that they were actually doubling down on their highly aggressive marketing campaign.[5]

Upon learning that their company was doing such immense harm, one would imagine a reasonable response by Purdue that they were causing such suffering and death would be to reevaluate, pull back, and establish precautions for the sale of opioids. Given the devastation OxyContin was wreaking, it appears the company would want to do everything possible to save lives. From their pattern of behavior, it seems that Purdue had chosen a different path and was not deviating. They intended to continue to ride OxyContin to the moon. From their actions, it appears that profit had so entrapped their hearts and values that they wouldn't or couldn't loosen their grip on that moon ride.

By 2007, it was not only Purdue that was choosing profits over life. By then, most of the major players in the pharmaceutical industry had observed the gains Purdue was amassing through its sale of opioids. They were pushing and shoving for their share of that market and were to use the formidable resources of their powerful industry to bulldoze any entity that attempted to interfere with that. They, as Purdue, were powerless in resisting the overwhelming pull of huge potential profits.[6] In retrospect, it seems naïve to expect Purdue and the rest of the drug industry to value lives over profits.

The Big Players Choose Profits Over Lives

Most of the pharmaceutical industry operates under a division of labor. There are manufacturers of the pills who sell to distributors, who in turn market and deliver to pharmacies. Of course, pharmacies sell to customers and patients. All these parts of the industry jumped into promoting opioids to the fullest extent possible regardless of the human cost.

Mallinckrodt and Actavis were two of the major manufacturers of opioids. In 2008, Mallinckrodt produced 4.3 billion doses of generic oxycodone, more painkillers than any other company. That same year, Actavis made 3.6 billion pills. (Cartel 36). Mallinckrodt's 4.3 billion pills were more than ten times what Purdue had manufactured that year.[7] At this point, due to their size, the larger companies were having a more significant destructive impact than Purdue.

Three major pharmaceutical distributors buy from the manufacturers. These three distributors ship nearly 95 percent of all drugs in the United States. They are all large, powerful companies. Cardinal Health, Inc., is the nineteenth largest company in the country, AmerisourceBergen Corp. is the twenty-ninth largest, and McKesson Corporation is the eighteenth largest. These three companies were shipping enormous amounts of opioids to the drug store pharmacies and so-called pain clinics that were prescribing and sometimes selling the pills themselves.

In the early 2000s, it was extremely easy to purchase opioids online. In 2008, congress ended that by passing the Ryan Haight Online Pharmacy Consumer Protection Act. It was named after Ryan Haight, a teenager who died after overdosing on opioids he had purchased online. He hadn't seen a doctor and didn't have a prescription. The new law put up firm guidelines to restrict online sales of opioids.[8]

When online orders were shut down, alleged pain management clinics cranked up. For the authors of *American Cartel,* these clinics were essentially "pill mills," dispensing large quantities of opioids pretty much to whoever wanted them. [9] Florida had very lax laws for opioids, so for several years, the clinics thrived there. The clinics operated through doctors who had no qualms about prescribing vast amounts of opioids to almost anyone who wanted them. The examples abound, but one was a doctor in Delray Beach in Palm Beach County who prescribed 1000 tablets to a single customer. The same doctor prescribed 20,000 pills over ten months to another alleged patient.[10]

South Florida became flooded with these pain clinics to the extent that drug dealers would come from West Virginia, Ohio, Alabama, Tennessee, and other states. The clinics began to take on the appearance of open-air drug markets with buyers in long lines who would then move from one pain clinic to the next. After prescribing, the clinics would sometimes sell the pills themselves, or if not, the dealers could fill the prescriptions at drug stores. Certain drug stores were open to filling large orders without questions. The dealers then returned to their respective locations loaded with pills to sell on the streets.[11]

The pain clinics created so much devastation and suffering that the Florida legislature shut them down. As the opioid supply from Florida was restricted, people in the locations where many of these pills had been headed figured out how to open pain clinics in their own regions. Portsmouth, Ohio, became one of many areas where these clinics opened, supplying not only the Portsmouth area but surrounding states. One of the most notorious clinics in that city was called "Legitimate Pain Care," owned by Margaret Temponeras, a family physician. Over six years, she ordered 1.6 million pain pills.[12] Eight people she dispensed pills to died.

At another pain clinic in Portsmouth, a doctor illegally distributed millions of painkillers. Between 2003 and 2005, he purchased more oxycodone than any physician in the country. Four of the people he treated died of overdoses.[13] Both of these doctors were arrested and sentenced to prison.

The Appalachian area was particularly hard hit, but this type of situation was happening nationwide. In October 2015, the Charleston Gazette-Mail published a story about the drug epidemic in West Virginia. During six years, some of the country's largest drug companies had shipped 780 million prescription pain pills to the state. The shipments were enough to provide 433 pain pills to every person in the state. During the same time period, 1,728 people in the state overdosed.[14] In 2007, McKesson shipped 3 million pain pills to a pharmacy in Baltimore while shipping 2.6 million pills to two pharmacies in Houston. These kinds of huge shipments in the opioid industry became common.[15] The corresponding overdoses, broken families, deaths, and suffering due to these shipments also became common.

The Companies Use Their Muscle—and Their $Millions

By 2007, under strong leadership, the DEA vigorously attempted to get on top of the problem. They were aware of the opioid epidemic and were highly motivated to bring the pharmaceutical industry into compliance with the law. When the distributors sent shipments of pain pills to pharmacies that were obviously more than the pharmacies could legally sell, the DEA started shutting down the warehouses making those deliveries. In response, the companies would sometimes negotiate with the DEA and agree to discontinue making illegal shipments. The companies would then ignore the agreement and continue sending huge shipments as before. The DEA would respond by taking the companies to court, and in these early court cases, the DEA usually won.

The drug companies were determined not to be blocked from a large chunk of their profits, so they abandoned attempting to negotiate with the DEA and instead developed a war plan to undermine the agency. The Healthcare Distribution Alliance (The Alliance) was the lobbying organization for the pharmaceutical industry organization. The industry chose it to organize, plan, and lead the attack against the DEA. As the industry was mobilizing to neuter the DEA, The Alliance was the vehicle they chose to lead the assault. The members of The Alliance were normally fierce competitors, but to take on the DEA, they joined forces. They created a united lobbying front and established an enormous war chest to achieve their goals.

A significant part of the industry's plan was to capture and harness the power of the US Congress to achieve two primary objectives. Since the companies couldn't get around the law that allowed the DEA to stop opioid shipments and prosecute them, their first objective was to defang the law so it would be powerless to disrupt their sales. Since the DEA was the agency with the power to prosecute them, the companies' second objective was to manipulate Congress into gutting the DEA.

The pharmaceutical industry was shrewd in that, over time, it had used its deep pockets to hire executives away from the DEA. These former DEA executives had inside knowledge of the agency and were exceptionally effective sabotaging its work. These former DEA employees were well-informed about who to contact in Congress and how to approach them to block the DEA from following through with their regulation of the industry.

The pharmaceutical coalition effectively followed through with its plan. The industry was very calculating in choosing which members of Congress would be open to their requests and how to approach them. They injected $60 million into specific congressional campaigns to facilitate the process. The industry was entirely successful in achieving its goals. (Cartel. 145) They had the director of the DEA removed, resulting in the agency being reduced to a shell of its former self. Congress also changed the law the DEA used to prosecute the companies so that it was powerless.

On the surface, the drug companies were winning. They had won significant political victories in clearing out the obstacles blocking their excess sales. However, as they cleared the way for greater opioid profits, they were simultaneously clearing the way for more addiction, suffering, and death.

Ostensibly, the pharmaceutical industry's goal is to improve health and well-being. However, in their compulsion to maximize profits regardless of human cost, the industry had lost sight of its fundamental reason for being. Instead of being in the business of health and well-being, the industry chose the business of death. Like Purdue, the other pharmaceutical companies were tightly clutching their ride to the moon.

In this story, there is a law of inverse proportions at work. As the companies cleared the way for greater profit, they became more deeply entrapped in their greed. They were traveling the same road that the owners of enslaved peoples had been on centuries earlier. In striving to increase profits, they were blinding themselves to being able to empathize with the suffering of those abusing their products.

The people becoming addicted to opioids were losing their physical lives; those in the opioid industry were losing their souls. From a spiritual perspective, the industry executives were not winning. They had become captives of their desire for profit. Their inner light was being extinguished.

Lawsuits Force $Billions in Payouts, but Are Powerless to Change Hearts and Values

A few lawsuits began to be filed against the companies. In some of these early suits, the companies were ordered to pay sums like $30 - $40 million. At first glance, this seems like a lot of money. However, the companies had gross sales that dwarfed these numbers. McKesson had $93 billion in annual revenues, and AmerisourceBergen's yearly income for 2019 was $179,589 billion. For giant corporations like these, losing a $30 million lawsuit is sometimes seen as a cost of doing business.

However, by February 2022, the slap-on-the-wrist occasional lawsuit settlement for $30 or $40 million had ended. The time of serious monetary payments had arrived, accompanied by bankruptcies and restrictions on how the companies could sell opioids.

Due to the magnitude of suffering, multiple prominent law firms began to sense that there was big money to be made by suing the drug companies. The number of lawsuits filed against the pharmaceutical companies had risen to at least 3000, with more expected to be filed. Both the law firms and the pharmaceutical companies were consolidating the suits. On February 25, 2022, it was announced that AmerisourceBergen, Cardinal Health, and McKesson had agreed to pay a total of $21 billion to thousands of communities all over the United States. Johnson & Johnson committed to pay out $5 billion as part of its settlement. Johnson and Johnson had already announced that it would no longer be marketing prescription opioids.[16]

Purdue Pharma and the Sackler family agreed to pay a $5.5 billion settlement. The company is also under a bankruptcy plan that mandates it to be sold or dissolved by 2024. Under the agreement, the Sacklers were not allowed to manufacture or sell opioids. The agreement also stipulated that the institutions carrying the Sackler name on their buildings and programs would be permitted to remove the name.[17]

Drug maker Teva agreed to pay more than $4.3 billion to settle lawsuits against it.[18] Mallinckrodt PLC settled its opioid suits by agreeing to pay $1.7 billion. It, like Purdue, has been in bankruptcy proceedings. [19]

An agreement in principle was announced on November 2, 2022, that CVS Health and Walgreen Co. would each pay approximately $5 billion to settle lawsuits related to how they had marketed opioids. These payments will bring the total legal settlements to roughly $50 billion.[20]

On November 15, Walmart followed closely behind in agreeing to settle thousands of lawsuits for their role in the opioid epidemic for $3.1 billion. The money will be paid to states, local governments, and tribes.[21]

These are significant settlements. However, observers believe that the actual damage these companies caused ranges in the $trillions. Of course, there is no adequate compensation for the more than 564,000 deaths the CDC attributes to prescription and illicit opioids between 1999 and 2020.

However, there is some justice in these court rulings. Much of the money in these settlements is dedicated to preventing and treating opioid abuse. Many people will benefit from these services. Indeed, we can celebrate that these companies are being blocked from continuing to operate like drug cartels. However, if one shifts from a monetary perspective and views this story through the lens of faith, there is little evidence of any substantial change in the attitude or values of the people running these companies.

In these several thousand opioid court cases, when a settlement is made against the companies, it is standard practice that the companies don't admit wrongdoing or accept responsibility for the opioid problem. Once, when pharmaceutical executives were called before a

U.S. House Energy and Commerce Committee oversight panel hearing and were asked if their companies had contributed to the opioid problem, all but one denied any responsibility. Another executive chairman admitted that he was sorry his company was so slow in blocking the millions of hydrocodone and oxycodone pills shipped to a couple of small pharmacies in West Virginia but still denied any responsibility. The executives shifted the blame to doctors for overprescribing painkillers and to pharmacists who distributed them.[22]

The pharmaceutical executives changed the way they were doing business solely because they were starting to pay out such vast sums of money in legal settlements. Also, they were required to change how they were doing business by the court settlements. However, there doesn't appear to be any fundamental voluntary change in their values and attitudes. In contrast, in Jesus and Zacchaeus' story, Zacchaeus underwent a total inner and outward transformation as he promised to return money to those he had cheated. Of course, he was also excited about pledging to give generously to the poor.

Similarly, when John Woolman asked enslavers to free those they had enslaved, he was challenging them to give up a large part of their wealth. Implicitly, he also challenged them to change their values, attitudes, and how they did business. He was asking them to bring the values of their faith into the way they lived and operated their businesses.

There doesn't appear to be evidence of these pharmacy executives following Zacchaeus' example in contributing part of their personal wealth to help rectify the damage they had wreaked. Similarly, the enslavers Woolman met with made significant voluntary, costly life changes. In contrast, the drug company executives only made changes they were compelled to by the courts to stop being sued. The changes they made were more like those made by enslavers who were forced to relinquish enslavement only after being defeated in a long and bloody civil war.

Sadly, there is little evidence that drug company executives went through a change of heart and values. The evidence suggests these executives and companies would continue operating in the same way they had earlier if it were not so costly.

NOTES

[1] In recent years, some of these institutions have wanted the Sackler name removed. The reason will become clear later in this chapter.

[2] Andrew Joseph, "A blizzard of prescriptions: Documents reveal new details about Purdue's marketing of OxyContin," *STATnews.com*, January 15, 2019, https://www.statnews.com/2019/01/15/massachusetts-purdue-lawsuit-new-details/.

[3] Abby Goodnough, *Study Links Drug Maker Gifts for Doctors to More Overdose Deaths, New York Times*, Jan. 18, 2019, https://www.nytimes.com/2019/01/18/health/opioids-doctors-overdose-deaths.html.

[4] Barry Meier, *Pain Killer: An Empire of Deceit and the Origin of America's Opioid Epidemic*, 2nd ed. (New York: Random House, 2018), 41.

[5] Ibid. pp. 83-109.

[6] Scott Higham and Sari Horwitz, *American Cartel: Inside the Battle to Bring Down the Opioid Industry* (New York: Hachette Book Group, 2022), 19, 101-123.

[7] Ibid. p. 36.

[8] Ibid. p. 29.

[9] Ibid.

[10] Ibid. p. 39.

[11] Ibid. pp. 44-45.

[12] Ibid. p. 52.

[13] Ibid. p. 53.

[14] Ibid. p. *4*.

[15] Ibid. p. 22.

[16] Brian Mann, "4 U.S. companies will pay $26 billion to settle claims they fueled opioid crisis," *NPR,* February 25, 2022,

https://www.npr.org/2022/02/25/1082901958/opioid-settlement-johnson-26-billion.

[17] "Attorney General Formella Announces Up To $6 Billion National Settlement with Purdue Pharma and Sacklers; New Hampshire to Receive $46 Million if Agreement Approved," *New Hampshire Department of Justice: Office of the Attorney General,* March 3, 2022, https://www.doj.nh.gov/news/2022/20220303-settlement-purdue-pharma-sacklers.htm.

[18] "Drugmaker Teva latest to settle opioid lawsuits nationally," *Politico,* July 26, 2022 https://www.politico.com/news/2022/07/26/drugmaker-teva-opioid-lawsuits-nationally-00048088.

[19] Dietrich Knauth, "Court OKs Mallinckrodt restructuring, $1 billion cut to opioid settlement," *Reuters,* October 10, 2023, https://www.reuters.com/legal/transactional/mallinckrodt-wins-approval-restructuring-plan-opioid-deal-2022-02-04/.

[20] Georff Mulvihill, "CVS, Walgreens announce opioid settlements totaling $10B," *Associated Press.* November 2, 2022, https://apnews.com/article/health-business-lawsuits-rhode-island-epidemics-50f3aa9cbe82b775cd3d7520c286ef25.

[21] Jan Hoffman, "Walmart Agrees to Pay $3.1 Billion to Settle Opioid Lawsuits," *New York Times,* November 15, 2022, https://www.nytim es.com/2022/11/15/health/walmart-opioids-settlement.html.

[22] Katie Zezima and Scott Higham, "Drug executives express regret over opioid crisis, one tells Congress his company contributed to the epidemic," *The Washington Post,* May 8, 2018, https://www.washingtonpost.com/national/drug-executives-to-testify-before-congress-about-role-in-opioid-crisis-one-is-deeply-sorry/2018/05/08/f4d91536-5259-11e8-a551-5b648abe29ef_story.html.

| ten |

Capitalism Made Me Do It

At the end of every seventh year you must cancel the debts of everyone who owes you money. This is how it must be done. Everyone must cancel the loans they have made to their fellow Israelites. They must not demand payment from their neighbors or relatives, for the Lord's time of release has arrived... "But if there are any poor Israelites in your towns when you arrive in the land the Lord your God is giving you, do not be hard-hearted or tightfisted toward them. Instead, be generous and lend them whatever they need. Do not be mean-spirited and refuse someone a loan because the year for canceling debts is close at hand. If you refuse to make the loan and the needy person cries out to the Lord, you will be considered guilty of sin. Give generously to the poor, not grudgingly, for the Lord your God will bless you in everything you do. There will always be some in the land who are poor. That is why I am commanding you to share freely with the poor and with other Israelites in need. "If a fellow Hebrew sells himself or herself to be your servant and serves you for six years, in the seventh year you must set that servant free. "When you release a male servant, do not send him away empty-handed. Give him a generous farewell gift from your flock, your threshing floor, and your winepress. Share with him some of the bounty with which the Lord your God has blessed you. Remember that you were once slaves in the land of Egypt and the Lord your God redeemed you! That is why I am giving you this command. (Deuteronomy. 15:1-15)

Once every forty-nine years on the tenth day of the seventh month, which is also the Great Day of Forgiveness, trumpets are to be blown everywhere in the land. This fiftieth year is sacred—it is a time of freedom and of celebration when everyone will receive back their original property, and slaves will return home to their families. This is a year of complete celebration... (Leviticus. 25:8-11a)

Are We Captives of Capitalism?

Jason Hickel, author of *Less is More: How Degrowth Will Save the World,* argues that terrible atrocities like the ones committed by the countries and corporations in the accounts above are not the results of just a few bad actors. He maintains that at the root of these crimes is the growth by capitalism. He insists that the structure of capitalism requires that corporations cannot be "... satisfied with a steady-state approach; if you don't push to expand, you'll get gobbled up by your competitors. *Growth becomes an iron law to which all are captive*" (emphasis added). It forces industries to grow or die. "The reality is that these firms, and the CEOs who run them, are subject to a structural imperative for growth. The Zuckerbergs of the world are just willing cogs in a bigger machine."[1]

In 2013, Michael Moss of the New York Times Magazine won a Pulitzer Prize for a well-researched article, *The Extraordinary Science of Addictive Junk Food.*[2] In it, he depicted how our economic structure dictates how the food industry functions.

Around 1990, after extensive scientific analysis, Kraft created a product called Lunchables, targeting children and parents rushing to get their kids a lunch prepared before dashing to work. The research was focused on a taste that would attract children while at the same time demanding a minimum of work for parents scrambling to get their kids ready for school as they were trying to get to their own jobs. Lunchables was a huge monetary success. It was also one of the least healthful lunch products on the market as it was loaded with sugar, fat, and salt. Obviously, these are some of the primary ingredients creating heart disease, diabetes, obesity, strokes, hypertension, fatty liver disease, and other significant health problems.

An article commenting on Lunchables stated that the most nutritious part of Lunchables was the napkin. Geoffrey Bible, CEO of Phillip Morris when Philip Morris owned Kraft, didn't dispute that and also acknowledged that the lunches had large amounts of sugar, fat, and salt. He was quoted saying, "Well, that's what the consumer wants, and we are not putting a gun to their head to eat it. That's what they want. If we give them less, they'll buy less, and the competitor will get our market. So, you're sort of trapped." At that time, Lunchables was bringing in around $1billion a year; there were no plans to change.

In the same article, Bob Drane, who played an instrumental role in creating Lunchables, said, "Our limbic brains love sugar, fat, salt…so formulate products to deliver these. Perhaps add low-cost ingredients to boost profit margins. Then 'supersize' to sell more, and advertise and promote to lock in 'heavy users.'"

A critical part of the quote above is when Geoffrey Bible states that if Kraft didn't continue marketing as they were, a competitor would take over his market. Then, he succinctly expresses his dilemma, "So you're sort of trapped." He is acknowledging his captivity. The article also states that Bible would later make an effort to encourage Kraft to diminish its reliance on sugar, salt, and fat. One way to understand this is that Bible was attempting to struggle against his own captivity. Paraphrasing Hickel, it appears that Bible was a cog in the corporate growth machine but not a wholly willing cog.

In an earlier chapter, we remembered that Jesus started his ministry by saying he had been sent to free the captives. Interestingly, Hickel describes capitalistic growth as creating a form of captivity. It is striking that Jesus started his ministry by saying that he had come to free the captives and that Hickel declares that we are all captive to the growth ideology of capitalism.

In chapter three, we saw how, during the enslavement of Blacks in this country, not only were enslaved people captives, but their owners were also captive to the brutal system they were enforcing. In enslaving other human beings, the owners were committing terrible crimes but also were enslaving themselves and cutting themselves off from God. In like manner, when the enslavers set their captives free, they freed themselves from participating in a system based on kidnapping, torture, beatings, rape, intimidation, murder, and destruction of families. When Zacchaeus goes through his transformation by giving half his property to the poor and returning four times what he had cheated others out of, Jesus tells him he and his family are saved. In like manner, as the Quakers that Woolman visited freed those they had enslaved, they were participating in this salvation. Both captors and captives were freed and made more whole. As those who owned enslaved people did not allow themselves to be aware they were captive to that terrible system, is it possible that we, in our time, are also unaware of being captive to a similarly destructive system?

Peter Maurin, while developing the Catholic Worker with Dorothy Day, wanted to build a society "where it is easier for people to be good."[3] We could paraphrase Maurin to say we need to create an economic system that would make it easier to do business ethically. Hickel implies that what we have is the opposite. He implies that the economic system we have makes it almost impossible to do business ethically on the corporate level. The demand for constant growth drives individuals, industries, and corporations toward destructive, unethical choices like those in the accounts above.

The goal of the Jubilee/Great Day of Forgiveness scriptures at the beginning of this chapter was not wealth creation. In contrast to our culture's goals, the purpose of these verses was actually to stymie wealth accumulation. For those immersed in the free market theology, this will seem terrible and the opposite of what an economic system should do. It might help to realize that this was what John Woolman was doing. In dedicating his life to freeing those who were enslaved, he was blocking the accumulation of wealth by people who enslaved other human beings. The enslavers were becoming less wealthy and the formerly enslaved were still at a disadvantage but had the opportunity to start earning money, own property, and start businesses. Equality was being given a foothold.

When the Jubilee/Great Day of Forgiveness scriptures were lived out, they leveled society so that all God's people had the basics to live. They freed people from economic oppression and debt that was robbing them of their future. The enactment of these verses restored families while creating new possibilities for them. These verses saved people from a life of destitution. These scriptures also build community. If these scriptures don't exist or are not lived out, gaps balloon between the rich and the poor. Class divisions, resentments, and injustice grow. In contrast, when these scriptures are lived out, and wealth becomes more equal, divisions and resentments recede. An environment is prepared for a sense of community to thrive.

In addition to saving the poor, these scriptures also save the wealthy. They block wealth accumulation and support the wealthy in resisting the temptation to love wealth more than their God. For the time when they were written, these scriptures were guardrails shaping the culture toward making it "easier for people to be good."

The Maximizing Profits Theology Is a Trap

A few years ago, a younger friend started graduate school in business. On his first day in class, the instructor said, "When you get your degree and go to work for a business or corporation, your responsibility will be to maximize profits for your employer." In a free-market/capitalist structure, that is what corporations are expected to do–maximize profits. In this country, it's not just something that is expected, but at this point, maximizing profits is the law of the land. The stockholders can sue if a corporation does not do everything possible to maximize profits.

So, what does maximizing profits mean? It means that making as much profit in as little time as possible is the overwhelmingly dominant goal. It infers that the profit objective overrides all other values and considerations. The stories about the countries, industries, and corporations in the previous chapters show that it is not unusual for profit to be valued more than life itself.

In the chapter about Great Britain's colonization of India, Mike Davis called Britain's rigid adherence to Adam Smith's free market economics their theology. It was their belief system, complete with a god and values. The god of this belief system was profit, and the values of their theology led them to allow tens of millions of human beings to die.[4]

We don't usually think of a rigid adherence to profit as a theology or a religious belief system. This book argues that it is. When an individual or a culture relentlessly pursues profits, knowing that the drive for those profits will cause death and destruction, profit has become their god. When profit has become what is most important for an individual or a culture, that is their god. In this theological system, wealth and accumulating more wealth is salvation. Of course, people don't think in those terms, which will confuse some, but that is what has happened.

As stated above, we saw that those who enslaved other human beings were also captive to that deadly system. The same dynamic was going on with Great Britain, King Leopold, the tobacco industry, DuPont, and the opioid industry. As their singular drive for profits dominated their actions, they, like the enslavers, became imprisoned. As with the slaveholders, human life had ceased to have value for them except as a means for further increasing their wealth. As these people, countries, industries, and corporations pushed forward in their drive for ever-increasing profits, millions of lives were lost and wrecked, including their own. In their drive for profits, even at the expense of human life, they had unwittingly become enslaved to the values of that system.

These entities and the people running them had chosen their treasure. Their hearts were unquestionably captured by their insatiable thirst for greater and greater profits.

As we remember the crimes that people have committed, we need to continue to remember that there are:

> Many American companies, owned and managed by genuinely caring people, good people, try to achieve some degree of fairness and to show genuine respect for workers in their businesses, but the structures of our economic system, built to increase profit and wealth, are heavily weighted against any significant mobility of those who live and work near the bottom or even the middle of the economic pyramid. Tax laws, banking regulations, health care costs, insurance premiums, pharmaceutical expenses, and education costs are among the many variables in our society that work together to generate and secure wealth and poverty.[5]

The Good Samaritan Should Have Let the Robbery Victim Die

Most of us don't spend much time thinking about the belief system underpinning capitalism. But the more we examine the hard-core principles of the free market, the clearer it becomes that these dogmas are antithetical to the Gospel.

James M. Buchanan spent his adult life promoting a pure form of free-market capitalism. In 1975, he wrote an article entitled *"The Samaritan's Dilemma."* [6] The Samaritan story is one of the best known in the Bible, not only teaching how to treat one another but also how we are to love those of other ethnicities. It is also an example of how to love our enemy. It is a foundational piece of scripture. For Buchanan, however, the story of the Good Samaritan was not a dilemma. For him, Jesus' parable of how we are to love one another teaches an entirely false message.

In his article, Buchanan argues that Jesus got it all wrong in the parable. He maintains that if we follow that teaching, it encourages the one receiving the aid to exploit the one offering the help rather than to solve his own problems. Buchanan saw this act of mercy and love as creating a potential parasite in society. In the story, the traveler who had been attacked on the road was helpless and probably would have died. However, Buchanan believes receiving help would encourage him to exploit the giver and become a parasite on society's producers. Getting help is a disincentive for the dying man to solve his own problems.[7]

Lester Thurow, in his book *The Future of Capitalism,* is concerned about the tension between capitalism and democracy. He doesn't address the conflict between Christianity and capitalism. However, what he says is relevant. He states:

> Democracy and capitalism have very different beliefs about the proper distribution of power. One believes in a completely equal distribution of political power, "one man, one vote," while the other believes that it is the duty of the economically fit to drive the unfit out of business and into economic extinction. "Survival of the fittest" and inequalities in purchasing power are what capitalistic efficiency is all about. Individuals and firms become efficient to be rich. To put it in its starkest form, capitalism is perfectly compatible with slavery. The American South had such a system for more than two centuries. Democracy is not compatible with slavery.[8]

Thurow was formerly a professor of economics and dean of Massachusetts Institute of Technology's Sloan School of Management. His statement is descriptive and shows the conflict between democracy and capitalism. This is the type of pure capitalism in which the weak are left behind on the side of the road.

Tyler Cowen is another economist working with think tanks advocating for unregulated capitalism. Cowen predicts that as unregulated capitalism takes place, the U.S. will look more like Brazil and Mexico. Cowen not only envisions but welcomes income and wealth gaps that will continue to widen. He recognizes that this will result in parts of the U.S. becoming like the favelas of Rio de Janeiro. He predicts shantytowns emerging to provide housing as the wealth inequalities increase.[9]

Incomprehensibly, for Cowen and the people working to put this belief system in place, this is not a problem. It is the way the world and society should work and be ordered. When we realize that there are now about 759 billionaires in the U.S. while simultaneously acknowledging that homelessness has become an intractable problem across the country, it's evident that those promoting pure capitalism are making alarming progress in realizing their goals. Shockingly, many people who understand themselves to be followers of Jesus are sometimes fierce advocates of capitalism.

Liberty has a precise meaning for the people promoting unrestricted capitalism. For these people, liberty means that corporations are free to do whatever they need to make ever greater profits, regardless of the consequences. Bertrand Russell's way of stating this is that "Advocates of capitalism are very apt to appeal to the sacred principles of liberty, which are embodied in one maxim: The fortunate must not be restrained in the exercise of tyranny over the unfortunate."[10]

If we want to visualize how this definition of liberty works in pure capitalism, the five examples above give a glimpse of that. Great Britain's colonization of India, King Leopold II's colonization of the Congo, the tobacco industry's continuing to find ways to make enormous profits, Dupont's continuing to pollute with forever poisons, and the drug industry's pushing opioids despite the deadly consequences are entities that have either operated with no restraints or have done everything possible to come as close to that as they were able.

The tobacco industry, DuPont, and the opioid industry weren't operating under pure capitalism. However, their ongoing, unyielding resistance to any regulation and constant lobbying for deregulation was an effort to create the "liberty" to increase their profits regardless of human and environmental costs. All these entities demonstrated by their actions that they wanted the "liberty" to maximize their profits without interference, even though they were causing unimaginable suffering and death. When corporate conglomerates gain and exercise liberty in the way they like, their singular commitment to profit assaults people and leaves them suffering on the side of the road. Great Britain, in its colonization of India, and King Leopold, in his colonization of the Congo, were consciously and purposefully operating under a capitalistic system about as pure as possible. They were living out Bertrand Russell's assertion that they didn't want to be restrained in their tyranny over the unfortunate.

Scholars like Buchanan and Cowen use their brain power to lobby so that corporations have as much "liberty" as possible to increase profits. Others are deeply concerned that corporations already have far more power and control than most people realize.

The Freer the Market, the Greater the Inequality

In the mid-nineteenth century, Milton Friedman and others at the Chicago School of Economics created their theory of a largely unregulated market-driven economy. Implementing this theory was a practical way of creating unqualified "liberty" for corporations to be unfettered in their pursuit of maximizing profits. This philosophy was adopted and strongly promoted by the Ronald Reagan administration. The idea was that this framework would generate wealth for the wealthiest of Americans, but there would be so much wealth that it overflowed and trickled down, filling the pockets of everyone so that even the needs of the poorest would be met. To sell the theory, the Reagan administration made ample use of the claim that "A rising tide lifts all boats." It was a captivating slogan. It was also a lie.

There was no trickle-down. The chasm between the rich and the poor steadily widened, bringing to mind a different slogan. "The rich get richer, and the poor get poorer." The theory of unfettered regulation, trickle-down, and a rising tide lifting all boats was a way of transferring unimaginable wealth from the average person and the poor to the already wealthy. Carter Heyward calls it a scam. She says, "Ever since Reagan's economic revolution of the rich, our country has been on a downward spiral economically, in which the rich truly are getting superrich, with yachts, planes, mansions, great art, and low (sometimes, no) taxes while the poor are increasingly struggling simply to survive." [11] One sees this very dramatically with the proliferation of billionaires. Ronald Reagan became president in 1981. According to Forbes magazine, in 1982, there were 13 billionaires in the U.S. By 1986, that number had doubled; by 1988, 68 individuals and families owned more than $one billion.[12] By 2024, the country had 813 billionaires.[13]

We have all seen pictures from the past of a merchant putting his thumb on a scale. We instantly know this is theft. In our day, a thumb on the scale is small potatoes. Today, the wealthy tip the scale by establishing laws and rules that allow them to steal. They do it legally since they make the laws. The super-wealthy tip the legal scale in a way that shifts billions to a few while pulling that wealth away from millions of ordinary people.

The other side of that picture is easy to see. One only has to walk around any city in the country and witness the overwhelming homeless population to realize that their boats did not rise while the billionaires were gaining obscene wealth. We don't know what Reagan and those in his administration thought would happen to these people. However, Tyler Cowen and the others writing the policies for billionaires knew exactly what would happen. They knew that parts of the U.S. would become like the favelas of Rio de Janeiro, just as Cowen had envisioned. We see that scenario playing out all over the country.

"There Is No Such Thing as Infinite Growth on a Planet of Finite Resources" [14]

Matthias Schmelzer states that a critical component of capitalism is the "growth paradigm."

> *'Economic growth' is widely regarded as a key goal of national and international economic policies, not only across the political spectrum but also in all countries, and it has been dubbed the most important idea of the twentieth century...*[15]

Schmelzer says that, according to the prevailing belief, the growth of a country's gross domestic product is a magic wand that can solve all kinds of critical challenges for a country. Following this theory, economic growth is indispensable to a society's progress, well-being, and national power. A crucial part of the paradigm is that economic growth is limitless.[16]

The theory is so powerful that the drive for constant economic growth is in the DNA of virtually every government. The belief is that jobs and society's well-being depend on growth. If the economy is not growing, there is the threat of economic stagnation, recession, and depression, all of which strike dread in the heart of every politician unless, of course, the politician's party is not in power and wants the party in power to lose.

Endless economic growth depends on ever-expanding markets, meaning ever-increasing numbers of consumers. Through advertisements, corporations program consumers to believe they have to own more and more possessions to be happy. To satisfy their stockholders, corporations must keep growing and their profits increasing.

Many groups, organizations, nonprofits, and Political Action Committees are committed to this belief system. To be very clear about its values, one very powerful group names itself The Club for Growth and advertises itself as made up of a "network of over 500,000 pro-growth, limited government Americans who share in the belief that prosperity and opportunity come from economic freedom. (We are) The leading free-enterprise advocacy group in the nation..."[17]

Amid this widely held belief proclaiming the absolute necessity of economic growth, warning signs are flashing. There is the disconcerting question of whether ongoing economic growth is, in fact, limitless. I have a friend whose signature at the end of each email asserts, "There is no such thing as infinite growth on a planet of finite resources." If this statement is true, we who inhabit the planet are on a suicidal path.

Constant growth exacts a corresponding, ever-increasing demand for more resources. More water, land, minerals, and food supplies are essential, but on a finite planet, these resources are limited and diminishing. A world economy five times larger than a half-century ago accelerates this diminishment.[18]

A system founded on greed and mandatory growth is inevitably a system that destroys life on earth. In a novel, one of Barbara Kingsolver's characters states it very succinctly when she says, "The free market has exactly the same morality as a cancer cell."[19]

The unlimited growth paradigm is dangerous enough in itself, but when population growth is added to economic growth, the picture becomes catastrophic. .It's frighteningly obvious that if the world population keeps growing at the rate it has for the last century, at some point, there will be no place for all of us to live. If this is not obvious, visualize the earth as flat. Then imagine the human population relentlessly multiplying on it, year after year.

As the world population continues to escalate, those committed to the unlimited growth ideology are furthering that doctrine by ensuring that all these people are converted into the belief system that they can only be happy by consuming more and more, whether they have the resources or not (obviously billions do not). The goal of those believing in unlimited economic growth is that they want as many people as possible to consume more of their products. Obviously, these products are made of the world's finite resources, finite being the keyword.[20]

If some foreign power were putting us on a trajectory leading to our destruction, we would instantly start planning for war. However, it appears that when short-term economic gain is the dominant goal, we cannot see that the planet's future and humanity are imperiled.

Neither major political party will be stating that unlimited economic growth is a suicidal path for the planet. The voice that says greed pushes us into self-destruction will not come from our politicians. They aren't going to tell us to limit our consumption or that being locked into ever-greater profits is suicidal. Both political parties are clinging to the economic growth paradigm for their short-term survival. Every president wants economic growth and knows that reelection depends on that growth.

Thank God we have people lifting their voices about the destruction of the environment, global warming, and what that means for life on the planet. Environmentalists are doing excellent work to honor God's creation. However, for the most part, they are not addressing how the drive for limitless consumption, ever-increasing profits, infinite growth, and population growth drives us toward the cliff.

That voice stating that greed, growth, consumption, and capitalism have put us on a death march should have been and still needs to be the voice of faith communities, both those who aspire to follow Jesus and other faith traditions who have corresponding values. All major religions have teachings confronting the greed ideology. God's voice has always been there to save. It has never been more needed. The world's fate desperately depends on our being attentive to that voice to save us from our self-destructive path.

A few decades ago, many of us believed that, at certain times, lemmings had an uncontrollable urge to march toward a cliff and then to hurl themselves off en masse to their death. We wondered what possessed this little creature to do something so crazy. As it turns out, lemmings don't have that urge, and they don't do this outrageous, suicidal thing. It appears that Disney Productions and some writers made it all up and then created a film to show what they had imagined.[21] Lemmings don't commit mass suicide.

However, given that infinite growth on a planet of finite resources is impossible, we humans are the new lemmings. We are hurling ourselves toward the cliff. This time it won't be a Disney movie.

What Is the Water We Drink and the Air We Breathe

I grew up in the South, graduating from high school in 1960. It was a segregated, prejudiced, racist culture. It was a disrespectful, unjust, and hurtful system to African Americans. However, as I was growing up in that culture, I didn't think about the way we lived as being wrong, sinful, or hurtful. It was more like, that's just the way things were. It was like the water we drank and the air we breathed. We were so immersed in racism that it was all but invisible to us. We didn't have the eyes to see it.

The civil rights movement was coming into full bloom in my high school and young adult years. In the back of my mind, there started to grow a voice that said something was wrong with the way we were living. As I increasingly paid attention to that voice, I wanted to separate myself from the values of the culture in which I had grown up. I consciously set out to do that.

The question for us is, are we blind to the evils of capitalism in the same way I was blind to the evils of racism? Are we living in a system that is destructive in the way racism is but so immersed in it that we are unable to see the evil?

Our culture celebrates what capitalism celebrates. We look at those at the top of the wealth pyramid as those who have made it. Wealth is the goal of capitalism and is how we measure success. To be a billionaire is what many aspire to be. It's taken for granted that this is the way the world works. Prestige, honor, admiration, respect, status, and power automatically accompany wealth. Movie after movie has either the theme or subtheme of being wealthy or gaining wealth. Being poor is a failure. The accumulation of more and more material wealth is capitalism's salvation. To not have wealth is the equivalent of being lost.

Companies desire, as the Sacklers did, to "bury the competition." Those who do this and whose stocks rise are envied. The companies that gain market share, dominate, and gobble up other companies are those that make the news and create fortunes. Countries maneuver to protect their national interests, which are nearly always identical to those of the country's corporations and business interests. Countries work to dominate in the same way corporations do.

Consumption is a crucial component of capitalism. We are surrounded by a corporate culture that uses its enormous resources to convince us that they are on our side and acting in our interest by selling us its products, which can fulfill our every need, relieve our deepest anxieties, make us successful, and bring us happiness. We are inundated with advertisements designed to convince us to consume more, live more luxuriously, increase our status, make us more comfortable, improve our sex life, and ensure that we will be more popular and envied. Our lives are filled with enticements promising to make us more prosperous, multiply our assets, increase our wealth, and make us more secure. These invitations to buy and consume increase our fears, play on our anxieties, and inflate our insecurities while promising to be the cure for all these maladies. The advertising industry knows that children as young as two are developing brand loyalty, so the goal is to shape their consumption patterns as early as possible.

Capitalism is an upward path. Wealthier families do all that's possible to get their children in a position to accumulate more wealth. Parents want children to have more than they had and to "get ahead in life." In our culture, the desire for upward mobility is automatically a given.

It is logical that we are seduced by capitalism. It lands squarely on our weak points as human beings. We are all concerned about our basic needs for food, shelter, security, and how we will survive financially. Beyond that, we usually have the more complicated cravings to be comfortable, admired, important, influential, and envied. We desire status, and many of us want the power that goes with that. A part of the human condition is that capitalism pulls directly at our real economic needs while simultaneously igniting our ego's yearnings and insecurities. The capitalist mindset is a powerful adversary because it settles where we are undefended. Part of being human is to have the needs, desires, fears, and ambitions that make us vulnerable to this way of believing and seeing the world.

Most of us have a built-in greed gene, as evidenced by the compulsion to increasingly accumulate more. Greed has always been a human problem. In our Christian past, greed was seen as one of the seven deadly sins to be confronted. In our time, however, instead of seeing greed as a problem, we have institutionalized it as the solution to our problems. Our economic system not only legitimizes our greed but celebrates it. It seduces us into believing that it is not only the lifestyle we should be living but that it is compatible with Christianity. Some succinctly state the problem as "We have blessed greed and called it a virtue."[22] We are blind to the reality that we have adopted the enemy's ideology.

The wealth of one CEO was recently estimated at $269 billion. Our culture blesses that by seeing him as astronomically successful. That reality illustrates how completely our culture and capitalism's values have taken over our faith. For Christians, material wealth is not success. From a spiritual perspective, to own even $one billion is a disastrous failure. For Christians to see wealth as success represents a profound disconnect from the core of our faith. Part of extricating ourselves from the grips of greed is to realize that this is not only failure but sin and inevitably destructive to God's creation.

Just as we in the South couldn't see the evil of our racism, we today are not aware that our attitudes about money are very different from what Jesus taught. For those of us who live in this time, the greed of capitalism is the water we drink and the air we breathe. This is the culture, milieu, and belief system in which we are immersed.

It helps to clarify how the goals of capitalism and Christianity differ. The goals of capitalism are wealth accumulation, maximizing profits, economic growth, status, power, and dominance. When Richard Sackler was rejoicing that he was going to bury the competition, he was in the mainstream of capitalistic theology. Capitalism promotes the individual or the corporation in becoming as wealthy as possible. What happens to others is irrelevant. Care and compassion for those left behind is sometimes scoffed at. Class divisions, resentments, and injustice are the fruits of capitalism.

In contrast, Christianity holds that giving, sharing, and generosity, are at the core of the faith. Accumulating wealth is not valued and is even a problem. Christianity holds that economic justice is critical so that all have the basics, and especially the weak and poor have their needs met. The hope is that none have too much and none have too little. Shared abundance is the lifted up. It is held that all human beings are valued, important, loved, and that all flourish and none are left behind. These values create an environment that prepares the ground for a sense of community to thrive. Relationships deepen and flourish.

If We Weren't Immersed in It and Could See It Clearly, Would We Say Our Corporate Culture Is Pathological?

As we have seen, for some, capitalism, maximizing profits, and unlimited economic growth represent a picture of how the world should function. For these people, it is their belief system and their ideal. However, there is a countercultural theory stating that our corporate culture and some of its leaders represent the worst of humanity. This theory holds that our corporate culture behaves like psychopaths, sociopaths, and narcissists.

One who has spent much of his career in the corporate milieu states that many of the terrible problems in the world,

> *...connect back to a common root that is nourished and guarded by the extraordinary power of corporate "persons" who are legally obligated to act like sociopaths...Sociopath? Yes. The corporate entity is obligated to care*

> *only about itself and to define what is good as what makes it more money. Pretty close to a textbook case of antisocial personality disorder.*[23]

David Niose, writing for Psychology Today, states that:

> If corporations are indeed "persons," their mental condition can accurately be described as pathological. Corporations have no innate moral impulses, and in fact, they exist solely for the purpose of making money. As such, these "persons" are systemically driven to do whatever is necessary to increase revenues and profits, with no regard for ethical issues that might nag real people.[24]

We Have Chosen the Opposite of the Early Church

The early church would be shocked that Christians today would see capitalism and Christianity as compatible. It would be incomprehensible to them that many who understand themselves to be followers of Jesus would be proponents of a system based on greed and accumulating wealth. The following scripture from Acts depicts how people in the early church were beginning to live their faith.

> *The group of followers all felt the same way about everything. None of them claimed that their possessions were their own, and they shared everything they had with each other. In a powerful way the apostles told everyone that the Lord Jesus was now alive. God greatly blessed his followers, and no one went in need of anything. Everyone who owned land or houses would sell them and bring the money to the apostles. Then they would give the money to anyone who needed it. (Acts 4:32-35)*

Astoundingly, these early Christians actually believed Jesus was serious about selling what they had and giving it to the poor. Evidently, they believed the other similar scriptures that Jesus taught about money.

For the early followers of Jesus, the goal was not to accumulate as much wealth as possible but to give, to want less, to live more simply, and to share their belongings with those in need. The goal was for all to have enough and for their basic needs to be met. Doing this was a way of loving God and loving their neighbor. Their purpose was not to accumulate wealth but to use their financial resources to relieve suffering and to love their neighbor. It appears they understood that by doing this, they were furthering the reign of God during their time.

The early church would have been incredulous that Christians now would use cliches like "money is what makes the world go around" or "the one with the most toys wins." Jesus' early followers would have automatically understood that cliches like these are antithetical to God's kingdom. In contrast, Jesus' early followers didn't believe money makes the world go around. They believed that "The love of money is the root of all evil." (I Timothy 6:10)

As per the scripture above from Acts, for the early faith community, a large part of what it meant to be a follower of Jesus was to develop values about money, property, and wealth completely different from the culture. In later centuries, as Christian communities were being formed, most of the time, there was a vow of poverty built into the "rule" for the community as a way of living out these teachings and values.

Part of what made the early church so dynamic was its powerful transforming presence to free people from greed and the worship of material wealth. The church had the spiritual power and values to transform the culture. In following Jesus, the early church was becoming free from the captivity of money, property, and wealth.

In our time, that pattern has been reversed. Now, instead of being a presence transforming our culture around the teachings of Jesus around money, we who understand ourselves to be Christian are the ones being shaped by our culture. We are not only immersed in the milieu of capitalism and greed; our culture and economic system have transformed us into accepting the values of material wealth and capitalism. We are so immersed in these values that, for the most part, we are unaware this has happened.

NOTES

[1] Jason Hickel, *Less i10s More: How Degrowth Will Save the World,* 86-7.

[2] Michael Moss, "The Extraordinary Science of Addictive Junk Food," *New York Times Magazine,* February 20,2013, https://www.nytimes.com/2013/02/24/magazine/the-extraordinary-science-of-junk-food.html.

[3] "The Aims and Means of the Catholic Worker," *Catholic Worker Movement* (Reprinted from the Catholic Worker newspaper, May 2019), https://catholicworker.org/aims-and-means/.

[4] Davis, *Late Victorian Holocausts,* 31 and 37.

[5] Carter Heyward, *The Seven Deadly Sins of White Christian Nationalism: A Call to Action* (Boulder, New York Lanham, and London: Rowman & Littlefield, 2022), 111.

[6] Nancy MacLean, *Democracy in Chains: The Deep History of the Radical Right's Stealth Plan for America* (New York: Penguin Books, 2017), 142-3.

[7]Ibid.

[8] Lester Thurow, *The Future of Capitalism: How Today's Market Forces Shape Tomorrow's World* (New York: Penguin Books, 1996), 242.

[9] MacLean, *Democracy in Chains,* 213.

[10] Bertrand Russell, Sceptical Essays, Ch. 13, 1928.

[11] Heyward, *The Seven Deadly Sins of White Christian Nationalism,* 110.

[12] "Number of Billionaires," *The Physics Fact Book An encyclopedia of scientific essays,* https://hypertextbook.com/facts/2005/MichelleLee.shtml.

[13] "Billionaires by Country," *World Population Review,* Retrieved March, 2025, https://worldpopulationreview.com/country-rankings/billionaires-by-country.

[14] I became aware of this quote through Jeremy Love. The source of the exact quote seems to be unknown though Sir David Attenborough penned a similar one. "Anyone who thinks that you can have infinite growth on a planet with finite resources is either a madman or an economist."

[15]Matthew Schmelzer, "The growth paradigm: History, hegemony, and the contested making of economic growthmanship," *Ecological Economics,* October 2015, https://www.sciencedirect.com/science/article/abs/pii/S0921800915003201

[16]Matthias Schmelzer, "The growth paradigm: History, hegemony, and the contested making of economic growthmanship," *Ecological Economics,* Volume 118, October 2015, Pages 262-271, https://www.sciencedirect.com/science/article/abs/pii/S092180091500320.

[17]About the Club for Growth," *The Club For Growth,* https://www.clubforgrowth.org/.

[18 Riccardo Mastini, Degrowth: the case for a new economic paradigm, *Open Democracy,* June 2017, https://www.opendemocracy.net/en/degrowth-case-for-constructing-new-economic-paradigm/.

[19] Kingsolver, *Unsheltered,* 412.

[20] *Population Matters,* https://populationmatters.org/the-facts/the-numbers.

[21] Riley Woodford, Lemming Suicide Myth: Disney Film Faked Bogus Behavior, *Alaska Fish and Wildlife News,* September 2003, https://www.adfg.alaska.gov/index.cfm?adfg=wildlifenews.view_article&articles_id=56.

[22] Delio, *Care for Creation,* 162.

[23] James Gamble, "The Most Important Problem in the World," *Medium,* March 13, 2019, https://medium.com/@jgg4553542/the-most-important-problem-in-the-world-ad22ade0ccfe.

[24] David Niose, Why Corporations Are Psychotic: These 'people' are not healthy," *Psychology Today*, March 16, 2011, https://www.psychologytoday.com/us/blog/our-humanity-naturally/201103/why-corporations-are-psychotic.

| eleven |

Capitalism Converts Christianity

You are the salt of the earth. But if the salt loses its saltiness, how can it be made salty again? It is no longer good for anything, except to be thrown out and trampled underfoot. You are the light of the world. A town built on a hill cannot be hidden. Neither do people light a lamp and put it under a bowl. Instead they put it on its stand, and it gives light to everyone in the house. In the same way, let your light shine before others, that they may see your good deeds and glorify your Father in heaven. (Matthew 5:13-16)

What Happened to Their Hearts, to Their Spirits?

Reading about the abuses of Great Britain, King Leopold II, and the corporations depicted above, it's easy to be harsh. It's almost impossible not to be judgmental. However, from a Christian perspective, we should also have a deep sadness that, from what we can see, the countries and corporations in the previous chapters lost so much of their humanity. These different entities certainly gained the world's wealth. However, from a spiritual perspective, they appear to be profoundly lost. The pull of wealth so ensnared them that they were numbed to the suffering of legions.

Unfortunately, it appears they joined the enslavers in becoming captured by their greed. In living out their single-minded dream of unbounded profits and all the obvious perks that come with that, they themselves became prisoners.

As these countries and corporations' material success flourished, their inner life of the spirit was dying. Their hearts and souls were becoming atrophied. As they gained their fortunes, the true light in their lives was being extinguished. Unfortunately, they exemplify the scripture, "For the love of money is a root of all sorts of evil, and some by longing for it have wandered away from the faith and pierced themselves with many griefs." (I Timothy 6:10)

At every turn, these entities and individuals did everything to grasp their wealth tightly. The hope for them is to follow Zacchaeus' example and do the exact opposite of clinging to their treasure. Hope for them lies in using their wealth to make restitution to the people they have hurt so badly. They, like Zacchaeus, are being called to turn away from their love of wealth to a path of love. Like the enslavers John Woolman visited, they need to let their hearts be transformed so that they let go of their material treasure. Just as Jesus celebrated salvation coming to Zacchaeus' house, he is waiting to celebrate that salvation coming to their houses. (Luke 19:10).

It's sad the people in these stories fell so far and that so many innocents were devastated by their actions. However, we in the Christian church need to be slow to judge. We may be closer to them than we think.

What Happened to <u>Our</u> Hearts, to <u>Our</u> Spirits?

It's easy to cast stones at the people in these earlier stories. However, we must be careful because those stones will inevitably boomerang back at us. To the extent that Christians and churches adopt the free-market belief system, we also worship at the altar of greed. To the extent that we are believers in the theology of maximizing profits, we are on the same path as the corporations. When we embrace the god of capitalism, we are complicit and compromised. At some level, that includes nearly all of us. Perhaps we are not as fully captured by the system as the corporations above. However, in this country, it's virtually impossible to escape participating in the capitalistic belief system to some degree. In multiple ways, our churches have become ensnared in the greed system.

We participate in that system when we are employed by corporations that are deeply committed to maximizing profits. Our whole economic system depends on growth, which is in lockstep with maximizing profits. Stockholders buy shares in corporations that are doing their utmost to maximize profits. If the corporations perform poorly, we penalize them and move our money to those who do a better job maximizing profits. Profit and growth are the measuring stick for everything in our economy. If we have the monetary resources to invest, nearly all of us participate.

A near-universal challenge is that of financially providing for ourselves as we age. We turn to investments, retirement plans, 401ks, annuities, and other financial instruments. Obviously, all of these are part of the maximizing profits game plan. However, if we have the financial resources, few of us choose to trust God to provide for our future as Jesus says God does for the birds. We don't want to live that out any more than we choose to become perfect by giving everything to the poor and following Jesus. (Matthew 19:21)

People at the bottom of the economic scale may not participate in this system's investment side because they lack income. Probably, they are being exploited by it, whether they are aware of it or not. Even then, there is the likelihood that they envy those who are benefiting from maximizing profits. Their minds are captured by the profit theology even as they are suffering from a system designed for the more affluent.

Churches are investing in the same value system in which the tobacco, opioid, and forever chemical companies are flourishing. The church has enabled this value system based on greed to flourish. When the church supports a system based on greed, we who understand ourselves as Christians are guilty. We are complicit.

There has always been a remnant of the church that has raised the issues of justice and injustice. Parts of the Christian church focus on justice issues around wealth inequality, war, militarism, global warming, racism, and the interconnections of these issues. Particular churches, groups, or individuals, primarily in some mainline Protestant churches, stay faithfully focused on these justice issues. Consistent with their history, the Quakers are more uniformly aware and continue to struggle with these concerns. In this country, the Catholic Worker movement has raised these problems for nearly a century. The Unitarian-Universalist Church certainly has had a strong voice related to justice issues. The Catholic Church, particularly in Latin America, has had what might be called a prophetic movement rooted in liberation theology. Pope Francis has called out the abuses of capitalism.

By and large, though, the Christian church is entangled in maximizing profits through free-market theology and practice. Many Christian churches have invested in the maximizing profits belief system in the same way that many churchgoers were comfortable with, promoted, and profited from slavery. It is very difficult to consider, but is it possible that the crimes in which we are participating are just as evil as slavery was in its time? Are we as lost spiritually as the enslavers were?

Incomprehensibly, one part of the Christian Church has even adopted a prosperity gospel or prosperity theology. Unquestionably, there are good people in these churches, and some of their work is laudatory. However, the fundamental thrust of this type of theology is absurd and, at its worst, predatory.

From his home in Dallas, Ben Kirby began paying attention to the clothes worn by TV evangelists and others helping lead worship in megachurches. One pastor was wearing a pair of sneakers that would sell for $5,600 on the resale market. Another was wearing a $3,600 Gucci jacket, another a $1,250 fanny pack, and still another a $2,541 Ricci crocodile belt. Out of this awareness, Kirby began an Instagram account called Preachers and Sneakers. He states:

> ... these pastors who have enormous social media followings aren't simply pastors anymore, he writes. Often they are motivational speakers, corporate coaches and leadership consultants. Kirby said he has heard of churches where a volunteer was designated solely for the purpose of carrying the pastor's Bible. Often, he writes, these pastors have private entrances, reserved parking spaces, security details and a gaggle of personal assistants or handlers. And, often, they promise blessings from God to their followers if their followers bless the church.[1]

Of course, it's not just expensive designer clothes that these pastors are sporting. One pastor was raising $65 million for a new Gulfstream G650 private jet. In another situation, a pastor lives in a $1.8 million-dollar house and bought his wife a $200,000 Lamborghini.[ii] Since we all are flawed in this area of money, we must be careful about throwing stones at religious leaders behaving like this. (John 8) Nevertheless, religious leaders profiting from churches in this way and modeling these values are on shaky ground. Maybe they could be blessed to find a sycamore tree they could climb with the intent of seeing Jesus. Hopefully, Jesus will pass by, invite them down, and they can experience the kind of transformation Zacchaeus went through. (Luke 19) Maybe they could sell their expensive toys like the people of the early church sold houses and property and then follow their example in distributing the money to those in need. (Acts 2) .

NOTES

[1] Sarah Pulliam Bailey, "Preachers and their $5,000 sneakers: Why one man started an Instagram account showing churches' wealth," *The Washington Post,* March 22, 2021, https://www.washingtonpost.com/religion/2021/03/22/preachers-sneakers-instagram-wealth/.

[2] Daniel J. Gross, "Relentless Church bought John Gray a $1.8M house in Simpsonville. Here's why," *The Greenville News,* Jan 20, 2019, https://www.greenvilleonline.com/story/news/2019/01/19/john-gray-house-relentless-church-pastor/2360826002/.

PART THREE: TRANSFORMATION

This section is written with the conviction that we all are captives, frequently in ways we are unaware of. Following that is the belief that Jesus came to free us all. It turns toward the vision that we might escape our own captivity with the aspiration that we could become instruments capable of partnering with God in freeing others from their imprisonment.

Jesus said that he came to free the captives/the prisoners. Could we who aspire to follow him be freed enough of our own captivity to become agents of transformation for others, even others who seem to be outside the scope of redeemable? Is it possible that we could be transformed, deepened, and love enough so that we might become agents of change in those situations? With that in mind, part three of the book focuses less on money, wealth, and property and more on transformation than the book's first two parts.

In any conversion story, we could find different ingredients that are important for change to take place. These stories help us start thinking about the components that are helpful for our and others' conversions.

| twelve |

The Prophets, Jesus, and Woolman

Jeremiah declares, "You have been allowing people to cheat, rob, and take advantage of widows, orphans, and foreigners who live here. Innocent people have become victims of violence, and some of them have even been killed. But now I command you to do what is right and see that justice is done. (Jeremiah 22:3)

He went to Nazareth, where he had been brought up, and on the Sabbath day he went into the synagogue, as was his custom. He stood up to read, and the scroll of the prophet Isaiah was handed to him. Unrolling it, he found the place where it is written:

"The Spirit of the Lord is on me,
because he has anointed me
to proclaim good news to the poor.
He has sent me to proclaim freedom for the prisoners
and recovery of sight for the blind,
to set the oppressed free, to proclaim the year of the Lord's favor."

Then he rolled up the scroll, gave it back to the attendant and sat down. The eyes of everyone in the synagogue were fastened on him. He began by saying to them, "Today this scripture is fulfilled in your hearing."

All spoke well of him and were amazed at the gracious words that came from his lips. "Isn't this Joseph's son?" they asked. (Luke 4:16-22)

Prophets Courageously Speak Truth to Power

The verses above from Jeremiah are similar to many scriptures by other courageous Hebrew prophets. The prophets were delivering unwanted messages that made them unpopular, even putting their lives in danger. People frequently think of the prophets as foretelling the future. However, their primary role was to speak for God, and a large part of that was to proclaim God's justice, particularly for the poor, vulnerable, and weak.

The prophets were wonderfully daring and articulate in calling out injustice and shining a light on the wealthy and those cheating the poor, some even killing to satisfy their greed. The prophets risked their lives to be faithful to their call to speak out against these injustices. Through the centuries and into our day, the voices of the prophets have advocated for justice. Jewish, Christian, and others seeking justice have held up their wisdom and seen them as models. We are deeply indebted to them.

In our day, a small fervent segment of mostly mainline Christian denominations has been active in following the prophets and God's commands, struggling for the weak, poor, vulnerable, and the foreigner. These modern-day prophets raise their voices about racism, homelessness, workers' rights, peace, immigrants, LGBTQ people, and protecting God's beloved planet. We are all blessed by their courage, activism, and witness.

In previous chapters, we celebrated the tenaciousness of lawyers who exposed some of the terrible behavior of corporations and stood on the side of those being victimized. They probably didn't think of themselves as prophets, but nevertheless, they took on the prophetic role. They are different from modern-day Christian prophets, given that they stand to make millions by suing these major corporations. Nevertheless, like the Christian activists, they take on the burden of exposing crime and injustice.

Rob Bilott confronted DuPont's crimes and the company's unwillingness to be responsible for the poisons they spread worldwide.

In his enormous commitment, he took significant risks, put himself in a challenging position, and sacrificed his health. He made his money but courageously and sacrificially stood for justice as he took on his prophetic role. Other attorneys working similarly have taken on the responsibility of exposing injustice and doing everything possible to hold corporations accountable in the legal system. They are to be celebrated and thanked.

The corporations and their leaders, however, even when confronted with evidence that lives are being destroyed, remain unrepentant and unchanged. Apparently, they still hold on to the same values and would be committing the same crimes if they could, and when they are able, some are already doing that.

If one views this story through the lens of faith, there is little evidence of any substantial change in the attitudes or values of the people running these companies. No transformation took place in them like Zacchaeus declaring that he would return four times what he had cheated people out of and give half his wealth to the impoverished. This is true even after these corporations are repeatedly confronted with the damage and suffering they are inflicting. One must conclude that profit is what is sacred for these executives and board members, not lives.

John Woolman and Rob Bilott lived centuries apart and confronted different kinds of wrongdoing but carried out a similar mission. They both confronted people captive to their greed and destructiveness. Both men were successful. Woolman was instrumental in freeing enslaved people even though it would cost their enslavers a substantial part of their wealth. Bilott won his cases against DuPont and diminished the spread of forever chemicals. Eventually, DuPont and its corporate spinoffs paid several $billion in fines and settlements. Both Woolman and Bilott brought relief and at least partial justice for the oppressed and suffering. However, there is a critical difference.

For all his Herculean commitment, courage, work, and sacrifice, Bilott did not bring about a change of heart or attitude in the people running DuPont. Similarly, as noted earlier, after the Civil War, for many in the South, there was no change of heart in those who enslaved people before the war. The South suffered 258,000 deaths, tens of thousands more were wounded, and the region was devastated. Even after such enormous suffering, there was no change in the hearts of those who had enslaved people. After the war, most of the South still clung to the same values and beliefs they had before the war. Just as the powerful Northern army had no power to compel those who fought for slavery to change their values, Bilott, and the legal system had no power to change the hearts and attitudes of the decision-makers at DuPont.

Jesus Frees a Captive

The story of Zacchaeus has frequently been our guide through different parts of this book. In chapter three, we listened to him as he told of his life and encounter with Jesus from his perspective of being liberated from his captivity and his life being transformed. We return to the Zacchaeus story with the emphasis shifting to what was going on from Jesus' perspective and how this story fits with Jesus' mission of freeing captives, releasing prisoners, and setting the oppressed free.

Probably, if it had been one of the prophets having an encounter with Zacchaeus instead of Jesus, the meeting would have been more judgmental, confrontational, and condemning. Zacchaeus was the kind of person the prophets were talking about when they accused those with power of cheating, robbing, and taking advantage of widows, orphans, and foreigners. In speaking for God, the prophets understood that a significant part of their call was to promote justice for the oppressed. They would have unequivocally condemned Zacchaeus' behavior but would have probably done it much more harshly than Jesus.

Jesus had the same concerns about the poor being abused as the prophets. However, in this story, he had the atypical stance of being for the vulnerable and poor that Zacchaeus was exploiting but was also concerned about Zacchaeus, the abuser. Even as Jesus was standing with the oppressed, he understood that the oppressors who were perpetrating suffering and injustice were also loved by God.

Jesus is coming at this encounter with a completely different worldview from those around him. He knows Zacchaeus has exploited his power and wrecked the lives of vulnerable people. He knows that the people hate Zacchaeus. Nevertheless, Jesus is communicating acceptance of Zacchaeus.

Jesus is clear that his mission is to those who are lost and to free the captives. He sees Zacchaeus as among the lost. When Jesus meets Zacchaeus, his goal is to separate him from the power that is controlling his life. He intends to free Zacchaeus from the grip of being lost in greed and perpetrating the destruction of his neighbors. In Jesus' words, "The Son of Man came to look for and save people who are lost." (Luke 19:10) Zacchaeus is profoundly lost.

When Jesus calls out to Zacchaeus, he doesn't come scrambling out of the tree because he feels judgment, anger, or self-righteousness emanating from Jesus. If he sensed those feelings and attitudes, he would have retreated into an entrenched, argumentative, defensive position. Perhaps Zacchaeus glimpses the possibility of acceptance rather than rejection. Surely, he is shocked to be singled out and invited to host Jesus instead of being called out as a cheating tax collector. He intuits something unusual about Jesus and dares to risk that this encounter could be different. Maybe, instead of sensing judgment in Jesus, he feels compassion.

When Jesus calls Zacchaeus out of the tree and tells him he wants to go home with him, he does not condemn the tax collector in front of all the people. He is not treating Zacchaeus as an enemy. (Dr. Martin Luther King, Jr. and Gandhi did this extraordinarily well) Jesus wanted people's hearts to change. On Zacchaeus' side, we imagine he might have felt the possibility of being loved and accepted. He may not have been able to verbalize it, but given his despised tax collector status, he desperately needed this.

Conversion is Jesus' goal, but not conversion in the sense of joining a church, or of "taking Jesus as his personal savior," or adopting a different belief system. Jesus' objective is that the extortionist in Zacchaeus die, so that he turns away from the devastation he is inflicting on his neighbors and the community. Zacchaeus is letting go of what had been his god. His heart has been transformed.

After encountering Jesus, Zacchaeus abandons the cheating and fraud that had made him a rich man. He is healing wounds in the community he has created by returning wealth to those he has defrauded and becoming generous to the poor. He becomes a new person.

In today's language, Zacchaeus is disbursing reparations. He is repairing the breach he had created. (Isaiah 58:12) This action is not just returning money to the rightful owners; it is rebuilding the broken lives and the devastation he had inflicted on the community. The community is being restored. Of course, embodied in this is Zacchaeus turning into the full embrace of his Creator. Zacchaeus abandons his old behavior, allowing it to die so that the rupture in his primary relationship with God may be repaired.

Jesus is reaching out to Zacchaeus and calling him to be the human being he has been created to be. Jesus understands that his call is to love people like Zacchaeus, and in loving him, he wants a very different life for him. The light of God in Zacchaeus, which has been struggling to survive, is suddenly revived. As Zacchaeus is converted, a sliver of the Kingdom of God starts to sparkle through him. Justice comes, but also healing, reconciliation, hope, love, community, and joy break out as Zacchaeus makes reparations and shares his wealth. In every place that Zacchaeus spreads his material wealth, God's Kingdom of peace and love will flourish. God's reign is breaking out.

Two opposite ways of being in the world are battling in this story. Zacchaeus has been living the gospel of wealth accumulation. Jesus is not joining Zacchaeus in that lifestyle. Jesus had already gotten rid of any wealth he might have had. It's evident that Jesus' goal is Zacchaeus' transformation and for Zacchaeus to share his wealth with the poorest. Jesus is modeling and telling Zacchaeus this is the path to salvation. Zacchaeus is looking at the world through new eyes, but more importantly, he is going through a radical change related to wealth and how he lives. He is moving from love of wealth to love of God. He is becoming born again.

As Zacchaeus becomes free, he immediately sets out to free those he has oppressed. He returns money to those he has defrauded, thereby releasing them from at least part of their poverty and desperation. By freeing Zacchaeus, Jesus also frees those Zacchaeus had driven into poverty and hopelessness. As well as freeing people from his economic oppression, Zacchaeus liberates them spiritually from their anger, fear, and hatred of him.

We associate the phrase "let my people go" with Moses and his delivering the Hebrew people out of slavery and captivity. In a different way, Jesus is delivering people from captivity. In his encounter with Zacchaeus, he is living out the words he read at the beginning of his ministry. He is delivering from captivity both Zacchaeus and the people he has exploited. It seems there is a natural sequence; when those captive to evil are freed, they free those they have imprisoned.

In the Jesus/Zacchaeus story, it would be easy to glide by the part when Jesus says, "Today salvation has come to this house." We probably have many different concepts of salvation, but whatever they may be, Jesus inextricably connects salvation to our choices about money, property, and wealth. (Luke 16:13)

John Woolman Follows Jesus' Example

There is a remarkable similarity between what Jesus did with Zacchaeus and what John Woolman did with the enslavers some 1800 years later. Jesus invited himself to Zacchaeus' house and dinner. This meeting resulted in a profound transformation in Zacchaeus, changing the entire trajectory of his life along with all the people he had been extorting as a tax collector. Very similarly, Woolman got himself invited into the homes of Quaker enslavers. In these encounters, Woolman inspired the enslavers to make the extremely rare, revolutionary step of liberating those they had enslaved.

Before Woolman, and those working with him, the Quaker enslavers were following a path similar to how Zacchaeus had been living before he met Jesus. The enslavers, like Zacchaeus, abused people for profit regardless of the human suffering it caused. But as Jesus freed Zacchaeus, Woolman was God's catalyst in freeing the enslavers from this evil system, motivating them to free those they had enslaved. Wherever the enslaved were freed, God's Kingdom was flourishing. God's reign of peace and love was bursting out.

It's hard to comprehend how Woolman could have been so effective. Maybe a hint about how he was so successful is that his concern was not only that slavery was immoral but that he set out on his mission fearful for his fellow Quakers. He was deeply concerned about the spiritual welfare of the enslavers and, in his belief system, was afraid they were going to hell.

It appears that he was able to communicate to the enslavers that he was on their side. He was not voicing condemnation but salvation, and he was doing that respectfully in a way they could accept. One has to believe that he communicated love and concern for these people.

Woolman was effective in this role with the Quakers because, in his own life, he continually searched for and invited deepening spiritual transformation. Woolman didn't just visit and advocate; he, like Saint Francis, was constantly committing his own life to being more deeply converted into a vessel for God's spirit. He was committed to removing any spiritual impediment in him that blocked him from freeing his fellow Quakers from their entrapment in enslaving other human beings. His ongoing transformational process was critical in being effective in his mission with his fellow Quakers. Without this being part of his commitment, it's easy to imagine his visits with the enslavers deteriorating into frustrating exchanges culminating in polarized arguments and anger, which we have all experienced.

It's also notable that Woolman was a vessel not only for God's spirit but God's power. We pray in the Lord's Prayer, "...for thine is the kingdom, the power, and the glory," but sometimes we wonder where God's power is. It seems to be absent or nonexistent. We pray for a loved one to be healed and they aren't healed, or for a friend not to die, and they die, or we question why people are left suffering. Wars and violence proliferate, and we wonder where is God and God's power to make these people whole, to heal the suffering, and bring peace. In contrast, Woolman makes God's power visible. We reflect on his life and become aware that God's power is very real.

As we attempt to be Christian, we know we are very imperfect and flawed. In reflecting on that, some hope they can be like an old rusty leaking pipe that manages to at least be clear enough to allow dribbles of God's spirit to pass through them. Woolman was much more than that. He was about as clear a passageway for God's power to flow through as possible.

Arguably, Woolman, and those working with him, were renewing the Quaker movement resulting in a reformation of their faith. Before Woolman, a substantial part of the Quaker movement had accepted slavery as compatible with the practice of their faith. Like other enslavers, they had grown accustomed to the increasing wealth and less demanding lifestyle that came from owning other human beings. Woolman, and the people aligned with him, pulled the movement away from slavery so that it evolved into a force for abolition.

If not for Woolman and his companions, the Quakers could have gotten swallowed by greed and slavery, as other Christian groups did. They could have followed other Christians who accepted slavery and even used their Christian faith as a tool to subjugate enslaved people. Like other Christian movements, they could have continued to use the scriptures that call for enslaved people to obey their masters. Quakers could have stayed with that betrayal of their faith in order to enslave other human beings and accumulate more wealth.

In most cultures, and definitely in ours, people celebrate wealth. In contrast, Jesus celebrated when people gave their wealth away. Woolman followed his example. In earlier parts of this book, we've seen that the goal for those in the colonizing and corporate worlds was to accumulate wealth and maximize profits. For Woolman and his Quaker companions, the goal was not to maximize profits but to maximize God's presence in people's lives leading to a change in behavior. The behavioral transformation Jesus envisioned for Zacchaeus and Woolman envisioned for the enslavers meant less material wealth, not more. Jesus and Woolman didn't honor affluence but celebrated when people became free from wealth's lure by divesting their assets. As Zacchaeus and the enslavers became liberated from the grasp of material wealth, they found real treasure. Jesus celebrates Zacchaeus dispensing reparations by telling the community that salvation had come to Zacchaeus' house.

Woolman's mission not only freed enslaved people but brought about changes of heart in the enslavers that renewed the whole Quaker movement. Woolman was a catalyst for transformations in values and behaviors that still reverberate into the present time. There was something exceptional about Woolman's spirituality that enabled him to be a conduit for God's power. He allowed God to transform him so that he could be God's instrument in touching the hearts of the enslavers so they could choose to change their lifestyles and voluntarily give up wealth. Woolman was extraordinary, but it wasn't his power. It was his willingness to be God's instrument in touching and transforming others that was so exceptional. God's power flowing through Woolman accomplished transformations in attitudes and behavior that the North's armies were impotent to match.

| thirteen |

Toward Further Transformation

Once again Jesus went out beside the lake. A large crowd came to him, and he began to teach them. As he walked along, he saw Levi son of Alphaeus sitting at the tax collector's booth. "Follow me," Jesus told him, and Levi got up and followed him.

While Jesus was having dinner at Levi's house, many tax collectors and sinners were eating with him and his disciples, for there were many who followed him. When the teachers of the law who were Pharisees saw him eating with the sinners and tax collectors, they asked his disciples: "Why does he eat with tax collectors and sinners?"

On hearing this, Jesus said to them, "It is not the healthy who need a doctor, but the sick. I have not come to call the righteous, but sinners." (Mark 2:13-17)

A Grand Dragon of the KU Klux Klan and a Black Civil Rights Leader Have a Series of Conversations

Jesus was the instrument of transformation for Zacchaeus, and Woolman was the agent of change for the enslavers. These accounts challenge us to wonder if we could be a catalyst in having a similar impact. For those of us attempting to follow Jesus, could we imitate him in freeing the captives and the oppressed? Is it possible to discern a path of breadcrumbs leading us to be instruments of freeing the captives and the oppressed, including those who have been destructive and hurtful to others?

This section of the book doesn't deal with money, wealth, and property like the previous parts. It is a conversion story and is included with the hope that it holds some insight into how we can be more deeply transformed into becoming agents of God's transformation.

Celeste Headlee is exceptionally accomplished in having conversations with people who hold sharply opposing views. She has been a speaker at Ted Talk and wrote a book called *We Need to Talk*. She strongly advises against trying to change someone in a conversation.

All of us have been in conversations in which the different sides hold very polarized positions. These conversations usually are not pleasant or productive. Neither side may think they are attempting to convert the other in these conversations. Nevertheless, if both parties are setting out to change the position of the other party on some political, social, or religious topic, they are attempting to convert the other to their belief. Frequently, our disagreements and arguments involve wanting the other person to see a particular issue as we see it. As stated above, this nearly always ends in frustration and anger.

Headlee tells the story of Xernona Clayton and Calvin Craig on the NPR TED Radio Hour. Clayton was a Black woman and a civil rights activist. Craig was a Grand Dragon in the Ku Klux Klan. In telling the story, Headlee says that starting in 1967, the two entered into a series of conversations that stretched over months. Then Craig had a press conference and said, "I'm leaving the KKK. My mind has been changed by Xernona Clayton."[1]

Headlee reports Clayton, saying, "I didn't try to change his mind. I just listened to him. There was nothing that I, a Black woman, would say to him that was going to make any difference." In this interview, Clayton also says that Martin Luther King, Jr. always said, "Just take the person where they are and accept them where they are." Headlee continues, "That's where you start. Let go of this idea that you are entering into a conversation to change someone's mind or educate them. That's always going to be frustrating, and that is probably where the anger comes from because that won't happen. Let go of that intention. Instead, enter into the conversation and say, I'm going to learn something from this conversation. That's something you have control over."[2] Headlee teaches others how to have difficult conversations and unquestionably is accomplished in doing this.

However, *Atlanta* magazine tells the story of the relationship between Clayton and Craig differently.[3] In that account, the relationship between Clayton and Craig began in 1967 when Atlanta Mayor Ivan Allen Jr. appointed them both to leadership positions in Atlanta's Model Cities Program. They both were given offices in the same building. Their first actual meeting came when Craig came by Clayton's office and introduced himself. Clayton started the conversation by asking, "Calvin Craig, now are you the one who heads the Klan?" He laughed and said, "Oh, Mrs. Clayton." Clayton says she could tell from that first meeting that he was a warm man; he was a very tall, handsome man, a well-attired man, and he had such a good sense of humor. Every day he would come by and make it his business to get into a discussion with me about race. Every time I asked him a question he didn't want to answer, he just laughed...."

She continues, "One Friday, he asked me what I was going to do that weekend. I said, "I'm having a dinner party this weekend, so I've got to get ready." He asked who was coming. I named people who were coming for dinner, and he said, "Those are white people." "Yes." "You mean they're coming to your house to eat?" I said, "Yes." And he said, "Oh, Mrs. Clayton, I could never eat at your house." "Well, Mr. Craig, people who come into my house have been invited. I haven't invited you to my home. But before this project is over, I'll not only have you eating at my house, I'll have you eating out of my hand. I will never forget that laughter."

In the Atlanta magazine version of the story, Clayton also found a way to gently challenge Craig about going to church while simultaneously being in the Klan. She reports saying, "They are diametrically opposed to each other—going to church, standing there at the congregation speaking obviously with the spirit of Christ who loved us all, and that underneath the skin we're all the same. And here you are practicing bigotry, and you have children along with you. I don't understand it." [She continues,] "I'd give him my spiel, and he would just laugh all through it." And I asked, "Why do you keep coming here? You and I don't agree on anything." He said, "Ha, ha. Oh, Mrs. Clayton, you're fun to talk to."

At a later date, after making his announcement of leaving the Klan, Craig reverted to his old ways and dabbled for a while in another racist organization. But as before, he pulled away and left it. Even with the relapse, this is a wonderful story. It's not as clean and neat as we would hope, but nevertheless, it's another beautiful transformation story.

Craig died in 1998. In 2011, this story was remembered when Clayton and Craig's daughter, Gail Craig Mayes, met. Clayton says during the conversation, "... my mind went back to the years when she was little. I used to say to her father, I'm concerned about these children, and especially this little girl. You're transmitting this bigotry and hatred. I just hope she'll grow up to be healthy, happy, sound, and grounded."[4]

In Headlee's account of Clayton and Craig, she says that Clayton didn't try to change Craig and that she just listened. Certainly, Clayton was a good listener at times, but in the *Atlanta* magazine account, Clayton describes herself as a very active participant in the conversations. In the magazine version, much more is happening in the encounters between the two of them than Clayton just listening. She may not have been trying to change Craig, but in the magazine version of the story, she unquestionably is challenging him.

Celeste Headlee says that when we enter into a conversation with someone with whom we strongly disagree, we need to let go of the intention that we are going to change someone's mind or educate them because that's just going to produce frustration and anger. She advises entering into the conversation to learn something because this is something we have control over. For most of us, most of the time, Headlee is right. For most of us, to function effectively in the manner that Headlee suggests would be a significant accomplishment. However, the stories of John Woolman and Xernona Clayton indicate that it is possible to reach a different level.

The Trail of Breadcrumbs Illuminating the Way to Transformation

One way of understanding Christian transformation or conversion is for a person to change from going in one direction to turning and going in the other direction. This transformation would involve not just a change in one's beliefs but a behavior change. Obviously, in the above story, Craig changed from being a part of a very racist organization oppressing Blacks to rejecting that behavior and belief system. He moved in the opposite direction as he was arranging to have a conversation with Dr. King. When King was murdered, Craig went to King's house to stand with the people who were there honoring him. He had turned from one mindset and behavior to a very different way of being in the world.

In looking for hints of how Clayton was instrumental in Craig's transformation, there is no evidence from these stories that Clayton was angry or rejecting; there is no evidence the conversation ever heated up. From their first encounter, she found things about him that she admired. It's astounding, but Craig found Clayton "fun to talk to." In contrast, in those times we have been in our polarized conversations, when would the other person have said that we were fun to talk to? When would we have said that about them?

In their encounters with people engaged in destructive behavior, both Jesus and Woolman started with care and acceptance of the other, as did Clayton. Of course, acceptance is totally counter-intuitive in these polarized situations. In the Clayton and Craig relationship, when Craig represents an ideology that has violated Black people for centuries, acceptance appears not only impossible but repugnant. Nevertheless, it appears the world can shift when seemingly impossible encounters start with an attitude of care and acceptance rather than condemnation. Astoundingly, if it can be achieved, an attitude of acceptance toward the other person seems to create an opportunity for healing, reconciliation, and transformation. Is it possible that acceptance tills the ground for miracles? Are we capable of acceptance in situations where each side has totally different beliefs?

In this particular conversion story, another important ingredient was humor. Clayton and Craig both had a great sense of humor. It's hard to imagine Craig's transformation without that ingredient. Clayton's opening statement to Craig was, "Calvin Craig, now are you the one who heads the Klan?" One could ask this question in an angry, accusatory way. However, in this situation, we have to assume that Clayton was being playful and teasing while communicating acceptance instead of judgment or anger. Had she started the conversation with the same question in an angry, accusatory way, the possibility of a positive relationship would have abruptly ended. Arguably, that first comment and how she said it set the tone for the entire relationship.

She started with acceptance and humor. It was an astonishing way for a Black woman to begin a relationship with a Klan leader. She could tease Craig in ways that he could join in the humor. We don't usually think humor facilitates the conversion process, but it was a crucial ingredient in Craig's transformation.

This conversion story parallels Zacchaeus' story in that just as Zacchaeus went to great lengths to see Jesus, Craig kept seeking out Clayton in the same way. He keeps coming back to engage in the dialogue. She says that every day, he would come by and make it his business to get into a discussion with me about race. One would assume that as a Grand Dragon of the KKK, Craig had rigidly fixed beliefs about race. However, that he came back daily to ask questions and hear a different perspective implies that wasn't true. It suggests that he had genuine questions about his beliefs and some discomfort with how he lived. That behavior challenges us to reevaluate the judgments we make about people with whom we strongly disagree.

Clayton asks Craig why he kept coming to see her, saying that they didn't agree on anything. He laughed and said that she was fun to talk to. It was great that she was fun to talk to, but clearly, Craig was not returning every day solely because she was fun to talk to. It appears that a part of Craig was uncomfortable with his life, and he was open to change if the right person and situation presented itself. One would never have guessed it, given his position and history, but it almost seems Craig was looking for a way to be a different person. He may not have been able to admit it even to himself, but everything indicates he was searching and had found someone he intuited could help.

Another intriguing part of this story is that as a Klansman, Craig would unquestionably have said extremely hateful and demeaning things about Blacks, both privately and as he led Klan meetings. However, with Clayton, he always respectfully addressed her as Mrs. Clayton. This behavior certainly would have been unheard of for someone in the South representing the Klan. Why did he treat her respectfully even though he was openly racist? It indicates that Craig knew something about Clayton and had decided to treat her respectfully before coming to her office.

These are the things we notice and wonder about related to Craig while leaving unanswered the questions of how Clayton was prepared to be the agent of change in this seemingly impossible relationship.

Out of the hundreds of thousands of people in Atlanta, why did Craig approach Clayton to push his questions about race? Beyond experiencing Clayton as fun, what about her drew him to her office initially and then kept him coming back? From the beginning, he seemed to sense something atypical about her and that she had something he needed. What was unique about her that he not only allowed but even invited her to challenge him?

Clayton was open to and accepting of this man despite his being a leader of an organization that had committed terrible hate crimes against her people. We don't know what Craig personally took part in as a Klan leader. We do know that the Klan instigated torture, terror, lynchings, mutilations, beatings, massacres, church burnings, and Jim Crow laws not just in the South but throughout the country.

Given that, when Craig came to her office, it would have been more typical for Clayton to have been angry and rejecting. She could have been afraid or formally polite but distant. Yet, from the beginning, Clayton was open to Craig and greeted him with playful humor. For her to welcome him in the way she did, Clayton had to have gone through her own process of becoming free from being trapped in the cycle of hate fueled by racism and the Klan. For her to relate to Craig in the way she did, surely, she had gone through her own conversion process of letting her fears and anger die. For this relationship to progress as it did, Clayton, following in the tradition of Jesus, Woolman, and Dr. King, had become free to be the instrument used in liberating a captive from his racism.

We have to imagine that Clayton's commitment to the civil rights movement and her relationship with Dr. King had been transformative in her own life. It would seem logical that in following Dr. King, she had been challenged by Jesus' and King's teachings of nonviolence and loving one's enemies. We have to imagine that she was deeply immersed in those teachings and had incorporated them into her being. Therefore, when Craig entered her office, her own transformation had prepared her to enter into the challenging relationship with the Klansman, leading to its very positive outcome.

Two very different belief systems were colliding in these conversations. Initially, Craig represented the vision of racial hatred, division, white supremacy, and the violence needed to carry out that worldview. On the other hand, Clayton held on to a vision of what King called the "beloved community," a community in which all are loved and valued. It was a vision in which all the oppression, hate, violence, suffering, and injustice that had gone before could be healed, and the beloved community could live in peace and unafraid.

Christians, adherents of other faiths, and people of good intentions frequently aspire to be agents of transformation in others' lives.

We admire people like Francis, Woolman, Day, and Clayton in their ability to be that type of presence, but living that out ourselves may seem beyond our reach. We see or experience hurt, or maybe we see others suffering because of some terrible injustice. Possibly, our perception that someone or some group is perpetrating something appallingly wrong and causing great pain may be accurate. However, that doesn't mean we have a clue about how to be God's presence in that situation.

The Light of God May Be Buried, but Still Smoldering

In looking at Craig before his relationship with Clayton and his transformation, many of us might write him off as not being a candidate for conversion from his racism. We might judge him as too entrenched in his racism to choose a different life. Part of his change suggests that those we might consider irredeemable may have a side we cannot see. Possibly, the side of a person's behavior that is most visible and repugnant to us hides a more authentic part of that person's totality that may be hidden and invisible to us, but nevertheless, alive. Maybe we could think of it as the light of God that the Quakers believe lives in every human being.

The Quakers believe that buried in each of us is a spark of God. When reflecting on this, it is easy to say it's a fine idea but then pass on without reflecting on its power. But if we stop to imagine that people who have committed some of the terrible crimes mentioned earlier in this book are carrying the inner light of God, we possibly start to take notice and wonder. Earlier in the book, we remembered people who have committed terrible crimes, like deliberately letting millions of people starve to death, cutting off the hands and feet of children, and poisoning the world. What happens if we stop to think that the people committing these crimes have living in them the light of God? What does that mean? If people with whom we are in conflict contain the light of God, does that change how we see and relate to them? Perhaps if we put the concept in a context where it seems completely impossible, the belief takes on more power. As that happens, maybe we are the ones starting to be transformed.

What was most visible with Craig was his being a leader of the KKK. For most of us, that side is repulsive, even reprehensible. However, the evidence is that Craig had a hidden side that was different from what he presented on the surface. Even as the Grand Wizard of the KKK, it appears there was a part of him that questioned the values and mission of the KKK. Perhaps in their conversations, Clayton could speak to and touch that part of Craig, even nourish that part of Craig's inner life, which may help explain how Clayton had such a transformational impact on Craig. Was Clayton speaking to and touching the part of Craig that was the inner light of God? Was it that side of Craig that kept him coming back to talk with Clayton?

Similarly, we remember the Quakers who came to Woolman in his early adulthood asking him to write their wills, and Woolman gently refusing to write the part of the will that involved passing on their enslaved people to their families. Woolman's gentle openness with them about his concerns around slavery prompted some of those who had come to him to acknowledge their own concerns about the practice of slavery, which had not been evident before. Then, some of those people came back at a later time asking to have their wills written in a way so those they were enslaving would be freed instead of being willed to family members. It appears Woolman had touched a part of these men that had always been present but had been suppressed.

As with Clayton and Craig, Woolman possibly touched a part of these men that was already uncomfortable with enslaving other human beings. It appears Woolman called out a truer, deeper part of their humanity and faith. These early experiences around writing wills likely gave him a model of how to have the challenging conversations he would have later in his travels.

In his journal, Woolman doesn't write about the light of God in the people he talks with, but as a devout Quaker, that concept had to have been part of his belief system. One has to believe that his deep spirituality guided him to speak to the truest part of the person he was addressing.

Suppose we approach a difficult conversation or relationship being aware of the light of God in that person. Does it create an opening for a better outcome than would have been possible otherwise? Is it possible that those who assist others in their spiritual transformations have the ability to speak to that hidden part of an individual? If one can reach the divine side of a person, would the odds of that person deciding to change increase?

The Catholic Worker Conversion

The type of conversion Dorothy Day precipitated was similar to but also different from Woolman. She modeled a vision and a life that people who understood their faith in a similar way to the way she did could imitate. Her actions inspired and attracted people who believed it was unjust for poor people to live in the way they were forced to. Instead of having a hidden side, they often knew they wanted to live their lives in a way that was truer to the gospel but didn't have the vision or the model to do that.

Dorothy and Peter's vision and way of being in the world inspired these people to change their lives and follow the Catholic Worker path. In doing so, these followers were not doing an about-face but were transformed by deepening their faith. Possibly, Day didn't inspire people to make such a radical about-face as Woolman did but gave them a vision that connected with what they already believed, giving them the opportunity to be what they wanted to be in their deepest hearts.

The people inspired by Day could come to her Catholic Worker houses and volunteer. Or they could begin their own houses of hospitality where they lived. Either way, in following her, they were being transformed into living their faith more authentically.

NOTES

[1]Celeste Headlee: “How Can We Have Civil Conversations With The Other Side?” *NPR TED Radio Hour,* October 27, 2017, https://www.npr.org/transcripts/560195583.

[2]Ibid.

[3]Maria Saporta, “Civil rights icon Xernona Clayton’s unlikely friendship with a KKK Grand Dragon,” *Atlanta,* May, 2011, https://www.atlantamagazine.com/civilrights/xernona-clayton-kkk-grand-dragon-calvin-crai

[4]Ibid.

| fourteen |

Extricating Ourselves

This fulfills the prophecy of Isaiah that says, 'When you hear what I say, you will not understand. When you see what I do, you will not comprehend. For the hearts of these people are hardened, and their ears cannot hear, and they have closed their eyes— so their eyes cannot see, and their ears cannot hear, and their hearts cannot understand, and they cannot turn to me and let me heal them. (Matthew 13:14-15)

To Be Transformed, We Need Eyes that See and Ears that Hear

I grew up in the South, graduating from high school in 1960. It was a segregated, prejudiced, racist culture. It was a system that was disrespectful, unjust, and hurtful to African Americans. However, as I was growing up in that culture, I didn't think about the way we lived as being wrong, sinful, or hurtful. It was more like, that's just the way things were. It was like the water we drank and the air we breathed. We were so immersed in racism that it was all but invisible to us. We didn't have the eyes to see it.

The civil rights movement was coming into full bloom in my high school and young adult years. In the back of my mind, a voice started growing that said something was wrong with how we were living. As I increasingly paid attention to that voice, I wanted to separate myself from the values of the culture in which I had grown up.

In the early 1960s, I began consciously attempting to extricate myself from the racism in which I was immersed. I was trying to separate myself from the air I was breathing and the water I was drinking. I started reading Black authors. I read radicals like Eldridge Cleaver, Malcolm X, and novelists like James Baldwin. I read a book called "Black Like Me" about a White man who found a way to darken the pigment of his skin so that he could go out and experience what it was like to live as a Black person. I listened to African Americans as I attempted to understand how they experienced the world and how they experienced racism. I was trying to have eyes to see what I had been blind to. It was an attempt to free myself from the milieu of racism. In retrospect, I would say I was trying to free myself from being captive to racism. While I was struggling to do that, it was enormously helpful that the civil rights movement was opening the country's eyes while I was engaged in that process.

Regrettably, we who think of ourselves as Christian are in precisely the same situation as Calvin Craig was before having the conversations with Xernona Clayton. He was immersed in racism and couldn't see the evil of it. Most of us are in the same quandary. We are submerged in an economic system based on greed and have adopted that belief system. As Craig was unable to see the evil of racism, we are unable to see that capitalism opposes everything Jesus taught and lived.

Uncomfortably, we are the people that Jesus and other Biblical writers are addressing when they teach about people who have eyes that don't see, ears that don't hear, and hearts that don't understand. (Isaiah 6:10, Ezekiel 12:2, Matthew 13:15, Acts 28:27)

It is very difficult to have eyes that see when we are immersed in what we need to see. Daily, we receive messages that indoctrinate us into the free-market belief system, but in a way that makes it appear as though this is completely obvious and normal. Even if we do manage to pry our eyes open to see the destructiveness of that way of life, starting to live those Biblical teachings about money is incredibly challenging. Even after our eyes are open, having hearts that turn to God and are transformed is an enormous undertaking.

At the beginning of Jesus' ministry, he reads from Isaiah about setting the captives free and giving sight to the blind. We see these verses in Luke, but it never occurs to us that we are the prisoners who need to be freed. It doesn't enter our minds that we are the ones who are blind and need to have our sight restored. We celebrate Zacchaeus' transformation, but it doesn't enter our consciousness that we are sitting up in that tree with Zacchaeus before Jesus passes by.

Extricating Ourselves

Obviously, there is no groundswell of people rising up to extricate themselves from capitalism, but rather just the opposite. In Buddhism, there is the concept of always being a beginner in one's spiritual journey. They understand that the further they go, the more they are just beginning in their spiritual journey. It's hard to state how true that is for most of us who entertain the hope of being free from the belief system of capitalism and of becoming closer to the teachings of Jesus.

Many of us can say with the "rich young ruler" that we have kept the commandments and have lived well following many of the precepts of our faith. Many of us can say that we have been genuinely "good" people. But most of us are barely beginners in living the life Jesus taught and lived about money, wealth, and possessions.

Today, the few voices raising the alarm about capitalism are relegated to society's remote, distant edges. An enormous megaphone promoting consumerism and wealth accumulation permeates today's world. The belief system celebrating the values of capitalism has infiltrated our minds like an invading army. We largely accept that these omnipresent voices are the way, as previous cultures accepted slavery.

For us, a start could be to follow Biblical theologian Walter Brueggemann's suggestion of separating our vision from the vision of the dominant society. Paraphrasing Brueggemann, the challenge is to imagine and live in a different reality from the culture in which we are immersed. He says we must develop our imaginations and separate them from those of the dominant society and from the powers that be. He implies that when we as Christians, accept the vision of those in power, we're finished. He is referring to not just political power but economic power, cultural power, and the power of those who can shape our thoughts and behavior.[1]

St. Francis, Dorothy Day, and John Woolman opened themselves to glimpses of an alternative vision. Their imaginations led them to concrete steps in transforming their lives. As their lives were changing, their new experiences provided more fuel for them to open their eyes further and continue expanding their visions. The interplay between action and imagination propelled them further into the reality of God's kingdom.

These were challenging transformations for Francis, Day, and Woolman. Not only their imaginations but their lives became increasingly different from the culture and from those in power. The changes they chose precipitated conflict and painful interactions with their families, friends, and respective cultures. They were unique in living out the phrase "being in but not of the world."

Getting Started

How to follow these saints in making these changes is beyond stating. However, a few basic principles are below:

We cannot follow Jesus' path concerning money with just our heads, thoughts, and good intentions. Francis, Woolman, and Day were continually turning to God for wisdom to make the right choices and to provide them with the strength and commitment to follow through. They were totally clear they could not move forward based on their own good intentions and intellect. They were fully aware of their dependence on God through prayer.

Most people start out with a built-in assumption that having more and accumulating more wealth is better. We need to understand that this belief is not only false and un-Christian, but suicidal. We can begin separating ourselves from that belief and consciously separating ourselves from its power and influence over us. At a minimum, we can make money suspect instead of automatically honoring and celebrating it.

To begin progressing in this area, we probably need to join with others who feel a similar need to draw closer to our faith path as we turn away from our cultural path. It's a demanding task. We need the encouragement, support, and insight of others. We need a place to make confessions and commitments. It's helpful to receive and share both our insights and struggles. There are few contemporary guides out there, but if we can find them, we need to pay attention. There are some writers in the secular world advocating for and teaching how to live a simpler life who can be helpful.

To live these counter-cultural values, the early church did it together. They knew they were going against a strong tide, so they pulled away and built strong alternative communities. Later, when the Christian church became the Roman church, the early desert fathers and mothers pulled away from the dominant culture and formed loosely knit communities. Even later in history, the communities became much more organized into monasteries and convents.

We need to turn away from making wealth our goal as we embrace generosity. Nearly all of us are automatically inclined toward wanting more. We want more wealth, property, comfort, and security. Wealth builds up our ego and the image we want others to have of us. It also creates how we want to see ourselves. This is part of our human condition. The values of capitalism strengthen these desires. In contrast, cultivating generosity, if done in the right way, confronts these tendencies and changes us.

We must realize that our identity as people of faith is the opposite of our culture concerning money. It seems impossible to extract ourselves completely, but we can search out and be creative about withdrawing and not cooperating with a structure that makes a god of profit and wealth. Together, we have to envision and create a system that makes it easier for us to live ethically concerning money. As much as possible, we need to abandon the treasure of the free market while allowing Jesus' way to become the treasure of our hearts.

Jesus was extremely radical concerning money. We need to acknowledge that and not deny or water it down. But for most of us, attempting to be as radical as Jesus or St. Francis is discouraging and feels impossible rather than helpful. In getting started, probably using John Woolman's choice to live more simply could be a more helpful model for us beginners. The important thing is to get started, set out on the path our scripture teaches us, and take steps in that direction.

Our Guides

Zacchaeus, St. Francis, John Woolman, and Dorothy Day rejected the dominant prevailing vision of the culture in which each lived. While extricating themselves from the belief and value systems in which they were immersed, they developed an alternative vision from those in power.

Jesus empowered Zacchaeus to extricate himself from being a person spreading poverty, distress, anger, mistrust, and dissension into someone creating God's kingdom by spreading justice, reconciliation, peace, and God's love. Francis went through an extremely difficult disengagement from his former life, which resulted in God's kingdom breaking out all around him. Woolman was very faithful in being transformed away from his culture's values and the greed embedded in it. As he incorporates the scriptures about money, wealth, and property in his life and ministry, a part of the world is repaired, restored, and healed. The kingdom broke through in the release of captives and the transformed lives of former enslavers. Dorothy Day had been seeking God's path since childhood. But it wasn't until Peter Maurin found her and began to share his vision that she could discern that path. Not only did her life change but so did the lives of thousands of others who followed her. By extricating themselves from their respective cultures, these faithful people lived out God's intent around the challenging scriptures about money, wealth, and property. We have all been blessed that they were able to live into those respective visions. They are our guides.

If those of us of the Christian faith take the scriptures about money seriously and allow those teachings to transform us, God's abundance will break out all around the world. Peace will spread seemingly miraculously throughout the earth. Hunger, poverty, homelessness, and the number of refugees will decline. The planet's ecosystem will start to heal. The verses about money and possessions are not just arbitrary teachings that seem impossible to live. If taken seriously, they are guides holding the truth and power to change us and transform the world.

NOTES

[1]Walter Brueggemann, *The Prophetic Imagination,* 2nd ed. (Minneapolis: Fortress Press, 2001), 3.

| fifteen |

Thy Kingdom Come

Our Father which art in heaven, Hallowed be thy name. Thy kingdom come. Thy will be done on earth, as it is in heaven. Give us this day our daily bread. And forgive us our debts, as we forgive our debtors. And lead us not into temptation, but deliver us from evil: For thine is the kingdom, and the power, and the glory, forever. Amen. (Matthew 6:9-13)

God's Kingdom Coming Is Dependent on Our Conversion Around Money, Property, and Wealth

When we pray the Lord's Prayer with the phrase "Thy kingdom come. Thy will be done on earth as it is in Heaven," we probably are not thinking about money, but to a large extent, God's kingdom coming depends on our choices about money.

When we pray the Lord's Prayer, we are saying that as followers of Jesus, we are asking that God's kingdom take place in us. However, no matter how much we pray the prayer, God's kingdom will not come until we become transformed around money, property, and wealth. God's kingdom comes on earth as we are transformed, and it will arrive to the extent that conversion takes place in us. To make a point, this book has a section on horrible crimes committed by some countries, industries, and corporations. Entities like these will not initiate the transformation the prophets and Jesus were calling for. If change is to happen in countries and corporations like the ones named above, it has to start with us. If God's kingdom of love, peace, justice, freedom, reconciliation, and equality is to come, we must begin to extricate ourselves from the kingdom of capitalism.

Our faith calls us to be the salt that transforms hearts, behavior, and culture. (Matthew. 5:13) However, we have allowed our culture to season and shape us according to its values, particularly around money. This leaves those of us who desire to follow Jesus needing to address the issue of money in our own lives. Few of us are ready to follow Jesus, St. Francis, and Mother Theresa in giving up everything. Few of us are filled with the spirit of the followers in the early church who sold their properties and gave the proceeds to be distributed to those in need. (Acts 2:44-46) Unquestionably, though, our scripture is leading, urging, and inviting us to take steps in the direction of these saints.

If we continue to embrace the values of our culture and if capitalism reigns, we are lost. If we stay committed to economic growth and maximizing profits, it's hard to see how God's kingdom can come on earth.

In recent chapters of this book, we changed from focusing on money, property, and wealth and turned our attention to conversion or transformation. This is where we have to start; God's kingdom begins with our own transformation. Earlier in the book, we recognized that when Zacchaeus began enthusiastically returning what he had cheated people out of and giving to the poor, God's kingdom was joyfully breaking out. We may not have individually cheated people in the way Zacchaeus did. Still, most of us have profited from an unjust economic system that deprives the poor and ravages God's creation. As we start to turn away from the values of that system, we are starting to usher in God's kingdom.

As we live into these verses about money and wealth, peace will spread miraculously throughout the earth. These transformational verses make God's vision real: each person living under their own vine and fig tree in peace and unafraid. (Micah 4:4) God's vision of the Peaceable Kingdom will blossom. (Isaiah 11:6-9)

Imagining the Kingdom (AKA Kin-dom, Commonwealth, Beloved Community, Kingdom of Heaven, Peaceable Kingdom, Commonwealth of Peace and Freedom, Reign of Unity, Reign of Peace

When we pray, "Thy kingdom come, on earth as it is in heaven," what are we praying for? How do we imagine that kingdom? Even if we don't see the kingdom come to its fullest, what does it look like when we see or experience glimpses of it? Below is a start toward imagining how God's kingdom might appear when we come closer to living out the scriptures regarding money, property, and wealth.

The treasure of God's kingdom is for all people and all creation to flourish. No one is left behind. In God's kingdom, there is no zero-sum game of winners and losers. There are no privileged or non-privileged groups. All races, ethnic groups, and countries are not only valued but loved. No groups are diminished or devalued. All are included, lifted up, welcomed, and embraced.

The kingdom is built on truth, the foundation on which all rests. All strive for it and recognize that without truth, the kingdom collapses. People dare to allow their eyes to see and ears to hear uncomfortable truths. They have the courage to see when they are spreading destruction and misery. They not only can see but choose to turn away from those destructive paths.

In God's kingdom, those with wealth have transformed hearts and do not abuse their power by creating systems that maximize their profits while impoverishing others. Accumulating material wealth is spurned. Success is measured by the material wealth we give, as opposed to what we've amassed. Following Zacchaeus' example, those with wealth share generously with those having less because that is what love does. Following the example of the early Christian community, those who had more now have less, and those who had less now have an abundance. Sharing, not accumulating, is honored in God's kingdom.

As the kingdom comes, billionaires recreate a modern-day Jubilee as they give away $billions creating common wealth. Those who had made captives of others by devising economic systems to enrich themselves while impoverishing others are freed from the captivity of those ideas, values, and beliefs. Instead of creating laws and structures to oppress, captivate, and impoverish, we join to make laws that release and lift up those who have been captive. The wounds caused by hate, envy, racism, injustice, and greed are repaired--in part through monetary reparations. Former captors and former captives are mutually liberated. The inhabitants of this kingdom choose behaviors and policies that heal the wounds of injustice. Neighbors and friends are no longer pitted against one another. In God's kingdom, each person values and nurtures a sense of community and unity. Joy abounds in the midst of Jubilee.

In the reign of God, people are no longer captive to and manipulated by greed. The pillars on which greed rests crumble as mutual flourishing and well-being are embraced and valued. There are no longer haves and have-nots. All flourish together in good times and suffer as one in challenging times.

Countries and individuals are freed from the captivity of consumerism and the compulsion to accumulate more. As they are freed, they can free others from the captivity of poverty and need. Abundance abounds. A sense of unity and community replaces the fear of struggling to survive.

When the kingdom of heaven comes on earth, the least of these, those who are homeless, refugees, disabled, members of different ethnic groups, and those of other races, are treated with kindness and respect, even honored. Astoundingly, they are loved as one loves Jesus. In this kingdom, those who had been first are now last, and those who had been last are first.

God's vision of justice will spread miraculously throughout the world, moving the world closer to God's intention and vision. Hunger, poverty, homelessness, and the number of refugees will decline. Those with more will have less, while those with less will have what they need. Community will flourish as envy and greed wither.

Countries under the thumb of more powerful nations are freed from their captivity. They are now liberated to create laws and cultures that benefit their own citizens and not the citizens of their more powerful neighbors. Debts between countries are forgiven, and wealth gaps between countries decrease dramatically.

In the Peaceable Kingdom of God, the lion makes community with the lamb. Our possessions, furniture, and garments are no longer our treasures. As they cease having power over us, they no longer nourish the seeds of war. God's reign of peace thrives amid mutual well-being. Swords are beaten into plowshares. Nuclear weapons, fighter planes, submarines, aircraft carriers, missiles, tanks, and land mines are transformed into playgrounds, schools, housing, health care, clean water, and a thriving ecosystem. Miraculously, as truth and love reign, people are astonished they are capable of loving those they hate. Each person rejoices in peace beneath their vine and fig tree. The peaceable kingdom thrives and blossoms.

Those driven from their homes by war, violence, and greed jubilantly return to their lands to live in peace. Families who had been ripped apart and displaced are reunited. Property that had been taken from them in the past is returned to them. All are freed from the principalities and powers of violence, injustice, greed, and fear.

People of every ethnic group, color, gender, sexual orientation, and ability are recognized as created in God's image and loved by God. The Beloved Community Dr. King envisioned blossoms. All are accepted, valued, included, and loved. The Kingdom of God becomes the Kin-dom of God. All are family in the truest sense of the word. Each realizes the truth that we are all connected and loved as kin.

Our divisions and polarizations no longer reign and terrorize us. Hatred is erased as the reign of unity replaces the polarities of division. Animosity withers; fear and envy diminish. The world relaxes in joy as former adversaries join with each other and the natural world. People and the earth alike relax and breathe more deeply. Humans and the natural world smile, joyful to be living in harmony.

In the kingdom, the planet's bruised and distressed ecosystem will start to heal as we become aware that creation is not a commodity to be exploited for material wealth, but a part of God's nature, an incredible gift being shared with us. All the different parts are created in the image of God and are part of God. Each part is an exquisite creation, sacred and honored. God is present in all the planet's magnificent, interrelated, intricate, and intertwined components. Following St. Francis' lead, in God's kingdom, we choose to be in a loving relationship filled with respect, appreciation, and tenderness for all these manifestations of God in creation. The planet blooms, regenerates, and heals. All creation celebrates in relief and joy.

In God's kingdom, some, like Francis, take Jesus literally and give everything to those in need. Saints like him are scattered across the earth as models of those who choose God's perfection. They remind the rest of us that we are unfinished and still have work to do on our own journeys of transformation. As we continue to be transformed, we become more capable instruments in converting others.

Our treasure is no longer material wealth but in being part of the kingdom. Our heart rests in loving, valuing, and working to realize God's vision. As God's kin-dom comes on earth, the divine celebrates with creation. In God's reign, joy is pervasive on earth as in heaven.

Epilogue

The beginning of the book focused on the teachings in the Bible related to money, property, and wealth, and how they seemed so impossible to live. They still seem incredibly difficult, but they are more understandable now. Jesus focused so strongly on money because it is such a huge threat to us as we attempt to follow him. The verses about money are about God's love to save and protect us from self-destruction. The purpose of the verses is to equip us to withstand the enormous power of money to save us from wounding others and abandoning our relationship with God. Just as Zacchaeus' salvation was dependent on what he did with money, so is ours.

God's vision of the kingdom can't come until we change our relationship with money. Concretely, God's kingdom can't come if we are starving people like Great Britain did in India. The African genocide in the Congo is more like the kingdom of evil than God's kingdom. Refusing to stop poisoning the world in order to earn billions blocks the kingdom. When corporations put their energy, power, and creativity into addicting their fellow brothers and sisters to tobacco or opioids is the opposite of God's kingdom taking place. Most of us are unaware of committing such terrible crimes, but as human beings, we are all capable of them. We sometimes participate in them without realizing it. In the Lord's prayer, we pray for God's kingdom to come. We human beings have to change in order for the kingdom to break through.

For that to happen, we have to depend on God's power to change us. As well as praying for the kingdom to come, we need to pray for our transformation so that the kingdom can emerge. We have to choose it, but the power for our transformation comes from God.

Reflection Questions

Chapter One: Jesus Chooses Poverty Over Wealth

1. Jesus rejected political power and wealth and chose spiritual power. Could we also have the potential to be a conduit for more of the kind of power that Jesus demonstrated?
2. Has there been a time when you have been particularly aware that you were struggling with evil? Were you aware of it at the time or in retrospect.?
3. In the story of the Rich Young Ruler, Jesus taught us to give away all of our wealth. He said that he didn't have anywhere to lay his head, implying he didn't have a home. (Luke 9:58) He taught that if you had two cloaks, to give one away. (Luke 3:11) His disciples said that they had left all to follow him. (Matt. 19:27) We have no evidence that he owned anything. How do these statements compare with the image you have of Jesus?

Chapter Two: The Saint Who Gave It All to the Poor

1. Francis and his small core group of followers grasped that if they were to love in the way Jesus taught, they had to allow their lives to be transformed by their commitment to the scriptures around money, property, and wealth. How would you feel about praying that these particular scriptures transform your life?
2. Some of us may admire Francis but are stymied by his seemingly impossible life and choices. In that case, maybe it's not helpful to focus on his seemingly unachievable poverty but to turn our attention to the impediments to our moving forward. What are your obstacles to loving God and your neighbor

more fully? What blocks you from treating the least of these as Christ?
3. What is your treasure? Where is your heart? (Matthew 6:21)

Chapter Three: The Quaker Miracle Worker

1. What would be the equivalent of enacting Jubilee values in modern times? What would be the result of that in society?
2. What are your thoughts about Woolman's choice to voluntarily become poorer? How do his choices about wealth compare to Saint Francis's?
3. By asking the enslavers to free their enslaved people, Woolman was asking them to give up a substantial part of their wealth. How would you respond to someone telling you that you were doing something immoral but that you could rectify that by giving away a significant part of what you owned?
4. Woolman believed that we go to war not for all the reasons our government tells us but to increase our wealth. When have you witnessed that?
5. How do you experience God's light being a part of you?

Chapter Four: Dorothy Day

1. Day's granddaughter states above that "the more affluent (we are) materially, the more destitute we are spiritually." Do you agree with that? How do possessions and material wealth help or hinder your spiritual life?
2. What would our culture say about Peter's belief that even though they had no money, that if they committed to launching the Catholic Worker, God would not be outdone in generosity? What are your thoughts about Peter's conviction? Have you ever lived like that? What was the outcome?
3. Have there been moments when you trusted God in a difficult time and felt that God provided for you?

4. Did you, like Day, leave the church at some point in your life? What precipitated that? What was the outcome of that decision?
5. Few people felt they could permanently live the sacrificial life that Peter and Dorothy lived, but many volunteered for a period of time. How would you feel about being a volunteer in a setting like this for a while? What would be your goal if you were to do something like that?
6. Had Dorothy and Peter never met, it appears that the Catholic Worker movement would never have begun; no one would have written about them, and we would never have heard of them. What type of person or group might you need to experience a growth spurt in your faith?
7. Do you believe the church needs to be reformed and that we should attempt to reform the church as Peter counseled? Do you, like Day, feel something is wrong with how Christianity is practiced?
8. Dorothy and Peter believed that capitalism is an unjust, oppressive system directly in opposition to our faith. Are Christianity and capitalism compatible?

Chapter Five: The "Late Victorian Holocausts"

1. During the famines in India, the British House of Commons agreed that the "...supreme principle was that India was to be governed as a revenue plantation, not an almshouse." What does this single declaration of intent say about the belief system undergirding British rule? How does it compare with the statements about money, possessions, and wealth in the Bible? Was the British philosophy different from the way countries generally function?
2. What if the "supreme principle" had been different? What if the supreme principle had been that Indian lives were as valuable as British lives? Suppose the British had believed that the

overriding value was that no human being should starve. How would the world have changed?

3. Under what belief system was the British operating that propelled them to commit such inhuman acts? What lies would the British have needed to tell themselves to ship grain out of India while millions were starving?
4. Countries define their responsibility as defending and expanding their national interests. This means there is a constant drive to increase their wealth, power, and influence worldwide. Given this, can one attempting to follow Jesus ever trust or be wholly committed to the values of one's country?
5. Many British who were involved in the colonization of India would have seen themselves as good Christians. Setting aside what these people may have believed was their god, what was, in fact, their god?

Chapter Six: The Belgian Holocaust

1. We can all recognize these accounts describing the colonization of the Congo as stories of terror. Take that awareness further and put yourself in the place of the Africans being massacred, whipped senseless, subjected to forced labor, or having their hand or foot cut off by foreign invaders. Most challenging, put yourself in the place of the parents who lived through having the invaders cut off the hand or foot of your children or grandchildren. If this happened to you, how would you react?
2. How did the terrible concepts propagated in the Doctrine of Discovery gain such traction and still have power in today's culture?
3. Probably, there were Europeans in the Congo who didn't want to participate in the violence against the Africans. Surely, most didn't know what they were getting into when volunteering to go to the Congo but found themselves there and were ordered

to do terrible things. When one is in a situation where authority, orders, and peer pressure push one to commit horrific acts like those described above, what options does one have? What might be the cost of refusing to commit these kinds of atrocities?

4. During the period of European exploration, discovery, and later colonization, the Christian church became the primary entity promoting war on peaceful people, enslaving human beings, plundering other lands, murdering millions, and establishing a theological underpinning for racism that has lasted for centuries. How do you understand the Christian Church becoming the very opposite of what the church is meant to be?
5. What is your understanding of how people can be so cruel in the ways they were during the age of discovery and colonization?

Chapter Seven: Defeating Regulation While Creating Death

1. What is the logic/thought process of people who invest in and commit to working for the tobacco industry even though they know they are creating disease, suffering, and death?
2. How does the system of capitalism contribute to the hardness of heart exhibited by the tobacco industry?
3. Both the Hebrew prophets and Jesus would have been dismayed at how the tobacco industry is indifferent to the human cost of promoting tobacco use. Even so, is there a difference in how the prophets would address the industry and how Jesus might address it? Would John Woolman challenge the tobacco industry differently from how the prophets might challenge these people?
4. In our day we seldom talk about idolatry. The scriptures about worshiping graven images, statues, etc., seem like silly hocus pocus. In our time, is it possible that profit is the real god of

the tobacco industry and other industries that don't value human life?

5. If enslavers can change, is it possible for captains of industry to do the same? For those of us who would like to see that happen, how could we facilitate that happening?
6. Do you have investments that might be supporting the tobacco industry? If so, what choices do you have about that? If you realize that you have money that might be invested in the tobacco industry, does it change the way you see people who lead and have committed their lives to this industry?

Chapter Eight: Poison

1. Wilbur Earl Tennant lost lifelong friends and became an outcast in the Parkersburg area for adamantly insisting that DuPont was poisoning the water. How does one find the courage to confront the most powerful economic entity in the area where one lives, as Tennant did? Has there been a time in your life when you have taken a strong ethical stance against a powerful opponent?
2. Let's assume that the people in this DuPont plant who are making the decisions are not "bad" people. Most love their family, care about their neighbors, are good citizens, and many would certainly understand themselves as Christians. Yet some covered up an atrocity, causing debilitating illness, intense suffering, and even death to others in the community. How does someone's heart get shaped so one chooses to cover up this kind of violence?
3. In the earlier chapters, some of the saints' choices about money seem crazy. However, when you look at what the colonial powers and some corporations did for wealth, do the saints' radical choices about rejecting money and wealth seem more rational?

4. As the enslavers Woolman visited voluntarily gave up part of their fortune, they were simultaneously becoming changed human beings. What do we learn from Woolman in that he could precipitate not only the freeing of enslaved people but also the freeing of people's hearts?
5. Do these stories about colonial powers and corporations being captive to profit make you look at money differently?
6. Are there ways that money, wealth, and property become the most essential thing in your life? What choices could you make to change this?
7. Have you sacrificed or suffered for refusing to do unethical things? For example, have you left a job or been terminated from a position for refusing to do something immoral?

Chapter Nine: Addiction

1. Does the economic system in which we are immersed make it harder for corporations to resist wrongdoing? Could a different economic system make it easier for businesses to function more ethically?
2. Have the decision-makers in these companies ceased to value human life?
3. Jesus said that he had come to free the captives. How would he describe the captivity of the decision-makers in these corporations? How would he address them?
4. Are the people in the tobacco, chemical, and opioid companies behaving similarly to the colonists in India and the Congo as they watched people die of starvation and cut off the hands and feet of children?
5. How do people become numb to the devastation they are causing other human beings? What is the role of the church concerning this condition?
6. It has been estimated that the loss of life from prescription and illicit opioids between 1999 and 2019 was over 500,000.

(https://www.cdc.gov/opioids/basics/epidemic.html) If the drug companies knew their product was unnecessarily causing hundreds of thousands of deaths, how is this not murder? How is it that the decision-makers are not charged with a crime?

7. The enslavers that Woolman worked with were transformed. If the people who were involved in causing the opioid epidemic were to be transformed, what would that look like? How would they be living differently? What would their being freed from their captivity look like?

Chapter Ten: *Capitalism Made Me Do It*

1. When an article stated that the napkins packed with Kraft Lunchables were more nutritious than the lunch, Geoffrey Bible, the CEO of the parent company of Kraft, didn't dispute that. He even volunteered that the lunches were also loaded with sugar, salt, and oil. He continued, "Well, that's what the consumer wants, and we are not putting a gun to their head to eat it. That's what they want. If we give them less, they'll buy less, and the competitor will get our market. So you're sort of trapped." If you were Geoffrey Bible, how would you, as a follower of Jesus' teachings, deal with this conflict. How would you deal with being "trapped"?
2. This book argues that rigid adherence to profit is functionally a theology or a religious belief system. How would you argue for or against this statement?
3. It's stated above that "When an individual or a culture relentlessly pursues profits knowing that the drive for those profits will cause death and destruction, profit has become their god... In this theological system, wealth and accumulating more wealth is salvation." How is this true? How is it false?
4. How would you respond to James M. Buchanan, who argues above that the Good Samaritan should have left the attacked man on the road to die?

5. This book argues that unlimited economic growth is suicidal. If this is true, what is the church's responsibility related to that?
6. It is stated above that many of us have become convinced that a life centered around greed is not only the lifestyle we should be living but also compatible with Christianity. Some succinctly state the problem as "We have blessed greed and called it a virtue." (Care for Creation, p. 162) To the extent this is true, what does it say about the Christian Church where this has happened?

Chapter Eleven: Capitalism Converts Christianity

1. We all live in a capitalist system, and none of us escape its influence, but is it possible to follow the teachings of Jesus while being an ardent advocate for capitalism?
2. How is capitalism trying to transform you?
3. Are there ways you consciously attempt to separate yourself from capitalism and its values?
4. We are told to love the least of these. How do we do that related to money?
5. Capitalism measures success in profit, economic growth, increased consumerism, and greater wealth. How do we, as Christians, measure success?
6. Is maximizing profits a euphemism for greed? If it is, is greed the law of the land?
7. We can get stuck thinking about how the scriptures around money, wealth, and property seem impossible to live. Nevertheless, how do they resonate with you? What steps do these scriptures call you to take at this moment?

Chapter Twelve: The Prophets, Jesus, and Woolman

1. Is it possible that, as followers of Jesus, we could become instruments in the type of transformation Woolman initiated? Could our faith so deepen that we could have the kind of impact that Woolman had?
2. Above, it says, "Jesus understands that his call is to love people like Zacchaeus, and in loving him, he wants a very different life for him." How much is it a part of our faith that we desire to love people who have cheated others, robbed them, split up families, and made others poorer and more vulnerable?
3. Is it possible that you have caused harm while seeking profit? Are there things that you need to make reparations for?
4. Woolman "...set out on his mission fearful for his fellow Quakers. He was deeply concerned about the spiritual welfare of the enslavers and, in his belief system, was afraid they were going to hell." When you have been in conflict with someone with beliefs very different from yours, are you concerned about their spiritual welfare? If not, how would the conversation change if you were? How would you be different if you were genuinely concerned for their spiritual welfare?
5. Woolman was determined to remove or allow God to remove any spiritual impediment that blocked him from freeing the Quaker enslavers. What would it look like if we were committed to eliminating any spiritual impediment in our lives to further God's kingdom?
6. Have you sacrificed or suffered for refusing to do unethical things? For example, have you left a job or been terminated from a position for refusing to do something immoral?

Chapter Thirteen: Continuing Toward Transformation

1. Imagine starting a conversation with someone with deeply held beliefs opposite yours. Then, imagine beginning that conversation with an attitude of acceptance.
2. If you had been in Clayton's position, how would you have started your first conversation with Craig? What would have been your attitude toward him?
3. Craig found Clayton "fun to talk to." In the polarizing conversations in which you have been involved, when would the other person have said that about you? Could you change in a way that would make that happen?
4. In your polarizing conversations, when would you have used humor to facilitate the process?
5. In remembering Craig repeatedly returning to Clayton's office to talk about race, does it appear that a part of him was seeking a way to become a different person? Why or why not?
6. How or when have you experienced the light of God in you? How have you experienced the light of God while working in a group?

Chapter Fourteen: Extricating Ourselves

1. Jesus rejected political power and wealth and chose spiritual power. Could we also have the potential to be a conduit for more of the kind of power that Jesus demonstrated?
2. Has there been a time when you have been particularly aware that you were struggling with evil? How did you become aware of what was happening?

Chapter Fifteen: Thy Kingdom Come

1. How would you write or alter this chapter about what the kingdom might look like? If you were to imagine God's kingdom coming, how would you visualize it?
2. If one asks, how can I act to bring God's kingdom to a particular situation, is that the same as praying, "Thy kingdom come"?
3. When you pray, "Thy kingdom come," in the Lord's Prayer, what do you envision your role to be in bringing God's kingdom into fruition?

Relevant Scriptures

Scriptures About Money, Wealth, Possessions, and Property

Leviticus 25
Deuteronomy 15:1-18
Deuteronomy 15:7-12
Psalm 82:2-4
Proverbs 3:9-10
Proverbs 22:22-23
Proverbs 31:8-9
Ecclesiastes 4:1
Isaiah 1:17
Isaiah 10:1-4
Isaiah 58:6-13
Jeremiah 22:1-3
Ezekiel 22:27-31
Ezekiel 34:16
Amos 5:10-16
Micah 2:1-2
Micah 2:7-11
Michah 3:9-11
Micah 6:6-16
Zechariah 7:9-10
Matthew 6:1-4
Matthew 6:19-21
Matthew 6:24-34
Matthew 7:12
Matthew 8:20
Matthew 13:22
Matthew 13:44

Matthew 16:24-26
Matthew 19:16-27
Matthew 25:34-40
Mark 4:18-19
Mark 10:23-31
Mark 12:38-4
Luke 3:14
Luke 4:16-20
Luke 6:20-37
Luke 12:13-34
Luke 14:25-34
Luke 16:13-15
Luke 16:19-31
Luke 19:1-10
Luke 21:1-4
Acts 2:43-47
Acts 3:1-10
Acts 4:32-37
Acts 20:35
Romans 13:8
Romans 12:19-20
2 Corinthians 6:10
2 Corinthians 8:1-15
2 Corinthians 9:1-15
1 Timothy 6:5-10
1 Timothy 6:17-19
Hebrews 13:5-7
James 2:1-13
James 1:9-11
James 2:14-17
James 5:1-6
1 John 2:15-17
Revelation 3:17-18

Bibliography

Andrews, Cecile and Wanda Urbanska. *Less is More: Embracing Simplicity for a Healthy Planet, a Caring Economy and Lasting Happiness.* Gabriola Island, BC, Canada: New Society Publishers, 2009.

Bilott, Robert and Tom Shroder. *Exposure: Poisoned Water, Corporate Greed, and One Lawyer's Twenty-Year Battle against DuPont.* New York: Atria Books, 2019.

Boff, Leonardo. *Cry of the Earth, Cry of the Poor.* Maryknoll, New York: Orbis Books, English translation 1997.

Brueggemann, Walter. *The Prophetic Imagination,* 2nd ed. Minneapolis: Fortress Press, 2001.

Coles, Robert. *Dorothy Day: A Radical Devotion.* United States and Canada: Da Capo Press, 1987.

Davis, Mike. *Late Victorian Holocausts: El Nino Famines and the Making of the Third World.* London – New York: Verso, 2001.

Day, Dorothy. *Loaves and Fishes.* Maryknoll, New York: Orbis Books, 1963.

Day, Dorothy. *The Long Loneliness: The Autobiography of Dorothy Day.* San Francisco: Harper and Row, 1952.

Day, Dorothy. *Little by Little: The Selected Writings of Dorothy Day.* Edited by Robert Ellsberg. New York: Alfred A. Knopf 1983.

Day Dorothy with Francis J. Sicius. *Peter Maurin, Apostle to the World.* Maryknoll, New York: Orbis Books, 2004.

Delio, Ilia, Keith Douglass Warner, and Pamela Wood. *Care for Creation: a franciscan spirituality of the earth.* Cincinnati, Ohio: Franciscan Media, 1989.

Frenkel, Sheera and Cecilia Kang. *An Ugly Truth: Inside Facebook's Battle for Domination.* New York: Harper, 2021.

Heyward, Carter. *The Seven Deadly Sins of White Christian Nationalism: A Call to Action.* Boulder, New York Lanham, and London: Rowman & Littlefield, 2022.

Hickel, Jason. *Less is More: How Degrowth Will Save the World.* London: William Heinemann, 2020.

Higham, Scott and Sari Horwitz. *American Cartel: Inside the Battle to Bring Down the Opioid Industry.* New York: Hachette Book Group, 2022.

Hochschild, Adam. *King Leopold's Ghost: A Story of Greed, Terror, and Heroism in Colonial Africa.* Boston and New York: Houghton Mifflin Company, 1998.

Kingsolver, Barbara. *Unsheltered.* New York: HarperCollins, 2018.

Larson, Kate Clifford. *Bound for the Promised Land: Harriet Tubman, Portrait of an American Hero.* New York: Ballantine Books, 2004.

Loughery, John and Blythe Randolph. *Dorothy Day: Dissenting Voice of the American Century.* New York: Simon & Schuster, 2020.

MacLean, Nancy. *Democracy in Chains: The Deep History of the Radical Right's Stealth Plan for America.* Penguin Books, 2017.

Meier, Barry. *Pain Killer: An Empire of Deceit and the Origin of America's Opioid Epidemic,* 2nd ed. New York: Random House, 2018.

Meier, Paulette. *Wellsprings of Life: Quaker Wisdom in Chant.* Paulette Meier Music, 2020.

Moulton, Phillips P. *The Journal and Major Essays of John Woolman.* Richmond, Indiana: Friends United Press, 1971.

John Woolman. *Quaker Spirituality: Selected Writings,* Edited by Douglas V. Steere. New York, Ramsey, Toronto: Paulist Press, 1984.

Sabatier, Paul. *The Complete Francis of Assisi: His life, The Complete Writings, and The Little Flowers.* Edited by Jon M. Sweeney. Brewster, Massachusetts: Paraclete Press, 2015.

Thurow, Lester. *The Future of Capitalism: How Today's Market Forces Shape Tomorrow's World.* New York: Penguin Books, 1996.

Slaughter, Thomas P. *The Beautiful Soul of John Woolman: Apostle of Abolition.* New York: Hill and Wang, 2008.

Tademy, Lalita. *Cane River*. New York and Boston: Warner Books, 2001.

ACKNOWLEDGMENTS

I once heard that none of us writes a book alone. That certainly is true for me. Many have helped this book come to fruition. I'm very appreciative.

I asked Maren Tirabassi to edit an early copy of the manuscript. After getting back her edits and suggestions, I realized the book was far worse and unfinished than I had realized. I spent at least two years attempting to correct the failings she pointed out. Conrad Kanagy, publisher of Santos Books, creates a place for many of us who are not big-name writers to publish our work. That is a gift. Chad Hale and Bob Jones are longtime friends I consult with and rely on for valuable feedback on a variety of things, including this book. John Tobin, Paul Levy, and LR Berger are also trusted companions who have given valuable feedback and encouragement. In wanting to make sure that I was being faithful to John Woolman and the Quaker tradition, I consulted with Mark Barker and was reassured that I had not misrepresented either. South Danbury Church allowed me to try out some of the ideas in the book on them in their worship services. Early in the process, I was a part of a writing group made up of Graham Mitchell, Jennifer Mitchell, and Michael Callahan, which was helpful as I was getting started. Toward the end of the process, John Gregory-Davis provided valuable proofreading. Elizabeth MacLellan has been very helpful with the technology, an area in which I need a great deal of help. From beginning to end, my wife, Helen Fitzgerald, has given feedback, been very supportive, encouraging, and created the space for me to invest the time needed to do the work. Thanks much to all and apologies to anyone I may have omitted.

Gray Fitzgerald has been active in lay ministry and social services for much of his life. He volunteered in Ecuador with the Peace Corps, was a lay leader in an Atlanta inner-city church, served with a nonviolent ecumenical group in wartime Nicaragua, headed up volunteer construction for an Atlanta inner-city housing program, visited inmates throughout the Georgia prison system, counseled individual and families coping with mental illness, and pastored two small United Church of Christ congregations in New Hampshire. In retirement, he continued to live in NH and was active in the UCC's peace and justice activities. In recent years, he has focused on writing a book concerned with his belief that, rather than the church converting our society to the values of our faith regarding money, property, and wealth, the culture has instead converted the church to the values of the culture in those areas.

www.ingramcontent.com/pod-product-compliance
Lightning Source LLC
Chambersburg PA
CBHW060127130626
46556CB00006B/2260